York Wilson

His Life and Work

York Wilson

His Life and Work

1907-1984

Lela M. Wilson

Edited by Sandra Dyck

CARLETON UNIVERSITY PRESS
&
CARLETON UNIVERSITY ART GALLERY

York Wilson: His Life and Work, 1907-1984 supplements the exhibition "York Wilson: The Mural Projects" at Carleton University Art Gallery, 30 May - 2 August, 1997.

Published by Carleton University Press with financial assistance from the Canada Council for the Arts and the Ontario Arts Council, and by the Government of Canada through the Department of Canadian Heritage and the Government of Ontario through the Ministry of Culture, Tourism and Recreation. The programme of Carleton University Art Gallery is supported by the Ontario Arts Council and the Canada Council.

Edited for the press by Sandra Dyck.
Typeset by Barbara Cumming.
Printed and bound in Canada by Trigraphic.

Cover art: *Castro Urdiales* (1977), acrylic on canvas by York Wilson. Private collection.
Frontispiece: *Self Portrait* (1981), oil on canvas by York Wilson. Collection of Galleria degli Uffizi, Florence, Italy.
Back cover photo: York and Lela on the opening night of the O'Keefe Centre for the Performing Arts. Toronto, 1960.

Canadian Cataloguing in Publication Data

Wilson, Lela, 1910-
    York Wilson : his life and work, 1907-1984

Includes index.
Co-published by Carleton University Art Gallery.
ISBN 0-88629-337-5

    1. Wilson, York 1907-1984. 2. Painters—Canada—Biography. I. Carleton University. Art Gallery. II. Title.

ND249.W54W54 1997   759.11   C97-901053-5

FOR YORK

ACKNOWLEDGEMENTS

My thanks to the people who contributed advice and encouragement to the publication of this book.

It is a pleasure to acknowledge those whose assistance and support aided the recording of a neglected but significant part of Canadian art history: Louise Slemin, Ian Montagnes, Jack McClelland, Michael Bell, Maxwell Henderson, Corinne McLuhan, and Virginia and Jon Kieran.

A special appreciation to Sandra Dyck, and to the Canada Council's support, for bringing *York Wilson: His Life and Work* to fruition.

CONTENTS

AGT   Art Gallery of Toronto
AGO   Art Gallery of Ontario (from 1966)
AIO   Art Institute of Ontario
CGP   Canadian Group of Painters
CNE   Canadian National Exhibition, Toronto
CPE   Society of Canadian Painter-Etchers and Engravers
CSGA   Canadian Society of Graphic Arts
CSPWC   Canadian Society of Painters in Water Colour
MMFA   Montreal Museum of Fine Arts
NGC   National Gallery of Canada
OCA   Ontario College of Art, Toronto
OSA   Ontario Society of Artists
RCA   Royal Canadian Academy of Arts
SSC   Sculptors' Society of Canada

Note: The publication date of some newspaper articles referred to in this biography is absent because the articles are not dated in the York Wilson papers.

It was a simple request. Lela Wilson sought a slide or colour transparency of For Peace, a mosaic mural designed by York Wilson and installed in Carleton University's Unicentre. I knew from the university art collection records that there was such a mural, and that it was likely that there was a slide of it somewhere on the campus, if not in the files of the collection, then in the teaching slide collection in the Art History Department. The slide was located, a copy made and sent off. And thus began our adventure with York Wilson and the devoted steward of his legacy.

I look for opportunities to build upon the University's past involvement with the visual arts. Here was an opportunity to follow-up. I met Lela Wilson at her home, the home and studio they built in Toronto. The entrance door is a work by York. Inside the house the evidence of his prodigious energy was everywhere, accented with the objects that they had collected over the years. The deep colours on the walls belonged to the same families that occurred in the paintings. This was a total environment, evidence of a unique partnership shared by the artist and his wife for over 50 years. It was a distillation, as I soon became aware, of the legacy of a singular career, little acknowledged by the next generation.

Lela, the steward of the legacy, showed me to the studio. It was filled with well-framed and systematically stored paintings and drawings. The studies for the mural projects, especially *The Seven Lively Arts* for the O'Keefe Centre, dominated the high walls of the studio. There was the library. There were the filing cabinets containing voluminous letters, clippings and other documents, the work tables, and the typewriters, manual and electric, that Lela had laboured with in her compilation of the narrative of their life.

Packed in a stationery box, the computer print-out was evidence that the several hundred pages of text had been entered on a computer, making the process of revision less onerous, but there was no computer to be seen to carry out the necessary work. Lela had made several attempts to have the story published, without success. In the course of our discussion about the desirability of showing the mural studies at Carleton University Art Gallery, it became more and more evident that the mural projects were the central feature of York Wilson's success. They were discussed in detail in the memoir; perhaps we should try to make the publication happen if the exhibition of the mural projects came to pass. It did.

Sixty-six years after York Wilson first exhibited his art and thirteen years after his death in 1984, the story of York and Lela's life together will be told. It is a personal memoir, presenting the things that were important to them:

finding a way to guarantee time to paint full-time; working hard to insure that there was a healthy art scene through leading the art societies of the day; supporting the few public art galleries; doing public talks; writing articles; and, struggling to rise above parochial visions.

York Wilson's early years as a commercial artist gave him and Lela an entrepreneurial edge in the world of the fine arts. Aided by Lela and assisted by Virginia, their daughter, Wilson made contacts, followed up with chance acquaintances, researched and used new media, completed commissions and systematically supplied his dealers in Toronto, Montreal, Ottawa and Hamilton with works for scheduled exhibitions. Businesslike and energetic, Wilson was certain to be wooed by the artists' societies to take on leadership roles. The same quality served him well in his dealings with corporations wishing to commission what at the time were among the largest commissions ever made to a visual artist. Approached methodically, from the research to the planning through to the final execution, the projects were all completed to everyone's satisfaction, including the artist's.

Rooted as they were in Toronto, York and Lela risked leaving the comfortable local art scene, sometimes for six months at a time, sometimes for a year or more. While these absences served the artist well in furnishing new inspiration for his work, it did distance him from the daily engagements so necessary to keep others' perceptions balanced and jealousies at bay. The art, of course, was of primary concern, and the right choice was made. The circumstances of petty parochialism will pass, but York Wilson's art will be always there to remind people of the material and spiritual achievement. And that achievement will be known, in all its richness and variety, because Lela Wilson maintained the records and the archives and dedicated herself to telling the story that follows. It is a story that is important, told first-hand, not by a professional writer who pulls out all the stylistic and rhetorical stops, but by someone who lived the life—"the design of the partners"—as one friend observed.

Michael Bell, Director
Carleton University Art Gallery

I

1925-1933

Eighty Cents Between Us

ON A BRIGHT, WINTRY NIGHT in 1925 at the Oakwood skating rink in Toronto, Ronald York Wilson, then eighteen, spotted a young woman gliding smoothly along on speed skates, hands behind her back as she kept time with the music. He decided he must meet her. When he did, he asked if he might walk her home. That girl was me, Lela May Miller. I was fifteen years old at the time, and a small-town girl. I lived with my parents in my hometown of Aurora, some thirty miles north of Toronto.

When studying in Toronto, I stayed with the Arthur Wells', old family friends. Their home was on Westmount Avenue, not far from York Wilson's home at 117 Mackay Avenue, in the St. Clair-Dufferin Avenue area. It didn't take long before we were seeing each other regularly. We were a couple of innocents but very much in love. We found great joy in just being together, exchanging stories and youthful dreams.

York was working as a lettering and layout artist at Sampson and Matthews, then considered the best engraving house in Toronto. York and his friend, Edwin Smith, had plans to go to the United States. Ed was slightly older and had been educated at Upper Canada College. He was brought up to admire and appreciate the Old Masters, and this appreciation he imparted to York. They intended to make a living at commercial art, devoting more time to fine art when possible.

Meanwhile, our companionship was beautiful as only young love can be. I often would invite York to my Aurora family home for the weekend. He was always welcome, and impressed my mother by his ardour and sincerity. He made many little sketches during these weekends; one, *Lela's Mother* (1938), is reproduced in Paul Duval's book *York Wilson* (1978).

Neither of us had much money so we sometimes went for walks, or skated with Art, York's younger brother. If we could afford it, we saw a movie. I would sit at the Wells' dinner table, hoping the phone would ring. Sometimes it did, and I would blush all the way to the phone, scarcely able to speak from self-consciousness.

YORK'S CHILDHOOD AND YOUTH

York and I talked about our lives and families. He spoke of his elder sister, Dorothy, whom he didn't care for at the time. When she took care of him as a toddler, she took him to the park and sat him on a bench doing dreaded spool-work (pulling yarn through the opening in a spool) for hours at a time, while she went off to play with her friends.

York often reminisced about his youth. His close friend, Reggie Leggett, possessed a vivid imagination, and would invent the weirdest tales. York's father sought to deflate Reggie's amazing tales by asking, "How many elephants does your pal have in his backyard?" Another friend was Barry Weatherstone, a tiny boy with a big St. Bernard dog that would lift Barry right off his feet and send him flying through the air. As Barry lived adjacent to the famous Dufferin racetrack, the two boys would climb up on the roof of a shed in the Weatherstone yard and watch the race horses stream by. It was a thrilling spectacle.

The Wilsons were then living on St. Helen's Avenue. They had a boarder, a Dutch man by the name of Boscher, whom the kids called "Boscher Washer." Northcott's, the corner grocery store on St. Helen's and Dublin Street, was adjacent to a big coal yard—a messy attraction for kids. One day while throwing a rock at another kid, York dispatched one through the window of the coal office. He raced home, trying to look as innocent as possible. He waited for the big knock on his father's door for weeks, but it never came. It was a lesson he never forgot.

The Wilson home was also close to the huge Christie's biscuit factory, a Toronto landmark. Everyone smelled the vanilla day and night, and joked about it. The area close to the railway was very dirty. The icehouse on Dora Avenue was a popular place to play, particularly in summer. The stable for the icehouse horses had a manure box; brother Art was often spanked for getting into it.

York's parents, William James (Will) and Maryanne Maude Wilson, were born and raised in England. Will was a designer; his window displays had won him many prizes. A well-educated man and great reader of the classics, he could recite any part of Shakespeare from memory. He was of a philosophical turn of mind and not at all ambitious.

York's mother, Maude York, came from a well-born family. Her father was a celebrated tea-taster who owned a chain of teashops. Maude's mother had died when she was young, leaving Maude to be raised by her aunt and uncle, the Kapernik Stokowskis, parents of Leopold Stokowski, the world-famed pianist and conductor of the Philadelphia Orchestra. Leo and Maude grew up as brother and sister. Leo's father was a celebrated cabinetmaker to royalty. Fascinated from birth by music, Leo became the organist in his parents' church at age eight. He never played with friends as a child, and his musical obsession made him such a frail child that his family built him a gymnasium in their home.

Although Will and Maude Wilson had little money when they immigrated with baby Dorothy to Toronto in 1903, they managed to live comfortably. It intrigued York that when the children hung their stockings up at Christmas, they received only oranges. One year, Dorothy's second-hand sleigh was repainted for her Christmas present.

The Wilson children always had pet dogs, usually mongrels with names such as Wolf and Taffy. Wolf, part collie, would run between toddler York's legs, knocking him flat. Taffy was mostly spaniel and a great pal. The Wilson family would walk to High Park on Sundays, sometimes taking the horse-drawn streetcars, which ran as far as Bloor Street and Lansdowne Avenue. This was probably about 1912. Bloor was not paved west of Lansdowne; a boardwalk on Lansdowne stopped about one hundred yards north of Bloor. When York was about eight, the family moved to 117 Mackay Avenue. York walked the ten blocks to and from Regal Road School four times each day. He would dream he found nickels and dimes on his way, or that a leopard or wild animal was chasing him into the house and out the window.

York's memories of World War I were limited to the fact that his parents couldn't obtain butter or sugar. He was a good student at Regal Road, always coming third or fourth in his class. He must have been all of eight when Agnes Nickle became his first girlfriend. She lived close by on Bird Avenue and would frequently call at the Wilson home to ask for York. This amused Will, who would call out, "Your five-cent girl is here again."

When York went to Oakwood Collegiate, his first-year drawings so impressed his instructor that everyone was convinced York should continue in art. Vernon Gross, York's close friend, would tear up York's drawings because they were so much better than his. York laughed it off. When Vernon failed to graduate, York convinced his parents that he should repeat his fourth year with Vernon.

York went on to win prizes in debating. He had an imaginative mind; given a subject he would tackle it non-stop until the bell sounded. He was in fact so high-spirited and full of devilment and practical jokes that he was threatened constantly with expulsion. The principal appealed to his father, who replied that as long as York was a top student, he would let the school worry about his son's behaviour. When the school year ended, the principal advised York to change schools because he had too many marks against him at Oakwood.

FORMAL ART TRAINING

During the summer of 1922, Maude took York's drawings to Toronto's famous Central Technical School and enrolled him in second year. York had entertained thoughts of entering medical school, being greatly impressed by the Wilson family doctor, William Fader. Maude's actions that summer started York on the path to his true career.

At Central Tech, the story was much the same as at Oakwood. York, however, came under the strong discipline of Peter Haworth, the new assistant art director who arrived from England in 1923. Haworth was a strict disciplinarian who was quick to anger. One day he caught York and two friends skipping life-drawing class, not liking the set school poses, and instead drawing from their own female nude model in an empty classroom. Haworth was so incensed that he marched the three students to the principal's office, demanding their immediate expulsion. On the way they met the principal, Alfred Howell, who chortled, "Ho, Ho, what have we here?" Before Haworth could finish his angry denunciations, York, with a quick glance at the unhappy faces of his friends, simply convulsed with laughter. Principal Howell relaxed and grinned. "Wilson," he said, "Your irrepressible laugh has saved you again. Go to your class."

York studied at Central Tech under Haworth. After two years, his mother confessed that, "We can't afford to send you back another year, you must try to get a job. If you try but don't succeed we will, somehow or other, send you back to finish at Central Tech." York thus left Central Tech in the summer of 1924, at the age of sixteen. Those two years at Central Tech were his only formal art training.

YORK'S FIRST COMMERCIAL WORK

York lost no time in trying to help his parents. He gathered samples of his artwork and applied for a job. His second call was at the art department at Brigden's Limited. The firm agreed to hire him, but as he was under-age, his father had to sign the contract. York, who earned $5 each forty-four-hour workweek, was pleased to contribute to the household. He continued sketching every weekend, and received criticism from Thomas V. Mitchell, art director at Brigden's. Charles Comfort, also employed at Brigden's, offered comments which sometimes conflicted with Mitchell's. York preferred Comfort's.

York cut mats, prepared frisket paper, and worked as a messenger boy. He soon realised that lettering men were always in short supply, so he decided to follow that route. He was told to forget everything he had learned at Central Tech. He copied Goudy's book on lettering in India ink, which took several months. This laid the foundation of his lettering knowledge, and he began work on real lettering jobs, eventually doing layouts with figures. He also attended evening classes at the Ontario College of Art (OCA), where he received criticism from Fred Finley, who had studied at the Académie Julian in Paris in the early 1920s. Finley was considered an expert on life drawing.

York's sense of the ridiculous and fondness for practical jokes never abat-ed. He was one of the main instigators of the nonsense that went on at Brigden's. One of his artist friends always kept a few raisins on his desk; York once decided to put a few dark lumps of rubber cement among them. Another trick was to put soap chips in galoshes, which, when damp, pro-duced more and more foam as the victim strode along. One day in 1925, an artist returned from lunch with a smart new hat, just purchased from Applegath's hat shop. That afternoon, the hat was spirited away, and a little stuffing was inserted under the inside leather band. When leaving that night, the proud owner was rather confused when the hat sat high on his head.

A catastrophe nearly occurred when one artist, Bob Mulholland, received a stiff note, ostensibly from Fred Brigden, which expressed his deep dissatisfaction with Mulholland's work. York was busy and had forgotten about it when suddenly Bob Mulholland went tearing past his desk, on his way to see Mr. Brigden. York dashed after him and, catching him on the stairs said, "Bob, I wrote that note, very funny, ha ha!" Bob stared and said, "I don't care who wrote it. He can't talk to me that way." It wasn't until the third try, just outside Brigden's door, that Bob finally realised the boss hadn't written the note.

York resigned from Brigden's after two and one-half years, while still under contract, because they refused his request for a raise. Brigden's retaliated by blackballing him with every other engraving house in the city, so he couldn't land a job. He then called on every store on Yonge Street, and got enough design work to last for six months, by which time the engraving houses had forgotten the Brigden's situation.

Sampson and Matthews was the best studio in Toronto at that time. York prepared a book of samples and made an appointment with Chuck Matthews, who gave him a job immediately. Franklin Carmichael, the art director, kept making York do jobs over and over again, which didn't build his confidence. A.J. Casson, then second in command, became art director in 1942. Carmichael was a founding member of the Group of Seven, which Casson joined in 1926.

After working at Sampson and Matthews for six months, York decided he was ready to go to the United States. The firm's partners were shocked, as no one had ever quit before. Mr. Sampson told York he was making a big mistake, as many artists who had tried going to the States ended up returning to ask for their old jobs. York replied that he would never want his old job back. Mr. Matthews responded by writing a testimonial on the firm's letterhead that read, "I wouldn't hesitate to recommend this man to anyone." York was very impressed, as he hadn't even asked for a recommendation; the two men became lifelong friends.

York always credited his pal Ed Smith for having aroused his interest in the Old Masters. York haunted libraries, studying the reproductions and reading all he could find by the great art authorities of the day, including Herbert Read. And so the day finally came in October 1927 when York and Ed left for Detroit, and we said sad goodbyes. York was then nineteen years old.

I missed York, but realised he had to establish himself and gain experience in his chosen field. I took a job at Canadian National Telegraphs, working with direct lines to stockbrokers' offices. The department manager, Miss Shortt, was pleasant and business-like and we got along well. The other operators were much older than I. Even the youngest, only twenty-seven, seemed so old to me. She told me about her love affair with a customs officer; their visits usually occurred on weekends. The concept of an affair was very advanced to me, and quite an eye-opener. I had a few casual boyfriends during York's absence, but none were as interesting as York, until I met an older man, charming and worldly. He proposed marriage and travel. I accepted, and off we went to Los Angeles. We had two very happy years together, during which our darling baby daughter Virginia was born in 1930. Our happiness came to a sudden end when it was discovered that he already had a wife and three children in Toronto.

I returned to Ontario, joining my mother in Aurora for a short visit before going back to Toronto, where Virginia and I stayed with my Aunt Ethel and Uncle Edgar Miller, who lived off Danforth Avenue. Aunt Ethel took care of Virginia while I worked for the *Toronto Daily Star* on King Street. Mr. Tate, the manager, devoted considerable time to enforcing the newspaper's strict rule of not employing married women, thus leaving more opportunities for men.

WORKING IN DETROIT

York gained invaluable design experience in Detroit. On arriving there, Ed and York had taken a room together to cut expenses. The next morning they were out looking for work. At the first stop, York was told he could start in two weeks, but he replied that his money wouldn't last that long. The art director kindly supplied him with a list of possible studios. At Meinzingers, the next stop, where he was told he could start work in about ten days, his reply was the same. Mr. Meinzinger said York could design a few Christmas cards for General Motors immediately. York asked what type of reproduction was required and Mr. Meinzinger replied, "Any kind." York went back to his room and designed several cards; he took them back the next morning and asked for $50, the agreed salary for a week. Mr. Meinzinger called a stenographer to make out the cheque, handed it to York and promptly tore up the designs, saying, "Now you won't look for any other work, will you?"

York returned to Toronto with Meinzingers' assurance that they would let him know his starting date. His second day back in Toronto brought a telegram instructing him to start work early the next morning. His first job was a twenty-four-sheet billboard poster advertising Pontiac. The art director told him, "Forget everything you thought was lettering in Canada. It's too old-fashioned." York learned the next day that he would alternate with the art director: they would compose a layout, get it approved by General Motors in the same building, and complete a used-car ad which would appear in the morning. It would take until midnight to complete the job, and the fact that they punched the time clock each morning made it a long day.

York stayed with Meinzingers at $50 per week for about a year, when he discovered that he had been redoing the work of a man who was earning $65 per week. He quit in disgust, only to experience difficulty getting another job. It took about two weeks—a long time. His next job was at Reid Smith Studios for $65 per week, where he stayed for eighteen months. Ed Smith was also working at Reid Smith. He had been working at a well-paid job in Toledo, but had soon given up the job because the city was so dirty. York did mostly layouts and watercolour illustrations, but that work ended with the stock market crash in 1929.

York later told me about his life in Detroit. Some of his and Ed's co-workers, who lived across the Detroit River in Windsor, often smuggled goods into Canada and liquor back into the United States, where prohibition reigned. When York first joined a group of poker players, he was asked if he had played much. He said no. It was his bad luck to win on the first night, whereupon his questioner, poking York's chest violently, threatened, "Don't say you haven't played much when you have. It might not be too healthy." York and Ed soon realised that some of these characters belonged to the underworld.

Windsor friends often asked him to help bring presents across the border. It was Christmas and they gave him a big doll to smuggle into Canada. He put it inside his shirt and trousers. At the customs they were told to get out of the car and as York bent over, the doll cried "M-a-m-m-a." The startled customs officer said, "What was that?" York said he had made the noise, and immediately made a few similar noises to bolster his claim.

GETTING ESTABLISHED IN TORONTO

York returned to Toronto in the spring of 1930, a victim of the Depression. Unable to find a job, he formed his own business with the designer Wesley Flinn, setting up the Flinn/Wilson studios at 100 Front Street West. It was York's job to bring in the work, making arrangements with the client, and doing his share of design work, while Wes remained in the studio. It was an amicable arrangement.

There were other art studios in the building, including one occupied by the Russian artist André Lapine, an expert on painting furs and lace who did a lot of work for the Eaton's catalogue. He was also a painter who exhibited with Malloney's Art Gallery and the various art societies. York enjoyed the company of this older artist, and was occasionally invited for dinner to André's home near the Humber River. André was an avid gardener and York would often find him in the garden on arrival. After dinner André would play the piano. André was later employed at Brigden's.

The Flinn/Wilson Studios had a joint bank account with a very small balance. Although York brought in most of the work, he didn't have many responsibilities and enjoyed working with Wes. Wes was slow and exact in speech, with a slight lisp. He eventually married Carolyn Davidson, whose father was dean of Emanuel College at the University of Toronto. He later taught at Toronto's Western Technical School when L.A.C. (Alec) Panton was principal. Alec, a stiff and officious man, had the nasty habit of talking down to his colleagues while blinking his eyes, balancing on his toes, and dangling a long, gravity-defying ash from his cigarette. Waiting for the ash to fall had an unnerving, mesmerising effect on people. He was not popular with his staff, and earned the nickname "Lacy" Panton behind his back.

York first exhibited with the Canadian Society of Graphic Arts (CSGA) at its Eighth Show in 1931. The exhibition's jury accepted four works: an etching, *F.S.* (1930); an etching of York's father *Bill* (1930); a chalk drawing, *Reverie* (1931); and a watercolour, *Three Heads* (1931). The same year he sent two watercolours: *The Ward* (1926), sketched from the roof of Brigden's; and *Richmond and York* (1926) to the Royal Canadian Academy of Arts (RCA). A selection from the show, including *The Ward*, went to the National Gallery of Canada (NGC) in Ottawa. The National Gallery wanted to purchase *The Ward* if York would lower his $45 asking price. The aspiring young artist refused. I think York later regretted his decision, as his first work only entered the National Gallery collection twelve years later, in 1943. He thus lost the potential distinction of being the youngest artist represented in their collection.

OUR MARRIAGE

York and I were reunited in 1932. He began visiting me at the home of my Aunt Ethel and Uncle Ed, who made him very welcome. York was a very different, worldly man; he had dated many women and had lost some of his boyish charm. I noticed he had acquired a few affectations such as calling most women "darling" but he was still the same earnest young man when it came to his painting and his values. His health had suffered, for he had played and worked hard. He might well have burned

out early, as many of the brightest artists had done, if he hadn't had a
steadying influence.

We saw each other almost nightly in the spring and summer of 1933.
One July evening he arrived, quite excited, and wanted to see me immediately. I was upstairs cleaning my white shoes, but he called for me to
come right down, as it was urgent. As I reached the bottom of the stairs
he asked, "Will you marry me?" I was taken aback but quick to respond,
"Yes, but can't you ask me better than that?" "I'm not very good at this,"
he muttered, and got down on his knees and made a lengthier proposal,
at which moment we both laughed. We decided to get married that
autumn. York started dissolving his three-year partnership with Wes
Flinn, as their business would not support a wife as well.

A few nights later York said, "Let's not wait till fall. Let's get married
right away." He had no money and I had only my $12-per-week job at
the *Toronto Daily Star*. I half agreed, realising that we would have to live
apart—he with his parents and I with my aunt. We agreed to meet at City
Hall the next day to get the licence. I think we both wondered if the other
would turn up! We did and, surprised at our audacity, wandered around
the building looking for the marriage licence bureau. A guard whom we
hadn't noticed said, "It's down this way." We said, "What's down this
way?" and he replied, "The marriage licence bureau, of course." We wondered how he knew, and we all laughed. We discovered we had to wait
three days. I suppose this allows people time to think it over sensibly.

That evening we went to my church on Danforth Avenue to arrange
for a small ceremony three days later, on July 13th. The minister was
kindly and helpful, asking us many questions to make us really think
about this serious step. Those partaking in our little ceremony included
York's parents, my mother in Aurora, and my Aunt and Uncle. York's
brother Art was best man.

Two of York's closest friends, Ethel and Fred King, themselves
recently married, made a generous offer. They would spend the night with
Ethel's parents and give York the key to their apartment. York's parents
drove us there after the ceremony, stopping en route for me to buy a
toothbrush. We discovered that we had eighty cents between us.

York opened the door of the Kings' apartment and carried me across the
threshold where, to our amazement, a path of rose petals led all the way to
the bedroom. Next morning I went to work at the *Star*, removing my wedding ring before entering the building, and York went out to search for work.

II

1933-1936

Places of Our Own

SEARCHING FOR WORK DURING THE DEPRESSION was a tough job. I went to work at the *Star* each day while York looked for a job, and we would meet at noon for lunch. I fell into the habit of slipping my wedding ring on during our meal and then removing it when I returned to the office. The day came when I forgot to take it off. The manager, Mr. Tate, called me into his office, stating, "It has been reported that you had a wedding ring on your finger. Are you married?" he asked. I said yes, whereupon he replied, "Well you know our policy," and gave me two weeks notice. York and I became so hungry at times that we would press our noses against the windows of shops displaying delicious food. I remember carefully counting prunes, or whatever, to make them last the week.

York persevered and soon landed a small job with Rolph Clark Stone, a big Toronto lithographic firm. Clutching his $45 cheque, he telephoned me at the *Star* to deliver the good news and suggested he would spend the rest of the day looking for a place to live. We reasoned we could be together as long as the money lasted. York found an apartment on King Street in the Parkdale district, a bed-sitting room for $7 per week. We moved in late that afternoon and proceeded to have our first disagreement. I picked up my unopened bag and started for the door. York made amends, and it soon blew over.

I never did return to the labour force. The $45 York had earned seemed to promise greater things. He didn't like the idea of his wife working. He had some other peculiar ideas as well. He seemed to think I should stay in the apartment all day, not visiting friends, even Aunt Ethel! There was little doubt that he thought the husband made all the decisions. I began to rebel, and one evening after a dinner of fish, I didn't move to do the dishes as quickly as he thought I should. He demanded I do them immediately. I didn't move, so he rubbed my face in the fishy plates. The one time he hit me, I hit him right back. He was so surprised he never did it again.

After a few weeks in our King Street quarters, York had found enough work to make life a little more comfortable. He decided to see how I responded to a little alcohol, as I had never indulged. He bought a 'mickey' of gin and mixed it with other things, thinking I might not like the taste. We started before dinner with silver fizzes, made with the white of an egg. After the first one he asked, "How was it? Do you feel anything?" I replied no. "Well, let's have a second...and a third." Still we felt nothing, and eventually finished the bottle. York was so intent on my reaction that he had no reaction either. He thought someone must have diluted the gin! Finally we pulled down the wall bed and crawled in, feeling the experiment had been a waste of time and money. The next morning, however, told a different story. Neither of us had a stitch of clothing on, and we never slept in the nude! That was the end of alcohol for a while.

Now that finances were a little better and I had stopped working, we took Virginia, now age three, from Aunt Ethel's home to live with us full time, instead of just weekends. She continued sleeping on pillows on two armchairs pushed together in our adjoining kitchen/dining area. York loved this dear little girl as his own, which turned out to be a great blessing over the years, as it had become a fact that he was unlikely to have children of his own. York legally adopted Virginia.

It was not long before York was again connected with Brigden's. For a retainer of $25 a week they had first call on his work, from which they would take 50 percent. York soon exceeded the $25 retainer, but Ronalds Advertising Agency through their client Glen Bannerman of Hudson Terraplane Motors, who started giving him car advertisement contracts, kept him busy. Things were looking up and we decided we could afford a larger apartment. An unfurnished one became available nearby at the corner of Queen Street and Dowling Avenue. Furnishing the apartment on a tiny budget was a great experience; York wanted colourful drapes for the windows. I responded with bright yellow and red, as I wanted to co-ordinate his ideas with mine. I too had been good at art in school!

A NEW STUDIO

With steady work, York decided he should leave Brigden's and open his own studio. He found a two-room, north-facing studio, owned jointly by the artist Dorothy Stevens and her brother Paul, at 145 Wellington Street West. The first room served as his office, the second his studio. Haunting used-furniture stores and auctions, we found a rosewood desk made from an antique piano, with elephant-sized legs. With only two drawers, it was not the most logical choice, but it was interesting and a wonderful conversation piece.

At about this time we purchased our first car, a used Plymouth with a rumble seat. We enjoyed our first holidays that summer with York's parents on a guest farm near Trenton, on Lake Ontario. We were halfway there when a great bang brought our car to a halt. The car had a broken axle and would take a few days and $30 to fix. We called York's parents, already at the farm and they came to pick us up. It was an idyllic setting. The thunderstorms across the great expanse of Lake Ontario were frightening, but the three of us were so happy and relaxed. The experience of joining everyone at the farmer's big table loaded with fresh produce was delightful. I will never forget the huge beefsteak tomatoes ripened on the vine. We spent hours wandering over the sand dunes and along the lakeshore, with York stopping frequently to sketch. It was the only two weeks we ever spent in this paradise.

A NEW APARTMENT

A larger two-bedroom apartment soon became available in the same building. It unfortunately faced Queen Street, a busy, noisy thoroughfare. At first we wore eyeshades and earplugs but quickly adjusted. The second bedroom became a much-needed studio. Virginia went to bed early in our bedroom; we moved her later in the evening, fast asleep, to the chesterfield. York worked many evenings at home and now had the space to employ a model. He had been using models posing for groups, but avoided professionals as they often affected set poses.

York was aware of a long-legged, well-proportioned girl we occasionally saw on our street but he was reluctant to approach her. He asked if I would try to arrange for her to pose. This I did, explaining it was necessary to pose in the nude, and that I was the artist's wife and would be present. Phyllis, a student, was interested, thinking she would learn something about art, but had to ask her mother. Her mother readily agreed and asked to accompany her daughter, which we thought was a reasonable request. After a couple of visits, the mother was satisfied that all was well and Phyllis turned out to be an excellent model. This marked the beginning of a lifetime practice. York drew from a model at least half a day each week, no matter where we lived.

As we prospered, York thought it civilised to enjoy a pre-dinner drink and begged me to have a cigarette with him, another new experience for me. We didn't know then how addictive and unhealthy these habits were. I remained a light smoker but York unfortunately was going through three packs a day, chain-smoking while painting. Classical music always played in the studio, a familiar environment for York, as his mother came from a musical family. While still at school, York spent the money earned from his first jobs (newspaper delivery and bakery work) on recordings such as Tchaikovsky's *Marche Slave*, Sibelius' *Finlandia,* and Debussy's *Afternoon of a Faun.*

MY CAREER AS A COMMERCIAL ARTIST

York was getting a fair amount of illustration work for magazine stories, including *Maclean's*, where Frank Sperry was art director. One day York arrived at 9:00 A.M. sharp with his finished illustration for Sperry. York was still sitting in the waiting room thirty minutes later when the editorial director, Napier Moore, stopped by to ask why he was waiting. Sperry finally arrived, obviously in a bad mood, as he had been reprimanded for being late. He started to criticise the illustration, wanting changes here and there. York, having waited forty-five minutes, was also annoyed and folded the card. Sperry said, "That's the last work you will ever get from us." York was sorry later that he had been so hotheaded for he needed the work.

He then devised a scheme. He would do samples, sign Lela May Wilson and I would present them as my work, not immediately to *Maclean's* but to other publications like *Chatelaine.* When the samples were ready he instructed me in terms used in the business, such as "a double spread," "proportioned to size," and "bleeding a page." I was extremely anxious; it sometimes took hours before I could bring myself to call to make an appointment to show my samples. Finally I managed to call Byrne Hope Sanders, long-time editor of *Chatelaine.* My story was that I was from California, and was stopping in Toronto and Montreal to do some illustrations for Canadian magazines.

Miss Sanders liked the samples and gave me work immediately. The completed illustrations pleased her so much that she gave me two more stories to illustrate. Things progressed to the point that I had three items in one issue, including the cover. Byrne was getting friendlier each time and one day said, "My husband Frank Sperry likes your work so much, he wondered if you would like to go sketching on the weekend?" I replied that I was very sorry, but I had another commitment. That was a close call, and I knew it could happen again. It reminded me of one of Socrates' conclusions, "If one could know all the ramifications caused by one lie, one would never tell a lie!"

Another time Byrne sent me in to discuss a point with the art director of *Chatelaine*. She thought a small change in an illustration would help. The art director agreed and suggested I make the change right there. I said, "Thank you, but I have an artist friend in this building, I'll use his materials and return right away." York was then renting space from Ronalds Advertising in the Maclean Tower. Fortunately he was there, and quickly made the change.

Eventually I did a three-part illustration, the third being a tailpiece for a long story. The tailpiece somehow ended up with an illustration by Kay Bell and was credited to her. York hit the roof and instructed me to object, telling me exactly what to say. Byrne listened carefully and said she would call me when she had more work. That was the last call I received. I learned years later from her secretary, Peggy Gay, who later married Ray Avery of Ronalds Advertising, that Byrne said, "We'll let Miss Wilson cool her heels for a while."

Another *Chatelaine* employee at that time was Lotta Dempsey, a young journalist from western Canada who years later became a great friend and fan of York's. When York was a fully established painter and muralist, he was invited to speak at the Heliconian Club, an association of professional women artists. The ageing Frank Sperry and his wife, Byrne Hope Sanders, were guests at this dinner. Mr. Sperry let it be known that he was anxious to meet the well-known painter, York Wilson. We were brought and presented to them, not without trepidation, I assure you. Mr. Sperry emphasised how much he had always enjoyed York's paintings. It was a beautiful, sincere appreciation and we felt a twinge of guilt. Byrne did not recognise Miss Wilson, her former illustrator from California. Byrne Hope Sanders was to have a distinguished career during World War II as head of the Consumer Branch of the Wartime Prices and Trade Board. She also wrote *Emily Murphy, Crusader* (1945), a biography of one of Canada's pioneers.

I took some of York's samples to the editor of *Canadian Home Journal*. He liked the samples and promised to watch for a story that required a woman's point of view. True to his word, he called in a few days, and I started doing story illustrations for *Canadian Home Journal*.

This work eventually ended as he realised there were so few stories that could be illustrated by a woman!

Much of York's work came from Ronalds Advertising Agency; Ray Avery was manager of the Toronto branch. Russell Ronalds, the owner and a prominent advertising executive, managed the head office in Montreal. Ronalds felt they had enough work to keep York busy and suggested he rent a studio in their offices. When they moved to the Maclean Tower in Toronto, York moved with them.

Ray and Peggy Avery became our close friends and York started doing their Christmas cards, as well as separate Avery/Wilson cards for a few special clients. In 1939 "Flit Insecticide" was a Ronalds Agency account, and the company president was a fun crony. York designed a card with Avery/Wilson heads on floating angels carrying a banner that read, "We Flit With Joyous Tidings." In 1940 York's boisterous sense of humour found expression in a poster offering a reward "For Information Leading To The Conviction Of A Person Generally Known As RonRay AveryWilson," with a frontal view of Ray and a profile of York. The poster looked authentic but the copy, signed by Sheriff Halfa Buck, was pure nonsense. York always signed Ron Wilson on his commercial work, but used "R. York" or later "York Wilson" on his fine art.

We made many other lasting friends at Ronalds. One of the writers, Charles Lee Hutchings, was the subject of York's painting *Hutch* (1941). Christine Connor, who later married Charles, posed for *Welfare Worker* (1940). As York had made Christine very unattractive in *Welfare Worker*, he later did a charming portrait of her. Other friends there were Glen Bannerman, and Cecilia Long, later the companion of Lady Henrietta Banting, widow of Sir Frederick Banting.

Claire Wallace was a well-known radio and TV commentator with a daily national program. Claire had a great sense of humour and a ready laugh. Her sponsor was the Bristol Myers Drug Company and she often interviewed pharmacists when giving the day's social news. If the specified pharmacist failed to turn up, she would summon York, who always had lots to say. It was sometimes hard for Claire to suppress her giggles at his antics. Claire once overheard York talking in hushed tones to someone at a party, and moved in fast. He stopped talking so she promised not to mention it on the air. York confided that when hosting a television program from the Art Gallery of Toronto one evening, he hadn't possessed black studs for his tuxedo so he had simply painted his white studs black. Claire aired the story the next night.

RAY AVERY'S ANTICS

I remember well the night Ray Avery, an inveterate prankster, brought a live goose to a party we were giving in the third floor Dowling Avenue apartment. He set the goose down inside the door, and it dashed around, squirting as it went. Ray was enjoying this immensely, in spite of our chasing around to clean up after the bird. Someone finally grabbed it and put it outside the door. There it was forgotten until someone went for cigarettes to the drugstore on the main floor. The goose was there, surrounded by a puzzled crowd. Peggy Avery apologised, saying she had no idea that Ray had a goose in the back seat of the car. She did admit she had wondered whom he was talking to as they drove to the party. She had given up taking any responsibility for her husband's misdemeanours.

On another visit, Ray slipped out, removed all the light bulbs in the halls and hid them in the flowerpots. The tenants were soon complaining about the dark stairs and hallways; the management was completely baffled and so were we. Ray brought a container of baby frogs to another of our parties. Unbeknownst to me, he set them loose in the large goldfish tank on the landing. Soon the frogs were jumping all over the place, even on the mantelpieces.

Another time Ray gathered the magazines on the coffee table and threw them into the blazing fireplace. I walked up to him and slapped his face. I had never done such a thing before, but I was exasperated beyond reason. Ray took it lightly and laughed nervously; he wasn't all bad, but just had a devilish streak. The last misdemeanour happened at a Ronalds Agency celebration, when Ray said, "With a twist of my little finger, I can decide what work goes to York or not." When I told York he confronted Ray: "What is this I hear about a twist of your little finger?" Ray said that he was only fooling!

Ray and Peggy had a cottage on Morrison Lake; we often joined them and did little repair jobs for Peggy's parents. Neither Ray nor York could resist putting a brush of red paint on the other's backside when temptingly close. The two of them would often clown in women's clothing and hats at parties on Morrison Lake. I would marvel at how two such talented men could have so many loose screws!

OUR FIRST HOUSE

It was now 1936 and we decided we needed more space, including a good studio for York and a room for Virginia. Our real estate agent said he would like to show us a house. It was so beautiful and an outstanding buy. It was at 28 Hambly Avenue in the Beaches area of Toronto. As it had been vacant for three years, the owner would let it go for very little. It was like new, built fifteen years earlier at a cost of $15,000, an enormous amount in those days. The owner's brother was in the lumber business and all the wood had been carefully selected. The vestibule had a handsome oak chest, while the large entrance hall, dining room and second-floor den were all panelled in oak. The house featured three fireplaces, three bedrooms and a sunroom on the second floor, and two enormous rooms on the third floor—one became York's studio and the other Virginia's bedroom. There was a brick garage with private drive and a small garden.

The price had been dropped to $7,500. The agent suggested an offer of $5,500 with $500 down, and we made the offer that night. York's parents offered to loan us the $500 down payment. If we sold our car and took in boarders, we could maybe swing it. Our first offer was refused; we then offered $6,500, which was accepted.

We soon sold the car and rented the second-floor bedroom to a young woman named Alva. Then a Mr. Pudifun rented the den. We all shared the one bathroom, which never seemed to present a problem with our different hours. Eventually Mr. Pudifun developed pneumonia and had to be moved to the hospital. He returned when he was well again, only to leave with a promise to pay many weeks overdue rent. That was the last we saw of him. The son of a well-known Toronto family then took the smaller bedroom next to Alva's and stayed for some time, always paying his rent on time. When he left, however, York's beautiful riding boots departed with him. We decided to get along without any more boarders.

III

1936-1943

Steady Development

FEW ARTISTS IN THE 1940S WERE ABLE TO LIVE by their work alone. The Art Gallery of Toronto (AGT) held a non-juried exhibition in 1943. York sent *Local Dance* (1943), which depicted an energetic group of dancers, including me. The reviewer for *Saturday Night* (April 17, 1943) called it "one of the liveliest of the paintings" in the show, and asserted that York was "an artist who can make his figures move (something unusual in Toronto)."

It was a great occasion when the AGT bought *Local Dance* that same year. The London Public Library and Art Museum also purchased three small works in the 1940s, including *Spring Thaw* (1944), *Port Credit Spring* (1944), and *Auction Sale, Belfountain* (1941), from which a silkscreen print was made during World War II. York was meanwhile getting the cream of commercial work; his paintings were used in advertising for clients like Elizabeth Arden, Yardley, Imperial Oil, Seagram's, Abitibi Pulp and Paper and various departments of the federal government.

In 1942 York was elected a member of the Ontario Society of Artists (OSA), and was soon serving on the executive. He was later invited to write an article for *World Affairs* (December 1942) entitled "There's Nothing Complicated About Art"; his *Welfare Worker* was reproduced on the cover. The caption explained that York disowned "any intent to caricature his subjects and only sets out to paint them truly. The hands of *Welfare Worker* were repainted five times to acquire the effect of softness and grooming in contrast to the harsh surroundings and the cactus plant."

The model for *Welfare Worker* was our friend Christine Connor, a social worker from a comfortable family. She had soft hands and long painted nails, which had just come into vogue. York added old-fashioned, steel-rimmed glasses and an unattractive hat, and placed her in a poor home. Her client, partly reflected in the mirror, had served her tea in a thick, cheap cup.

Welfare Worker caused a furore when it was later exhibited at the Winnipeg Art Gallery. The gallery's administrators ignored demands that it be removed from the exhibition. Years later, Leslie McFarlane, director of a National Film Board documentary called "Social Workers in Vancouver," spotted a reproduction of *Welfare Worker* hanging on an office wall in Vancouver. He asked why it was there and was told that it "reminded social workers not to be like that!" He sought York's permission to include the painting in the film, writing on August 20, 1949 that "your painting casts illumination on the contrast between the old...type of social worker and the practical, sensible and sympathetic type emerging here...." As a result of such interest, and in addition to many a reproduction in newspapers, *Welfare Worker* has become one of York's best-known paintings. The Ottawa owner of this painting says he will eventually consider giving it to an art gallery.

In late 1942 York presented a thoughtful gift to Ray and Peggy Avery at the birth of their first child, Lynne. As the *Telegram* (December 15, 1942) reported, Lynne's gift was "a framed blank canvas with a card appended in one corner and inscribed as follows: 'This space reserved for Lynne Gay Avery.'" York loved Lynne dearly, but he preferred older portrait subjects.

York and his friend Melville (Bud) Feheley often went sketching together. They preferred the Port Credit area, where they sometimes stayed overnight with the Blacks, a local farming family. In 1942 Mrs. Black announced their arrival in the local paper, claiming that York could spend a whole year in the Credit Forks vicinity without running out of subjects. Thomas R. Henry, art critic for the *Evening Telegram*, observed that although York was known mainly as a painter of urban subjects, he had "dealt with vigor and surely selective sense with various aspects out of the Ontario landscape and has been successful."

In 1943, York prepared *Dimout* (also called *Street in a Dimout* or *Early Closing*) for the OSA. The 1943 OSA exhibition catalogue showed a photograph of York at work on this painting. Sampson and Matthews, York's former employer, reproduced *Dimout* in their 1944 calendar, with the comment that York's "paintings of typically Canadian characters and situations have won him recognition as one of Canada's outstanding young artists." *Dimout* was earlier used on the North American Life Insurance Company's 1943 calendar, followed by four paintings on the theme of pioneer life in Canada. Sadly I have no record of the whereabouts of *Dimout*; it belongs with the war records in the Canadian War Museum.

Blood Donors (1943), shown at the 1943 OSA exhibition at the AGT, was reproduced in the exhibition catalogue and on the cover of *Saturday*

Night (March 20, 1943). As the critic for the *Telegram* observed, York was "doing his sketching from the vantage point of the kitchen sink, literally rubbing elbows with the two washers-up constantly at work at the sink which practically filled the tiny kitchen space." York unfortunately destroyed *Blood Donors*, felt by many to be a key picture of the home front in Canada during World War II. Only a slide and photograph exist to document this painting.

THE WILSON FAMILY

When York's parents sold their house at 117 Mackay Avenue, we suggested they move in with us. We were able to afford our first cleaning lady. Pop Wilson used to love gardening and polishing the brass on the front door. Mom Wilson had a bad heart; when in pain she became very religious and prayed for Pop to put his trust in God. Pop had become accustomed to this over the years, and would try to relieve her pain by making her laugh with the retort, "Yes, trust in God and keep your bowels open." It's easy to see where York got his mischievous nature. Mom was a dear little lady who sometimes sat on a park bench chatting with passers-by. People would tell her their troubles, and in some instances she would bring them home for a good meal.

The senior Wilsons never drank much. When York offered his father a scotch or beer, he also offered some to his mother. She usually replied, "Yes, dear, just a thimbleful," meaning just that. York would give her this tiny amount and she felt devilish, thinking she could feel its effects. In his youth, Pop sometimes made fig or elderberry wine, which he drank in moderation, perhaps when returning home on a cold night. He always advised his sons never to abuse alcohol. One might hope such civilised behaviour would become habitual but, alas, it did not. The Wilsons stayed with us for a few years, and then rented a small house in north Toronto. Finally they later went to keep house for York's brother Art, who was living alone in Orillia. When York's mother died in 1956, we brought Pop Wilson back to stay with us.

When York's wanderlust struck again in 1957, York's sister Dorothy invited him to stay with her and her husband, Ross Gillespie, the auditor for the city of Toronto. It became clear that Dorothy was a little too fussy for Pop. He smoked a pipe, so she placed a protective covering at the base of his favourite chair, should he spill tobacco when lighting his pipe. Pop eventually returned to Orillia, which was a worry for us, as Art worked all day and was seldom home in the evenings. Pop and Art enjoyed a good relationship, however, aided by a kind of telepathy. When Pop fell out of bed one night, Art claimed he "heard" it many miles away and rushed home.

Pop Wilson stayed with us again when he was in his late eighties and sporting a flowing white beard. We enjoyed taking him out with us in the evenings. Our long-time friends, Jean and Cleeve Horne, liked Pop and kidded him a lot. When we left on another painting trip abroad, he returned to Orillia to live with Art. One morning in 1958, Art found Pop had passed away in his sleep. He was sadly missed.

A NEW HOUSE

After seven years in the palatial Hambly Avenue house, we sold it to a large Québec family in 1943. We bought a new builder's house in north Toronto, at 8 Apsley Road in Armour Heights, for $8,500. Large open fields separated our house from the Toronto Cricket Club, where Virginia and her dog Suzi liked to roam. The house had a large recreation area with a fireplace. York invited his artist friends to dinner, a couple at a time; their "payment" for dinner was to paint a decoration of their choice on the recreation room walls.

Cleeve Horne painted a tremendous crack on the ceiling which looked so real that York's mother cried out, "Oh dear, whatever happened to your new house?" Syd Watson's creation, starting below ground level, depicted earth, worms, stones and garbage cans, with a *trompe l'oeil* broken wall in one corner. J.S. (Syd) Hallam painted a musician with puffed cheeks; the existing radiator pipe became a tuba that seemed to be coming out of his mouth. A.J. Casson copied the two windows on either side of the fireplace, creating a third over the fireplace, complete with a peeping Tom. York painted a framed nude emanating out of the corner. Jack Bush did a framed picture, complete with a cord, in the centre of a wall. Bill Winter painted a man coming out of the doorframe kicking his heels; his head came off with his raised hat! I can't remember what Angus MacDonald painted. When we sold the house twelve years later to the Stronachs, they insured with our agent, Wallace Clancy, who told the Stronachs they now owned the most valuable room in Canada. They understood and preserved the room for posterity.

Jack and Mabel Bush bought a house for $10,000 at about the same time in the Armour Heights area, where they raised their three boys. Jack and Mabel were having a bad time with their four-year-old son, who used the foulest language. Jack threatened him again and again, but to no avail. In exasperation, Jack finally put the boy over his knee and gave him a sound spanking. As the tearful little tyke was going out the door he turned to Jack and said, "You dirty old married bastard." Jack could barely suppress his laughter.

FRIENDS AND EXHIBITIONS

York was becoming an exponent of palette-knife painting in Toronto. In her review of the OSA's 1944 "Little Pictures Exhibition" at Avon House, Simpsons, Rose Macdonald of the *Telegram* wrote that Syd Hallam and York, "have had a happy and successful time involving the technique of the palette-knife. To the landscape of both it has given character, a sort of 'juiciness.'"

Jack Bush and York often sketched together. In 1944, the Women's Art Association invited them to exhibit together in their gallery on Prince Arthur Avenue in Toronto. One day in 1946, Jack did a quick little pencil sketch of York sketching at Thorold, Ontario, which he kindly gave to York shortly before his death in 1977. The AGO borrowed it for their 1985 exhibition, "Jack Bush: Early Work."

York sent *Burlesk No. 3* (1944) to the Canadian Group of Painters (CGP) exhibition at the AGT in 1944. The painting, which showed, through the open door of a dressing room, a burlesque actress applying makeup, near two other actresses descending the stairs, was reproduced in *Saturday Night*. York did the sketch for this painting at "Casino," one of Toronto's famous burlesque houses. The comedian Phil Silvers helped persuade the actresses to stand still while York quickly sketched. Robert Alda and Gypsy Rose Lee were other entertainers York encountered in Toronto's two burlesque houses of that period.

The University of Toronto invited York to mount a show at Hart House in the autumn of 1944. For this exhibition, his first at Hart House, he installed thirty-seven paintings. The reviewer for *The Varsity* (October 1944), the university newspaper, singled out *Zoot Suits and Gypsies* (1944), *Public Library* (1943) and *Burning Twitches* (1944) for special mention, and declared *Street in a Dimout* as "one of the finest works in the whole of Canadian art."

York was invited to speak at a luncheon on October 11. He later told me the students were a tough audience who put him on the hot seat. He was very honest and articulated clearly his views on the very essence of art. I often noticed how well he was able to engage his audience, giving them a glimmer of art's many meanings. He had a rare vision and did much for art, not only in Canada, but in the many countries we visited.

Among our friends were some fascinating characters, including most members of the Group of Seven. A.Y. Jackson, who later purchased York's *Banana Grove* (1949), often praised York's work in public. Our daughter Virginia was often seated on Arthur Lismer's knee while he taught children's art classes at the AGT. Arthur might argue fiercely with York at a particular art society meeting, but during a break would put his arm around him affectionately, as if to say, "Underneath it all, we're friends." J.E.H. MacDonald's son, Thoreau, was a friend whose woodcuts York admired. In later years Frank Carmichael became a good friend. Although York hadn't appreciated having to redo the lettering jobs while working under Carmichael at Sampson and Matthews, he later realised this practice had greatly improved his lettering ability.

After Fred Housser, author of *A Canadian Art Movement: The Story of the Group of Seven* (1926), lost his wife Bess to Lawren Harris, he married Yvonne McKague. Yvonne was an interesting, lively redhead and good painter. She later purchased *Whirling Dervish* (1976). Yvonne and Isabel McLaughlin spent much time together painting and studying in Paris. They were lifelong friends until Yvonne's death in 1996.

Fred Varley painted and drew many excellent portraits, including a drawing of Reva (Silverman) Brooks, an acclaimed photographer and wife of the Canadian painter Leonard Brooks. Varley's colour was always unusual and creative.

FRANZ JOHNSTON

Before our marriage, York had spent much time with Franz (Frank) and Florence Johnston because he was attracted to their daughter Wenawae. York soon became quite a favourite with the family. Franz was a little irresponsible with money; when he was to receive a cheque, Florence sent some of the children along to bring him directly home. It sometimes worked in reverse, and they would all come home outfitted in new clothes! Franklin (Archie) Arbuckle, then a promising young artist, was smitten with Wenawae's sister Frances Anne, herself an accomplished painter. The men became engaged to Franz's daughters before my time.

York and Wenawae were once engaged; I learned of this shortly before York and I were married.

Franz believed in Christian Science, but if he were seriously ill he would read the writings of Mary Baker Eddy and also call in the doctor. He once had a serious abscess, fatal if it should break inwardly. After the doctor's visit, Franz insisted York stay with him all night, talking and holding his hand until the crisis was over. York listened all night to some of Mary Baker Eddy, followed by a little pleading with God. Toward morning the abscess broke outwardly and subsided, and York was allowed to go home.

York remembered when the Schultz exhibition came to the Eaton's Fine Art Gallery. Franz spent a great deal of time studying Schultz's snow scenes, intrigued that they sold so well and at such high prices. Franz decided that if he painted a few snow scenes, enough to earn some money, he would return to his own painting. They began to sell so well, even at higher prices; the painting of snow scenes sadly became his established practice.

MORE EXHIBITIONS

In the mid 1940s, Eaton's Fine Art Galleries showed interesting exhibitions which featured top artists. Two memorable directors were René Cera and later Richard van Valkenburg. Fourteen artists from Toronto, Montreal and Québec City were invited to present their work in "Adventures in Art," a group show held there in October of 1944. Rose Macdonald of the *Telegram* (October 4, 1944) wrote that York had "the most catholic variegation in style. We find here some of his street scenes which are such keen and often amusing character studies, and we find also the most charming, luminous landscapes in quite lyric vein." Amidst the "alarums and excursions" of this display, wrote Pearl McCarthy in the *Globe and Mail* was *National Affairs* (1942), "a well-executed piece of genre by York Wilson."

The 1944 OSA exhibition was shown at the *Musée de la Province de Québec*; a selection from there went to Cornell University, including York's *Lovely Ladies of the Ensemble* (1944), a group of 'lovelies' at a local burlesque house. The 65th RCA exhibition at the AGT in 1944 included York's *Pie Social at Willisville* (1944). This painting was done from a scene York observed one evening at Willisville, in the La Cloche area, where he had come across a pie social in progress. Women were arriving by boat, pies in hand, walking up in the dark to the well-lit schoolhouse. The La Cloche region was the greatest distance York had travelled in Ontario to sketch. Parts of the area were surrounded by water, which made it unusually exciting, and he found it comforting to see evidence of members of the Group of Seven, who had cleaned their brushes on the rocks.

THE GIRLS

Florence Wyle and Frances Loring were two American sculptors who had spent time together in Paris, and had settled in Toronto. They were founding members of the Sculptors' Society of Canada (SSC) in 1928. They purchased an old church at 110 Glenrose Avenue; the basement provided living quarters for them and their cats. They had little money but always had time and food to help young sculptors like Dora de Pédery-Hunt and Francis Gage. Florence did beautiful woodcarvings; including lovely nudes carved from sumach wood, such as *Spring* (c.1951). Wyle and Loring were referred to as "The Girls" and we, among many others, enjoyed delicious meals at their long dining table. Frances was very feminine, with her long hair rolled into a bun. She later became extremely plump, while Florence remained slim and mannish, with cropped hair. Lilias Torrance Newton, the Montreal portraitist, did a fine portrait of Frances for the 1944 OSA "Artist Paints Artists" exhibition at the AGT. The portrait now hangs at the Women's Art Association gallery on Prince Arthur Avenue in Toronto. Lilias occasionally used York's studio when she had a Toronto commission.

Florence asked York if he would trade a sketch for one of her works. He was delighted to do so, and when they came to dinner Florence brought three or four carvings, each covered with a silk stocking. York chose one and Florence chose York's *Acambay, Queretaro, Mexico* (1950). The oil sketch is now in the London Public Library and Art Museum. Florence and Frances gave one of Frances' large white, clay tablets incised with a bird design to our daughter Virginia as a wedding gift.

The church, left in their will to the RCA, was sold to create a foundation which now serves many good causes, sometimes assisting elderly artists but mainly giving money to public art galleries to purchase art. Cleeve Horne, with Maxwell Henderson as treasurer and Meredith Fleming as legal adviser wisely managed this RCA Trust Fund. Two recent artists' bequests have added considerably to the foundation.

WAR WORK

During World War II, A.Y. Jackson conceived of the idea of producing silkscreen prints made from Canadian paintings to decorate officers' messes at home and abroad. He enlisted the support of the National Gallery of Canada; A.J. Casson oversaw the production of the 30" x 40" prints at Sampson and Matthews, where he was artistic director. York's *Auction Sale, Belfountain* was chosen. The print featured a brief biography and a caption which extolled York's picture as, "a faithful record, painted with insight and sympathy, of that rural civilisation which is still the proud and invaluable background of our country."

York received a letter dated August 30, 1944 from the office of the Minister of National Defence saying, "You have made a very generous gift of your talents," and that the prints would "bring beauty and colour into quarters where brightness is highly desirable." After the war ended, the prints began to appear in banks, schools and community centres. As recently as 1985, Christine Boyanoski of the Art Gallery of Ontario (AGO), requested one of York's prints. I wasn't too anxious to comply, as York had long since graduated from realism to pure abstraction. I saw in retrospect, however, that *Auction Sale, Belfountain* represents a certain period in York's long, slow drive to abstraction.

YOUNG HOPEFULS IN THE ART WORLD

Hedley and Ursula Rainnie, handsome and interesting artists fresh from England, soon became involved in the local art scene. The theme for the special section of the 1944 OSA exhibition was "Artists Paint Artists." Rose Macdonald of the *Telegram* felt that York's and Hedley's portraits of each other were informal, clever and "intimately alive." Paul Duval, art critic for *Saturday Night* (April 8, 1944), commented on the wide range of techniques evident in the show, "from the competent ultra-conservatism of Kenneth Forbes' portrait of Fred H. Brigden to the gay modernism of Yvonne McKague's double-portrait of Rody Kenny Courtice and the palette-knife expressionism of York Wilson." York's portrait of Hedley ended up in the collection of the Sarnia Public Library and Art Gallery, now called Gallery Lambton. Hedley, displeased with his portrait of York, destroyed it and planned to paint another. Sadly he never got around to it.

Hedley and Ursula became part of a group that included Lister and Alice Sinclair, John and Claire Drainie, Bernie and Barbara Braden, and ourselves. No one had much money, but the Sinclairs had a fine collection of classical music albums stored in boxes on the floor. We spent many pleasant hours listening to music there. Their downtown apartment was small and bare; a curtained-off section of the living room served as the bathroom. Hedley and Ursula had a small downtown apartment consisting of two studios.

The members of our group gradually dispersed. After a few years, the Rainnies left for New York, where Hedley did more acting and radio work than painting. They eventually returned to England where Hedley soon died because of his asthma, the main reason he had emigrated to Canada. John Drainie, a well-known actor, also died young, leaving Claire and his daughter, the eminent columnist Bronwyn Drainie. Bernie and Barbara moved to England, where Bernie hosted a popular program on the BBC and Barbara worked as a stage actress.

When Bernie's mother died, Bernie felt his father was spending far too much time at her grave, and asked York for a posthumous portrait, which York completed in 1948. He was rewarded with a letter from Reverend Braden, who wrote from Vancouver to say, "You have given me back my wife." York later did a portrait of the Reverend in 1950, after his death. Bernie was pleased to have these reminders of his parents.

York and I at home at
28 Hambly Avenue. Toronto,
c. 1936-43.

IV

1945-1946

Gains in Toronto; Trips North and East

IN 1945 YORK'S *Embarrassment* (1945), *Reflections* (1945) and the satirical *Head Table* (1945) were accepted for the OSA spring exhibition at the AGT. *Head Table* won the J.W.L. Forster Award ($100) for "the best subject painting." The *Telegram* art critic called it a "devastatingly clever satire," and the "most astute satirical comment in the show." *Head Table* was shown again, along with *The March Past* (1945) in the 65th RCA exhibition at the Art Association of Montreal. *New World Illustrated* (October 1945) published reproductions of *Welfare Worker* and *Head Table*. *The March Past*, which depicted a crowd discussing its bets at the old Woodbine Race Track in Toronto, was a favourite of Paul Duval's, who hung it in his studio until it was purchased by the Beaverbrook Gallery in 1959.

York was elected an Associate of the RCA in 1945. The ageing president was Ernest Fosbery, with the elderly Edmond Dyonnet as secretary. Dyonnet brought a large trunk filled with RCA documents to meetings. He would fish through the trunk looking for the required item, and then bang the lid down. York couldn't resist making a few quick sketches of these two dear "elderlies" plodding through RCA business.

"So-Ed," a Brantford art program of "social education" directed by the YMCA and YWCA, invited York in April to speak, do a painting demonstration, and judge their work. At this 1945 meeting, York painted a portrait of Frances Anita Kaminski, a woman selected from the audience. He painted her likeness in oils, explaining as he went, and stopping periodically to answer questions. Ms. Kaminski was presented with the completed portrait.

York's work was included in a group show with John Alfsen, Hedley Rainnie and William Winter at Eaton's Fine Art Galleries in April of 1945. The reviewer for the *Telegram* (April 16, 1945) noted York's landscapes, and decided his ballet scenes were, "his top-ranking canvases, these not altogether beyond the experimental stage, but sometimes brilliant in the solutions at which the artist has arrived."

York's approach to ballet was entirely his own. He always took front seats at ballet performances, often at Toronto's Royal Alexandra Theatre, making sketches, and hiring his own models. He had a great love of and real feeling for the ballet, which resulted in some colourful and unique work, such as *Beginners* (1948), *Ballerina* (1949), and *Ballerina Resting* (1951). Within two or three years York was defeated, as his ballet scenes became too popular. Some so-called art critics, misunderstanding York's intent, labelled these works "saleable," and "sweet." When people started to tell York that they would purchase his next—as yet unpainted—dance picture, he decided in 1951 that he had painted his last ballet picture.

"Postdimensions," the special section of the 1945 OSA exhibition, caused quite a stir. When the show travelled to London, York declared that viewers should not attempt to explain the meaning of a picture until they had studied it for at least fifteen minutes. Ironically, a local reviewer wrote in the London *Spectator* (April 20, 1945) that York's *Embarrassment*, all thumbs, clumsy hands and feet, was "one of the few modern pieces that the average individual could understand."

York was invited by the University of Toronto in March 1945 to demonstrate his palette-knife technique. York's portrait *Stanley S. Cooper* (1945) was included in the Canadian Society of Painters in Water Colour (CSPWC) exhibition, which toured to the Willistead Art Gallery in Windsor. The painting's "rich colours, good skin tone, and discerning characterisation" were mentioned in the *Windsor Daily Star* (July 7, 1945). York later gave the portrait to Stan, who did not like it, and may have even destroyed it. I tried to reach Stan's daughter after his death in order to locate the work, but my efforts were not successful.

Saturday Night Hop (1945), an animated dance group, and *Bus Stop* (1945), which shows a queue at a bus stop, were accepted for the CGP exhibition at the AGT in 1945. In March, the AGT ran a "Quiz Program" with a panel of experts: Florence Wyle (sculpture), the cellist Boris Hambourg (music) and York (painting). It was a lively evening with good questions. In 1949, York did an excellent India ink drawing of Boris, a founding member of the Hart House String Quartet.

Things were moving fast for York. He had risen quickly to very responsible positions in the OSA and RCA. It was obvious he was a natural leader who had much to offer. He stopped there, however, convinced that he should focus on painting. His leadership was thus expressed in his innovative paintings.

More exhibitions followed. The University of Toronto held a solo exhibition of York's work at Victoria College in 1945. Following the OSA exhibition in the spring, the London Public Library and Art Museum displayed eighteen of his paintings through the summer. He was invited to take part in an exhibition at the Women's Art Association in October and November; he sent seven paintings.

EXERCISE MUSKOX

In 1945, York heard about "Exercise Muskox," a government-sponsored initiative to test clothing and materials in the Canadian Arctic. York let it be known he was anxious to participate in this expedition. His friends at *Liberty* magazine chose York as their press representative, and made arrangements with the government to have his expenses paid. J. Tuzo Wilson, the well-known geophysicist, was appointed captain, York was official artist and Gilbert (Gib) Milne was official photographer. York and Gib tested their materials in a large, walk-in refrigerator in Toronto. Gib discovered that the oil in his cameras congealed and slowed the shutter. York found that the cold temperatures caused his oil paints to solidify; he decided to sketch in pencil outdoors and use watercolours inside.

York took the train to Gimli, Manitoba and then boarded a Hercules plane for expedition headquarters in Churchill. The unheated plane had metal seats, and York learned he was regarded as excess baggage, space being at a premium. He was squeezed between loose oil barrels, which slid around and pressed against him at times. When trying to land, the plane circled repeatedly in a raging blizzard. An experienced worker said quietly, "I will be glad to land." Another commented, "I will be glad if we land." Great comfort for a novice like York.

Once on ground, York was assigned to the officers' mess and promptly informed of the rules of survival in the Arctic. Gib and York had arranged a few commissions to augment their time on the expedition. York had arranged with the Provincial Paper Company to do some portraits later at one of their lumber camps. Exide Batteries supplied Gib with a giant thermometer, hoping to gain some publicity. The first morning, Gib hurried out to position and photograph this thermometer. When he checked it later, the mercury had shot right out the top. York, also out that morning, found it difficult to manoeuvre his pencil with his thick fur mitts, and had to hurry inside to record his impressions. During this chance visit to the Arctic, York hoped to beg space in the plane when supplies were being transferred north to Eskimo Point. When they reached the site by plane after a day of delay caused by bad weather, a ferocious blizzard prevented their landing. Only the supplies were dropped to the site. The plane returned to Churchill. An unhappy York missed his only opportunity to visit Eskimo Point.

The officers invented games to entertain themselves. In the mess some evenings, they would stand on the bar, drink in hand, and do a somersault to the floor, hopefully without spilling a drop. It was probably inspired by the generous rum rations. A makeshift theatre showed films. There were no seats, and the men stood around a great, solid mound of ice in the middle of the room.

"Mammas" was the only eating establishment, and Mamma decided where you could sit, even separating friends. If you protested, she would say, "If you don't like it, get out." One evening York was sitting next to Artie Oman, a man of mixed Inuit and Scottish descent. Artie, through subtle hinting, invited York to his home, a small one-room wooden shack, lined with paper to keep out the wind. The room contained one big bed, a table and little else. He met Artie's wife, three children and his wife's parents, all living in this small space. The south-facing side of the cabin was open. They were beyond the tree line; further south was the "banana belt." They sat and talked on the edge of the bed while York did a few sketches.

Always looking for new experiences, York persuaded Gib to spend the night in an igloo. They were given instructions to keep an oil lamp burning for warmth, as the Inuit did. One of them knocked it over during the night, and they had to return to the barracks. Another time, they listened to stories about the wonderful experience of having a sauna, dashing out in the nude and diving into the snow. Of course they had to do this, but made the mistake of not testing the snow beforehand. Not only did the snow have a hard crust, but there was an old hinged door hidden under the snow. They both limped indoors, grazed and bloodied.

Gib took many official photos of the terrain, people in their parkas, and the snowmobiles. York filled a couple of sketchbooks and did many small watercolours, including *Muskox Gnomes* (1945). He decided on walrus teeth and tusks as souvenirs, dismissing animal pelts in case they were not properly cured. On York's return, he was invited to relate his experiences on the CBC program "Cavalcade" and in the newspapers.

Back in his Toronto studio York painted many larger oils; *Arctic, Muskox Do* (1945) went to Jim Harris of *Liberty* magazine.

While en route home, York took the train, as directed by the Provincial Paper Company, to a certain station, where he was met in the middle of the night. They drove for some time, finally arriving at a lumber camp deep in the bush. All was silent and dark, as everyone had gone to bed. He was taken to a sleeping cabin, where his guide pointed to an empty bunk and shut the door. Two other men were already sleeping in nearby bunks. Early the next morning, he discovered his companions were German prisoners of war. York thus found himself at a top-secret POW camp, where the prisoners were employed cutting and preparing trees.

The management soon put York in touch with his prospective subjects, three camp bosses. He did their portraits and was off again in a couple of days. The portraits appeared on the covers of the monthly trade magazine *Provincial's Paper*, in January, March, April and October of 1946.

A SKETCHING TRIP IN EASTERN CANADA

In the summer of 1945, we went on a sketching trip to the east coast of Canada with Virginia and her dog Suzi Q in our old second hand jalopy. Québec was very exciting to us—the shapes and colours of the barns, the horse-drawn carriages, the haystacks, the challenge of coping with the language. When York saw something he wanted to sketch, we would stop. I remember sketches depicting such subjects as a horse-drawn carriage in the rain, the Laurentians, and the rock at Percé, and one titled *On the Road To Ste.-Cecile-de-Masham* (1945).

Next we crossed into New Brunswick, where we were astounded to find so many unpainted wood houses. We learned that unpainted wood lasted longer in the salty sea air. I remember the illusion of Magnetic Hill outside Moncton; we put the car in neutral and it seemed to back up the hill!

Along the coast of Nova Scotia York made many sketches at Peggy's Cove, Indian Harbour, Lunenburg and St. Mary's Bay. When the tide went out at Digby there was a great roar—"the Bore"—when the basin was calm. Suzi Q fell into the deep basin in her excitement. We needn't have panicked, as she swam safely to shore. On the way back we crossed briefly into Maine, and then continued on to Montreal.

We had been visiting many art galleries during the trip. While at the Dominion Gallery in Montreal, Mrs. Millman, the proprietor, asked to see York's sketches, and purchased one entitled *Carleton Place* (1945). This was a tremendous help, as our money was depleted from replacing our wartime tires with used tires every few miles.

BACK HOME IN TORONTO

The 74th OSA exhibition opened at the AGT and York sent an Arctic painting, *Forty-Six Below* (1945), and a portrait of *Jack Kent Cooke* (1946), then the owner of the profitable Toronto radio station CKEY. York painted Jack sitting at the piano with his music spread around him on the floor. The *Globe and Mail* critic thought it a "particularly clever portrait not in the formal manner," while in *World Views* (May 1946), it was said that, "York Wilson captured the mood and character of the sitter in a way that formal portraits could never do."

Jack Cooke assisted the OSA because of our long friendship. We were both from the Beaches area and when we lived in Armour Heights, the Cookes owned a house in the field north of us near the Toronto Cricket Club. Jack had sold his partnership interests with Roy Thomson in order to buy radio station CKEY from the Gooderhams. He had mortgaged and borrowed heavily in order to complete the deal. One night at 2:00 A.M. the station was transferred to Jack's ownership. We waited in the garden to celebrate the big event.

With no money to furnish the station offices, Jack went to the Robert Simpson Company and persuaded them to furnish his offices and give him their account. He invented the singing commercial, which he patented and franchised to other stations. He never looked back. He was now ensconced in a sumptuous Bayview Avenue home with his wife Jean, who had misgivings about Jack's ambition. She didn't want him to become wealthy and was happy as they were, but nothing would hold her husband back.

The 67th Royal Canadian Academy exhibition held at the AGT in 1946 included York's *Young Dancer* (1946) and *Indian Harbour* (1946). Viscount Alexander, Governor General of Canada, and his wife Lady Margaret Alexander came to open the exhibition. The RCA committee planned a dinner for the special guests at the Arts and Letters Club before the opening. It was learned that the Viscount enjoyed Irish whisky, so a bottle was found and taken to the club. A fine dinner was prepared, to which I contributed strawberry-filled meringues.

Dinner conversation flowed easily, as the Viscount was also an artist, and an amiable man. He was pleased to be in our Arts and Letters Club with his favourite tipple. On hearing that I was studying Spanish, Lady Alexander said she was too, but admitted feeling stupid in trying to converse. After dinner she complimented me on the meringues. When it came time to leave for the gallery, I was elected to carry the bottle under my cape. After an interesting opening speech the Viscount mingled with the artists discussing their paintings. Pearl McCarthy's *Globe and Mail* (November 23, 1946) review was appropriately titled, "Alexander Turns Critic at Academy."

York during his stint as official artist for Exercise Muskox. Churchill, Manitoba, 1945. Photograph by Gilbert A. Milne.

V

1946-1949

Return to the Arctic

THE MID-1940S CONTINUED to be a busy and productive time for York's work and career. The Willistead Gallery in Windsor held an exhibition of the work of York, John Alfsen and William Winter, opening in May, 1946. Several of York's Arctic works—*Muskox Gnomes, January at Churchill* (1945) and *Storm Clouds, Pogh Lake* (1946)—were included. The *Windsor Daily Star* (May 11, 1946) called York "a versatile clever painter, with sound technique and plenty of imagination." These same painters, with John Hall, showed their work at the Eaton's Fine Art Galleries in March of 1946, where they were presented as "Four Moderate Moderns."

The *Canadian Review of Music and Art* featured Hedley Rainnie's portrait of York on the cover of the October-November 1946 edition. York was the subject of C.L. Hutchings' lead article, "A Canadian Painter in Seven League Boots." Reproductions of *Indian Harbour, Head Table, Burlesk No. 2* (1938) and *Fourteen* (1944) accompanied the text. York received a great compliment from Graham McInnes, who wrote in an article on the Canadian Group of Painters in *Canadian Art* (February 1946) that the paintings of York and William Winter demonstrated "a certain timeless quality one normally expects to find only in a painter like [Edward] Hopper."

York was invited to deliver a lecture to the Women's Art Association of Hamilton. In his speech, reported in the *Hamilton Spectator*, York "blamed the fact of Canada having no place in the world of painters on this country's neglect of her people's talent and the lack of financial support to encourage leadership in this field." York presented an informal retrospective of the past three centuries of Canadian art, showing slides of representative works of forty-five Canadian painters.

In 1946, Dr. O.S. Pokorny of Sarnia gave York's *Port Daniel, Quebec* (1945) to the Sarnia Public Library and Art Gallery. Dr. Pokorny became a devoted collector of York's work; his 1946 donation marked the beginning of Sarnia's large and important Wilson collection.

Special effort was expended in the staging and touring of the OSA's 75th anniversary exhibition in 1947, to which York contributed *Backstage* (1946), *Telegraph Messengers* (1947) and *Ontario Village* (1947). Both a hard- and soft-cover catalogue were printed. The Honourable Raymond Lawson, Ontario's Lieutenant Governor, opened the show. York followed with his presidential address, and we hosted a supper for OSA members at our home that evening. York led exhibition tours at the AGT and opened the exhibition when it toured to St. Thomas. The show was installed at numerous Ontario venues; a selection was also shown in Manitoba, Alberta and British Columbia. The extra travelling stretched the small government grant, but increased catalogue sales and members' fees helped.

Both *The Standard* (March 1947) and *Canadian Art* (May 1947) reproduced York's *Backstage*, a work that Pearl McCarthy of the *Globe and Mail* thought, "brilliantly painted—a case where Mr. York Wilson's verve really came off." The *Evening Telegram* published a picture of York and Jack Bush painting in their studios and noted that the work of both men had "added very considerably to the distinction of OSA and other exhibitions in more recent years." Augustus Bridle wrote in the *Toronto Daily Star* (March 9, 1947) that when the OSA celebrated its 100th anniversary, the AGT would have to be enlarged! Such coverage hints at what artists can do when they have the support of their art galleries. Never had Canadians been so conscious of the visual arts and their art galleries.

York gained acclaim for his stage set designs for "The Mighty Mr. Samson," a play written by Virginia Coyne Knight and directed by W.S. Milne, in a performance by the Arts and Letters Club at Hart House Theatre for the Central Ontario Drama Festival in the spring of 1947. York's sets were favourably reviewed in the *Telegram* and *Globe and Mail* (March 28, 1947), where Pearl McCarthy reported that the noted English actor and critic Robert Speaight claimed that, "the best performance was undoubtedly given by the scenery," and that York was in his opinion, "one of three or four in Canada who have no betters anywhere in the world."

York sent the humorous satire *Beauty Contest* (1946) to the RCA's 68th annual exhibition, held in Montreal in late 1947. *Beauty Contest* was inspired by the many times York had been asked to judge such contests; the painting is now in the Winnipeg Art Gallery collection. *Young Ladies* (1947) went to the CGP exhibition, shown at the AGT in 1947 and in Montreal in 1948. The painting was reproduced in the exhibition catalogue and in *Saturday Night* (December 13, 1947) and later purchased by

Branksome Hall, a private girls school in Toronto. *Open Air Market* (1947), a watercolour York exhibited with the CSPWC at the AGT, was highlighted in the *Toronto Daily Star* as "an animated market scene" by a "lively and usually good-natured observer of humanity."

THE AGT WOMEN'S COMMITTEE

York and I took a motor trip to the United States around 1947. One rewarding discovery on that trip was a visit to the Philadelphia Museum, where we saw a large exhibition of the French Impressionists. Some of the artists had a complete room to themselves, an advantage in evaluating their work. The collection made a lasting impression on me, although I've now seen many great museums in the world.

Among the cities we visited was Cleveland, Ohio. At the Cleveland Museum of Art, we had a big surprise. The rooms were so crowded that it was difficult to see the exhibition, which included paintings, sculpture, crafts, ceramics and jewellery. The next surprise was that most of the work was already sold! It turned out that the Cleveland Museum had a Women's Committee, which had devised clever promotional schemes to support local artists. The buyers from a similar exhibition the previous year, for example, were given first purchasing priority the next year.

We brought the news back to the AGT, where it fell luckily on the interested ears of women like Lady Kemp, Mrs. Walter Gordon and Mrs. George Hendry. A group visited Cleveland, returned with all the necessary information, and started the first Women's Committee at the AGT, with York as adviser. Other art galleries across Canada followed suit. This promotion by Women's Committees made a big difference, as committee exhibitions made Canadians conscious of work by their own artists. The committee reserved a small percentage of sales and worked diligently behind the scenes, raising funds through events such as gourmet luncheons and art costume balls. One innovation was the silent auction, where bids were dropped in a box placed before each work, with a draw occurring on the final evening.

Eye-catching manufactured goods were made available for sale in a gift shop at the AGT entrance. Connie Matthews, a Board member, asked me to work in the shop on a time-share basis. I found little interest in the manufactured items and said, "If we had Canadian crafts to sell, I would be delighted." Connie said, "Oh we can't make any money on Canadian crafts." A few weeks later, she decided to give me a chance.

I took on the job, knowing the craftspeople had nowhere to exhibit their work. I searched out artisans across the country, starting with local potters like the Sadowskis, Harlanders and others. They told me about weavers, jewellers, and gave me the names of their contemporaries across the country. The shop was redone with glass cases, shelves and new lighting. Fine Canadian crafts immediately piqued much interest; where else could you find so much quality work in one place? The Gallery management was pleased; they permitted us to use the sculpture court for two big sales each year. Members and their friends flocked to these sales and the merchandise quickly disappeared, especially before Christmas. It was a new thing for many to purchase handmade goods and meet the artists. By 1949, Paul Duval reported in *Saturday Night* (November 15, 1949) that the success of that year's sale was "evidence of increasing active interest in art among Canadian laymen."

This was the beginning of the magnificent gift shop found at today's Art Gallery of Ontario. I had two assistants, Helen Watson, wife of the painter and OCA principal Syd Watson, and the sculptor Jean Horne, as well as gallery members like Signe Eaton, who put her car and chauffeur at my disposal to pick up works out of town. Back in the 1950s, the art societies, artists and their spouses worked closely with gallery staff. We were all one big family. My involvement in the gift shop continued happily until 1960, when York and I left for an extended sojourn to Paris.

I had gained some experience selling as a member of the Toronto Symphony Orchestra Women's Committee, working on their annual rummage sale. I founded and started the "Picture Department," a popular part of the sale with some astounding bargains. It wasn't unusual to find works by the Group of Seven and other prominent Canadian artists, which brought in big sums like $40! York and Cleeve Horne would appear at dinner time with a little drink and sandwich to revive Jean and myself. When the pictures were not all sold as the end of the sale neared, York and Cleeve, full of devilment, acted as hucksters, calling out special items, steering customers into our booth and creating much fun and excitement.

RETURN NORTH

In 1947, Standard Oil of New Jersey commissioned York to record the mammoth task of moving their refinery from Whitehorse to Edmonton. The whole refinery was to be dismantled and moved over the Alaska

Highway by truck. The operation occurred in winter, as an ice bridge had
to be built over the Teslin River to support the forty-ton digester.

York joined the convoy in a taxi; the entire trip cost $75! When the
digester moved off the highway to detour on to the ice bridge, it rolled off
the specially-built truck on which it was being transported. The horror-
struck team tried every device possible and finally managed to manoeuvre
it back on to the huge vehicle. It then passed over the ice bridge without
incident and everyone breathed a sigh of relief. All the while, York had
been sketching furiously. His painting, *Point 804 Alaska Highway* (1947)
was the result. Many of the paintings resulting from this trip, including
Teslin Bridge, Alaska Highway (1946), *Near Whitehorse* (1947) and
Dismantling Refinery (1947) are now in the permanent collection of
Standard Oil.

York had many interesting stories to tell on his return. Whitehorse
then consisted of one main street; the building's false fronts made them
seem more impressive. York worked from the window of his hotel in
freezing weather to record this scene. *Main Street, Yukon* (1947), the
resulting oil sketch, was purchased by Don McGibbon, an Imperial Oil
executive, and his wife Pauline, later Lieutenant Governor of Ontario.
Gambling was the main entertainment in town. York met a man who had
just won the entire town on the roll of a dice the previous night. He was
found in the local beauty parlour having his nails done.

The Vancouver photographer, Harry Rowed, recorded the refinery
move on film. He and York spent most of their evenings together. A big,
loveable dog called Bessie befriended them at their Whitehorse hotel. As
the hotel doors had no locks, Bessie would slip in to spend the night with
York or Harry. Years later, Harry had another commission in Whitehorse
and thought to create mischief by sending York a letter saying, "You
remember Bessie, well that little tramp is now sleeping with anyone who
will have her." You should have heard York trying to explain to me that
Bessie was in fact a dog!

In May of 1948, the AGT hosted "Oil," an exhibition of industrial
portraits drawn from the collection of Standard Oil of New Jersey and
arranged for exhibition in Canada by Imperial Oil. Of the twenty-two
artists featured in the show, York and three others, Arthur Lismer, Will
Ogilvie and Don Anderson, represented Canada. Of York's
contributions to the show, *Point 804 Alaska Highway* earned the most
attention.

A 1947 article in the *Telegram*, "Industry Helps Fine Art Earn a Living in Canada," mentioned one of York's paintings done for the 'Moulders of Canada Unlimited" advertising series sponsored by O'Keefe's Brewing Company. The painting was included in the 26th Annual National Exhibition of Advertising and Editorial Art at New York's Metropolitan Museum along with work by artists such as Salvador Dali and Thomas Hart Benton. It was also reproduced in *American Artist* (April 1947), and chosen as one of fifty works in the show to tour the United States.

"Portraits of an Industry," an article appearing later in the *Imperial Oil Review* (October-November 1948), pointed out the potential benefits of uniting art and industry. Each artist was "assigned subject matter sympathetic to his style and medium," and the collection was seen as representing, "a new kind of documentation based on a close relationship between art and industry."

MALTON AIRPORT MURAL, 1948-49

In 1948 York had entered a contest for a mural at the Gander, Newfoundland airport, but he came in second, with Kenneth Lochhead declared the winner. National Gallery director Alan Jarvis, H.O. McCurry's successor, assured York that other commissions would appear.

Before long the airport at Malton, west of Toronto, was to have a new terminal, and York was given a mural commission for the new building. York spent much time researching his working design, and decided that various forms of transportation over the ages would be the theme. When the sketch was presented to the committee, everyone was pleased except Controller Allan Lamport, who balked at the $4500 cost of the 12'6" x 28' mural. The *Globe and Mail* (January 13, 1949) reported Lamport's comment that it was "another case of a champagne taste and a beer pocketbook," and that "there are Toronto artists who would be glad to do it for nothing." During the city council debates, the project was accidentally called a "murial." From then on, the *Telegram* claimed, the mural was doomed.

The fight dragged on into early 1949, with all three Toronto papers reporting more grumbling by the town councillors. Although the Board actually approved York's sketch on January 12, Lamport's objections eventually won out and York never did do the mural. The *Globe and Mail*

(January 14, 1949) carried an article, which recommended the establishment of a cultural fund to finance worthy projects. With such a fund, "such regrettable silliness as the squabble over the mural might have been avoided." The artist Kenneth Forbes argued in favour of York, noting that "murals are important encouragement of art and beauty."

1948, A BUSY YEAR FOR YORK

The year 1948 found York going at a fast pace, which seemed to have become his lot. Toronto's Laing Galleries were now showing York's work regularly. The 76th OSA exhibition at the AGT included an important work of York's, *The Girls* (1946), inspired by the members of our "Thursknit" Club which we had formed years earlier to produce knitted articles for the soldiers during World War II. York found it amusing that we called each other "The Girls," as some club members were quite elderly. We met in each other's homes every Thursday with our finished articles— turtleneck sweaters, balaclava helmets, mittens, socks and other items. When we held fund-raising events, York would donate a painting as a prize. One year my closest friend, Christine Connor won the painting, which rather embarrassed us both, though a legitimate win.

Ross and Bess Hamilton, who founded the Doon School of Fine Art in 1948, invited York to teach there and chair their Board. It was an easy decision when York learned that Fred Varley and Gordon Payne would join him as the school's first teachers. They took their meals together, and spent the evenings talking about art. York, president of the OSA since 1946, was being groomed to succeed A.J. Casson as president of the RCA. Varley advised York not to waste his time on these positions—though prestigious, they were largely administrative and a waste of time for an artist of his talent. York thus turned down the RCA's offer, as well as an opportunity to head the OCA.

When A.J. Casson (Cass) was president of the OSA, York was his vice-president; when York was president, his vice-president was Jack Bush. Jack became ill and had to resign so Cleeve Horne replaced him. York, Cass, and Cleeve served many years on the executives and juries of the art societies, positions elected by the members. When Casson was asked what young artists to buy, Wilson headed the list. York, always out in front presenting something new, was one of the few figure painters of the period.

Preston Bauer of Waterloo purchased *The Girls*. While York was teaching at Doon, Mr. Bauer invited him to see the painting. York was surprised to find it placed on a large table with an *objet d'art* in front, but it looked well. Mr. Bauer had given much thought to placing his works of art. On Mr. Bauer's death, I received a call from a thoughtful man named Albert Miller, who told me he had purchased the painting. Al Rain, our accountant and himself an ardent collector, had asked Mr. Miller to call. Al had long been helpful to me in locating some of York's paintings. I gave him the main drawing for *Local Dance*, in the collection of the AGO.

York also sent paintings to other venues in 1948, including *Red Pyjamas* (1947) to the CNE that summer, *Children of Lac Mercier* (1947) to the First Winter Exhibition of the Hamilton Art Gallery, and a 1948 portrait of our friend Melville (Bud) Feheley disguised as a farmer to the 69th RCA exhibition late in the year. He also participated in a nine-person exhibition at the Gavin Henderson Galleries in Toronto. His delightful portrait of Boris Hambourg appeared in *Mayfair* magazine (March 1948). *Nursing Young Crops in the Garden of Canada* (1948) was one of two paintings created for a commission from the Heinz Company that year. York spent two hot days sketching tomato pickers in Leamington, Ontario.

York was invited to hold a solo exhibition at the Arts and Letters Club in 1948. He was elected to Club membership in 1942, having been proposed by Leonard Brooks, who has resided in Mexico since 1947. York agreed to the exhibition if the lighting and hanging space could be improved, and promptly helped make these changes. He was given credit at the Club for the improvements and also for instigating a jury system, thus raising the quality of the exhibitions.

York was invited to open the 54th exhibition of the Women's Art Association of Hamilton in the spring of 1948. At the gallery, the organisers had decorated the stage with tall plants, ferns and cages of canaries. With the strong lighting on stage, the canaries thought it was morning and started warbling. York, hidden amongst the ferns, became more perturbed as the evening progressed. When he was finally introduced he cut his talk short to give people time to view the exhibition. The evening was really a parody, the equal of George Bernard Shaw's "The Critic."

In the autumn, York had a solo exhibition at Eaton's Fine Art Galleries on College Street. Pearl McCarthy of the *Globe and Mail* (November 5, 1948) wrote that York was making "an artistic advance beyond even the cleverest things he has done in the past," and singled out his ballet studies for special mention. Don and Pauline McGibbon purchased *L'Entrechat* (1948). Rous and Mann Press, an engraving house, reproduced *The March Past* in full colour on their 1948 calendar.

York contributed a watercolour, *Madonna and Child* (1947), to a "Canadian Water Colours" exhibition, held at the National Gallery of Canada in late 1948. The NGC and CSPWC arranged to tour the show to New Zealand, where *Madonna and Child* received an honourable mention. The gallery there planned to purchase it, but a furore developed because people thought the Madonna—clad in shorts, walking down the street, reading a book and holding the hand of a child—far too modern. York had simply painted what he had seen.

1949

Cocktail parties were popular in the late 1940s. The parties were usually held in small living rooms, where people vied for space with big hats and long cigarette holders, then in vogue. This situation amused York so he painted *Cocktail Party* (1949), shown at the 77th OSA exhibition in the spring of 1949. Cleeve Horne devised a new system of voting by a five-person jury, which was first used in this exhibition. The *Evening Telegram* (February 18, 1949) explained how the jury members would, "register their individual vote on the panel of lights behind them by pressing a button, assuring a poll in which none knows how his or her companions have voted."

York taught at the Doon School of Fine Art during the summer of 1949. The prospectus for that year lists York's fellow instructors as Alec Panton, Yvonne McKague Housser and Gordon Payne. A photograph in the brochure shows three of York's students at work at their outdoor easels, not far from the picturesque old mill.

York was made a full member of the Royal Canadian Academy in 1948. He submitted *Dancing Class* (1948) as his diploma work to the 70th RCA exhibition at the Montreal Museum of Fine Arts (MMFA) in late 1949. *Dancing Class* then joined the other RCA diploma works in the permanent collection of the National Gallery of Canada.

In early 1949, York was one of eight people chosen to decorate a room, "the room I'd like to stay home in," at the Robert Simpson Company store in Toronto. The *Globe and Mail* (January 14, 1949) reported that York dreamed up "one of the most original rooms." York was also honoured that year by Cleeve Horne, who made a plaster portrait bust of York, first exhibited at the April 1949 Sculptors' Society of Canada exhibition at the AGT, and later presented to York. One of York's important early works, *Welfare Worker* was included in "Fifty Years of Painting in Canada," a retrospective exhibition held at the AGT in the autumn of 1949.

As I reflect back on the 1940s, I remember the house at 8 Apsley Road. There are so many memories there. Of the men who decorated our recreation room with such originality—A.J. Casson, Syd Hallam, Alec Panton, Cleeve Horne, William Winter, Angus MacDonald, Jack Bush, Sydney Watson and York—all have passed on except Cleeve.

Angel Descending the Stairs (1944), a charming portrayal of our daughter Virginia descending the stairs, was painted at that house. Virginia posed quite often for York at that time; the memorable *Red Pyjamas* was the result of one such sitting.

York (at far right) with students at the Doon School of Fine Art:
Jack Bechtel (standing centre) and John Labonte-Smith (standing right).
Doon, Ontario, late 1940s.

VI

1949-1951

Introduction to Mexico

THE YEAR 1949 HERALDED A BIG CHANGE in our lives. Leonard Brooks, an official war artist from 1944-45, took advantage of funding for veterans' study, and moved to Mexico with his wife Reva in 1947. Back in Toronto for a visit, he gave an enticing picture of Mexico to York during lunch one day at the Arts and Letters Club. York decided that we were going to Mexico as soon as we could get ready. That evening we began discussing arrangements.

Was this the moment to give up commercial art and try to live on painting alone? Only A.Y. Jackson, a bachelor, had been able to do this, and relatives and friends supported him. Would our savings last six months? Could we get by on the $1,500 that Canadians were then allowed to take out of the country? Could Virginia be taken out of school for six months? What about Suzi Q? We threw caution to the wind, and laid plans to depart in September of 1949, only a month later.

When Standard Oil of New Jersey heard of our plans, they contacted us to see if York would stop off in New York to do a little job. Our money problem was thus solved. Rose and Don Pringle, our neighbours, agreed to look after Suzi Q for six months. Bit by bit everything fell into place, and I rented out our house for six months.

Cleeve and Jean Horne gave us a send-off at their home. As people arrived, women were sent one way and men the other. The women emerged wearing *rebozos* (a long scarf draped over the head) and some were in bare feet. The men had rolled-up trousers, bare feet, and wore *serapes* (a poncho-like blanket with a centre slit for the head) and sombreros. The model stand in Cleeve's studio became a throne for us. It was decorated with iguana skins, *rebozos*, and *serapes*. There were three chairs, with a small chamber pot beside each in which our drinks would be served. The food, so hot that it burned our mouths, was supposed to prepare us for Mexico.

A.J. (Cass) and Margaret Casson appeared a little late. People were already eating, but Cass descended the long stairs into Cleeve's studio, clad in sombrero and *serape*, drink in hand. They were handed plates of food, and all eyes were on Cass as he took his first bite. He quietly announced, "If anyone would like to light a cigarette, I will breathe on it."

THE DRIVE SOUTH

En route at last in our car, we sang most of the way, we were so happy. In New York we settled into the Wellington Hotel and York called Standard Oil. He started working in the hotel room in watercolour, using a drinking glass as his water bowl. He wanted to be alone, so Virginia and I spent the day at the Bronx Zoo. We returned to find York getting along well and set to finish by noon the next day. Pushed out the next morning, we stayed in Central Park until noon. Returning at midday, York had just finished and was cleaning up. He was so excited that he grabbed his brush-cleaning glass and took a long drink! He delivered the job to Standard Oil right after lunch, and returned in high spirits with a cheque for $1,500. He cashed the cheque, and we hid the money and checked out.

It took an exasperatingly long time to get out of New York, but we stepped on the gas as soon as we hit the highway. I watched the route from our map, but the names of places turning up were not those marked! It was nearly time for supper, and we decided to have a celebration drink and a bite to eat. We discussed our route with the manager and suddenly realised that we had been heading back to Canada! It was such an inauspicious start, and we still had three thousand miles to go.

Through the Kentucky Hills, we saw actual hillbillies and wondered if they had stills in them thar hills! We were amazed at Louisiana's swamp land, with so much bird and animal life and Spanish moss hanging from the trees. The turnoff for New Orleans was tempting, but our goal was Mexico. Arkansas' cotton plantations appeared before our eyes. In Texas, the land of wonders, we saw tall cowboys with big hats and drove straight, flat highways for miles. Navajo Indians were selling their wares along the edge of the highway.

We settled for the night at Laredo, ready to cross the border in the morning. At the motel, there were trees with real oranges and we had to touch them. Huge brightly-coloured parrots were eager for conversation. At bedtime I thought I saw something move on the white sheets, so I investigated and found the biggest black insect I had ever seen. Other cockroaches were jumping in and out of my purse. We went in search of the management, who promised to spray right away. We spent an uneasy night and were up before daybreak. We later learned that it was far more unusual to find a place without cockroaches.

After crossing the border we found the scruffy little towns on the other side so different. Our Spanish consisted of a few poorly pronounced phrases. We knew that we must not drink the water or have salads, so we had beer and cooked foods, mostly boiled eggs. Driving down the Pan American highway towards Mexico City we passed distant thatched huts, but only rarely did we see figures amongst the bushes. We passed small towns and late in the day came to Ciudad Victoria, where we stopped for the night.

We learned from other tourists that we were about to have a day's drive in the mountains, with very tortuous and dangerous curves. We could not leave before 10:00 A.M. because the mist was heavy. However, it was a beautiful experience in these lovely mountains, with tremendous drops without protective barriers! The colours and forms greatly excited York, and at one point, the car radio was playing Bach, one of his favourites. This thrilling moment led to the painting *Bach in the Mountains* (1949). Coming out of the mountains towards evening, we entered the small town of Querétaro.

Starting out next morning we tried asking directions of peasants on the road or in the fields, but most seemed afraid of strangers and ran away. We finally saw a priest. We stopped and carefully asked, "Buenos dias, por favor, donde está San Miguel de Allende?" He answered in English, "This is San Miguel de Allende, where did you want to go?" Hearing English was such a shock that we thought we were beginning to understand Spanish! We had stopped just outside the town. We found John and Florence Johnson's house at Sollano 35, where Leonard and Reva were staying temporarily. Allen and Peggy Smart were staying with them while house hunting. Allen, a professor of English at Ohio University, had written a book-of-the-month selection, *R.F.D.* (1938). He later wrote *Viva Juarez!* (1963), a book on Benito Pablo Juárez, Mexico's first Indian president.

GETTING SETTLED

The Brooks' had a house ready for us on Calle Recreo. Complete with maid and gardener, it cost U.S.$50 a month. A two-acre estate built by an American, we learned later it was one of the best in town. Matilda, our maid, occupied the entrance house on the property. The gardener had a house out back and made his living growing produce on the land.

The stunning mansion had black tile floors, white leather furniture and sterling silver flatware. There were three bedrooms with baths. York quickly claimed the largest bedroom facing the mountains as his studio. We took the front bedroom in the other wing, with Virginia's adjoining. There was a large swimming pool with an overhanging pecan tree.

After we settled, we returned to the Johnsons' with our friends. A garden fiesta had been arranged to celebrate our arrival. The mayor was there among many others, Mexican and foreign. We were entertained by *mariachis*, Mexican musicians in their typical costumes—black with gold braid and epaulets, with matching sombreros. They sang their doleful, romantic songs about love and life. The food served included tamales, and guacamole which one scooped up with a piece of fried tortilla. *Jicama*, which looks like a white turnip, was served in pieces sprinkled with lime juice and paprika.

Here we met our next-door neighbours Sonia and Enrique Cervantes, both artists and agents for our American landlady. Sonia was English, with a Russian mother; Enrique was Mexican and a cousin of the great artist Rufino Tamayo. We also met Don and Mary Newton; Don was *Time* magazine's representative in Mexico and South America. The American artist Stirling Dickinson continued teaching Spanish at the *Instituto Allende* after it had incorporated the *Escuela de Bellas Artes*, founded in 1938 by Dickinson and Cossio del Pomar.

The *Escuela de Bellas Artes*, San Miguel's first school of fine arts, was then located in a building behind the old market, which later burned down. Enrique Fernandez, the governor of the state of Guanajuato, and Cossio del Pomar had an old convent in San Miguel restored, thus forming the *Instituto Allende*. Leonard Brooks, Jack Baldwin, Jim Pinto and a few others were teachers there. These men taught advanced painting, taking their students out in the marketplace or the surrounding hills. Arturo Suarez taught photography, Howard Jackson jewellery, and Judy Martin weaving. York never taught there, but his name was put on the board of directors without his consent.

We immediately began studying Spanish. This was essential, as no one in the marketplace spoke a word of English. Absorbed in his painting, York had little time to study, but he had a good ear and his pronunciation was excellent. He learned a few typical phrases, using them with a flourish, and occasionally someone would say to me, "Why he knows more Spanish than you do." He always basked in this praise, never admitting that I was much more proficient in the language, which I could read, write and understand. I never minded and laughed with York.

Most foreigners make a faux pas occasionally with the language. Often a suffix ending in 'o' or 'a' is added to an English word, and sometimes it works in Spanish. In trying to explain to a new model that it was necessary to draw from the nude and there was no reason to be embarrassed, York used the word *embarasada*, which in Spanish also means pregnant. The young girl looked surprised, to say the least. To excuse oneself, one might say *excusado*, which also means lavatory. The great British writer Max Beerbohm, after living in Italy for many years and never learning a word of Italian, said, "Genius doesn't have to learn another language!"

NEW FRIENDS AND EXPERIENCES

The light, the market scenes, and the mountains were new for York and he became absorbed in his surroundings. He went on occasional sketching trips near San Miguel with Leonard and Enrique but often ventured further afield to places like Pátzcuaro, Tzintzuntzan and Janitzio Island, where the fishermen still used butterfly nets and dugout canoes. We were amazed to see very young children painting charming designs on the dishes at Tzintzuntzan. The Indian women at Pátzcuaro wore black skirts with pleats piled one on top of the other in back, a style seen nowhere else. The men everywhere wore white cotton shirts and pants, and sombreros, which differed by region in colour and ribbons. Everywhere there were burros but few cars. The burros carried everything from bundles of firewood to bags of rich black loam for gardens, and pottery on its way to market.

Across the street lived Fleta and Mac MacFarland, who had arrived in San Miguel on horseback in 1933. There were five San Miguels in Mexico; they had visited some of the others before finding the right one! They built a charming large house on Calle Recreo, where they grew most of their own produce and had a beautiful flower garden. Fleta was a nurse who worked for many years for a doctor in Querétaro, going back and forth each day. In retirement she worked for the library and various charities and wrote a weekly gardening column for the local paper *Atencion*, until she died in her nineties in 1993.

Jim and Rushka Pinto became our good friends. Jim, a Yugoslavian with a Spanish grandmother, had immigrated to the United States in 1939, where he took up American citizenship in California. He was the most interesting artist in San Miguel. York's appreciation of talent in others had him wondering how he could show Jim's work in Canada, or snare him for a teaching job at the OCA. This seemed a good way to speed up the quality of art in Canada, but it never happened. Jim worked as an art teacher at the *Instituto* until his death in 1990.

Dr. Francisco (Paco) Olsina, another new friend, had left Franco's Spain to come to San Miguel. He was instrumental in founding the first hospital in town. His friend, the Spanish writer Paulino Masip Roca, settled in Mexico City. His daughter Carmen often came to San Miguel to visit Dr. Olsina, eventually settling there and marrying an American, Jim Hawkins. Carmen started an excellent language school in San Miguel and I was one of her first students. Carmen gave me a copy of Cervantes' *Don Quixote*, the first book I read in Spanish. She has now been director of the *El Centro Cultural Ignacio Nigromante*, generally referred to as *Bellas Artes*, for many years.

A young Mexican gentleman, Armando Garcia, became a good friend of the artists. He was from a prestigious well-educated family. Their home was on the central square, the *Jardin*, above where the Banco de Mexico is today, adjoining Casa Canal, the original home of the Counts of Canal. Armando often invited his friends to dinner or to watch a fiesta from their balconies. He gave many parties in the large pink-walled villa directly behind the Parroquia Church, where the bougainvillaea billowed over the scalloped pink walls, to a fountain below on Calle Cuadrante, at the corner of Aldama.

At one party as we stood talking with a group in Armando's garden, we overheard a conversation between a group of young men. One said, "Have you seen the beautiful redhead who has just arrived?" We realised they were talking about our daughter, Virginia, who seemed to be caus-ing quite a stir. Armando was a young, tall and handsome man, who could be seen each morning in his white riding breeches, entering town on his white horse after riding in the beautiful hills of the Atascadero. We were stunned when he died from leukaemia three years later.

Our maid Matilda began disappearing for part of each day. We even-tually discovered she was working part-time for someone else, sometimes setting up her own stall in the market. This was unsatisfactory and we had to get another maid. Enrique had a difficult time getting her and her family out of the house on the property. She had been there so long she felt it belonged to her. Our next maid was Lydia, a tall nice-looking young girl. York used her as a clothed model for many paintings. He paid her extra, so she was pleased to model. It wasn't long before models, often art students, were found and arrangements made to pose in the nude.

Most kitchens in Mexican towns at that time did not have gas or electric stoves. One cooked brazier-style, lighting a fire with charcoal and wood in a front opening of the tiled kitchen counter, which had a hole on top with a grate for the pot. Water for bathing was heated in an upright tank called a *calentador*, again lit by a fire underneath. No one seemed to mind, we were all young then.

Many of our friends had maids who came from homes with dirt floors. On cold nights, they moved their animals inside for warmth for the family. Amazingly these maids appeared spotless. They did their family's wash at their employer's house in a *pila*, a shallow, cement-ridged tub, where there was always a good supply of soap and water. Most houses had servants" quarters where they could bathe and wash their hair. Few had running water in their homes, and went to a public fountain with their pitchers and pails. There was a public *pila* near the waterworks in San Miguel, with separate *pilas* for twelve or more, where the maids dried laundry over the masonry walls or took it home wet. Often they washed their children, and occasionally themselves, in the tubs after the laundry was done. Sometimes York would discreetly sketch there for an interesting setting and a free model.

York had come to San Miguel to work but life was becoming too social. It was the custom of many ministers and ambassadors in Mexico City to come to San Miguel on weekends. Friends started asking if they could entertain their diplomatic personnel at our house, supplying all the refreshments. We made many lasting good friends but York needed as few interruptions as possible. We then implemented a strict rule that York was not to be interrupted until 5:00 P.M. Practically no one then had a phone, so that became an established rule.

NEW SKETCHING SUBJECTS

It was a joy for York to face each sunny morning knowing that he could go to his studio and paint the whole day long. The large glass doors were opened wide each morning, and as we were on a hill, he had long, interesting views of the town and distant mountains. Sometimes he would take his easel to the patio, where he would have Lydia pose by the fountain, or go into town and paint a market scene. It was more complicated sketching in the marketplace, as people always gathered. On one occasion, a policeman told him there was a fee for sketching. York, thinking to end it quickly, pretended not to speak Spanish. York finally reached into his pocket and gave the officer a peso, at which point the policeman said, "And one for my friend too."

Other diversions, apart from cocktails or dinner in the evenings were the bullfights, *Los Toros*. After seeing a few, I was spending most of the time with my eyes closed. However, York became quite an aficionado, likening it to ballet. He and Leonard Brooks usually went to fights in San Miguel and nearby towns. His excitement knew no bounds, and he often jumped into the ring and out again or behind boards if the bull came his way.

There were many fiestas with fireworks and dancing: the Blessing of the Animals, the Day of the Dead (November 1), *Candelaria* (February 2), Independence Day, school parades, saints' days and the *Peregrinations*. The fireworks were most ingenious; the huge two-storey-high structures had great horizontal arms and shapes like bicycles and human figures. One part was lit, with wheels spinning and great explosions. As one section finished, it lit the next, until the whole structure was spent. At the same time, rockets showered the sky with rainbows of colour. York and Leonard were always there, not missing a thing. The Blessing of the Animals found fantastically costumed animals and birds lined up at the church door, where the priest blessed them. York did at least one painting of this event, *Blessing of the Animals* (1954), which Hallmark used as a Christmas card in 1954. *Candelaria* was a great profusion of flowers and plants, filling the entire town square. Great truckloads of trees, shrubs, and potted plants were unloaded and assembled the night before. Everything that flowered was made to bloom for this occasion, making a fabulous display.

The *Peregrinations* (pilgrimages) were another great religious show. Most lost their maids, gardeners and workers for a few days, as this huge mass started out by foot to reach a shrine a few days distant. People cooked, fed their children, and slept en route, with some traversing the last mile on their bleeding knees. On arrival they bought whips with beads on them from the shrine and whipped themselves. Such is the religious fervour. The money made through the sale of religious objects went to the shrine.

We often started out on this pilgrimage with Leonard and Reva, Jim and Rushka, and others from San Miguel. The artists sketched furiously and cameras clicked steadily. At the river outside of town, Rushka, Reva and I were offered rides across on burros, while the men waded across. On the other side, out came the cooking pots and fires were lit. After a mile or two, our little group would return. The men studied their sketches in their studios for painting ideas.

The goal was sometimes the shrine at Atotonilco, a few miles from San Miguel. The religious came from afar to this village, which boasted a tremendous church, equipped to accommodate thousands. The church had co-ed toilets to handle a few hundred people at a time; there were many hot springs in the area, and row after row of toilets had hot water constantly flowing beneath. The long tortilla belts heated hundreds at a time. The great soup pots, heated from beneath, were so large that ingredients were added from a ladder set at the side. It was like a scene from the middle ages. York's *Penitantes* (1951), inspired by this scene, was included in "The Artists' Mecca: Canadian Art and Mexico," an exhibition curated by Christine Boyanoski at the Art Gallery of Ontario in 1992.

In 1949 the Mexico City daily paper, *Excelsior*, invited York to exhibit in its great outdoor annual exhibition in Chapultepec Park. He was pleased and sent *Ayer y Hoy (Yesterday and Today)* (1949), depicting modern and ancient buildings side by side.

THE BEGINNING OF ABSTRACTION

In early 1950 the meaning of abstract art suddenly became clear to York while he was painting in Acambay, a small town on a high point of land on the way to Mexico City. As he sat sketching a scene of the market, with canvas-covered stalls, women with *rebozos*, and mountains behind, he realised that all the shapes worked together—one complimented the other, taking on the same shapes, and suddenly the essence of abstraction emerged. This painting, *Sunlit Street, Acambay* (1950) was purchased by Park Jamieson, a Sarnia lawyer and strong supporter of the Canadian Drama Festival. On Jamieson's death he left this painting to Dr. O.S. Pokorny, who in 1966 gave it to the Sarnia Public Library and Art Gallery. While *Sunlit Street, Acambay* itself was not very abstract in comparison to York's later works, it was nevertheless a turning point for him.

MEETING SIQUIEROS

York was familiar with the work of *Los Tres Grandes*, Mexico's three great muralists: José Clemente Orozco, Diego Rivera and José David Alfaro Siquieros. They were strong painters, but he delayed seeing their actual murals until he had experienced Mexico on his own terms. When he did see their work, he wasn't too interested in the violent and brutal political subjects, but he admired their mastery of large spaces.

William Finlayson of *Western Home Monthly* asked York to compare Mexican and Canadian art in an article for their magazine. York chose to talk with Siquieros, who was delighted to oblige, and invited us for dinner. There was much rivalry between the big three painters and Siquieros was always well-armed and surrounded with bodyguards. We were given minute instructions on how to get to his home.

We followed Siquieros, surrounded by bodyguards bulging with guns, into his house. Inside we met his charming wife Angela, and were seated around a low, round coffee table with a tray of bottles. Angela knelt in front of the tray and poured our drinks. She was petite and beautiful. Right behind her was her huge portrait, done by her husband. It showed a gigantic, strong woman with great fist-like hands, such a contrast to the delicate woman in front of us. York showed Siquieros many reproductions of Canadian artists' works. Siquieros studied them carefully, asked questions and acknowledged that we had some very good painters. York made notes for his article and acquired some reproductions of the work of Mexican artists.

We were then invited to the dining table, the two bodyguards standing on either side of Siquieros. I was directed to the chair on his right, but with a bodyguard in-between. Angela, without protection, had York sitting on her left. Dinner conversation was lively. He showed us his current work, rather unimpressive portraits of movie actresses. York enjoyed discussing art with the Mexican master, and concluded that Canadian art compared favourably with Mexican.

ANXIETY IN MANZANILLO

Anxious to see more of Mexico in 1950, we travelled with Grant Powers, a cartoonist for a US army magazine during the war. We drove to Guadalajara, then boarded the train for Manzanillo, a port city. Upon arrival, the police, asking for our passports, which were back in San Miguel, confronted us. They warned us not to leave without the passports.

We had planned to stay only a week, considering our tight finances. We immediately wrote to Enrique Cervantes, hoping he might have a key to our house. More than two weeks went by while York did many sketches in small nearby villages. He would be up at daybreak while the rest slept, pick a banana or two en route to his first sketch and still be back in time to have breakfast with us.

After more than two weeks, a large envelope covered in drawings arrived for us, with our passports inside. One picture showed us behind bars, with Enrique handing in a loaf of bread with a saw sticking out the end. We didn't find his humour so funny at the time but packed immediately, checked out and headed for the station. We sat down on the train, delighted that no one seemed to be checking us. The train was about to pull out when two policemen entered, walked directly to us, examined our passports and left. They hadn't been fooling!

THE HORNES AND GRAHAMS VISIT MEXICO IN 1951

During the winter of 1951, York developed sores that would not heal. Dr. Olsina said that they were due to a calcium shortage, and sent his nurse a few times to administer calcium injections. I had mentioned this in a letter to Cleeve and Jean in Toronto. The Hornes had a farm at Claremont, Ontario where they spent weekends, often inviting friends. Wallace and Kay Graham were guests on the weekend my letter had arrived. They began to talk about York's problem and Wally, a doctor, said that he could cure it easily. After a few drinks, they decided they should all come to Mexico and fix up old York. They agreed to clear their calendars and leave as soon as possible. We agreed to meet them at the airport.

We decided to go into Mexico City a day early to arrange things. We told Jorge, the manager of Hotel Francis on the Reforma, about our friends coming to Mexico for the first time. Jorge arranged a luxurious three-bedroom corner suite with a good view of the Reforma, and invited us for dinner the first night. We picked up our friends at the airport and drove to the hotel. In the elegant suite we found a large tray of liquors, mixers, ice and a magnificent bouquet of flowers, compliments of Jorge. Cleeve said, "Well, we certainly feel sorry for the Wilsons, living under such hardships."

We invited Jorge for drinks and went down to dinner with him. He was great fun and everything got off to a good start. After dinner Jorge took us to a nightclub, where a bottle of rum was promptly put on the table. We headed to the park at midnight, where the mariachis gathered to play. We recognised "Poet and Peasant," and York requested "Guadalajara" and "Cumpleaños," the birthday song.

The next day we discussed what we could do for Jorge. It was decided that we would buy the materials and frame for Cleeve to paint his portrait. We invited Jorge again for drinks that evening and Cleeve got to work. Jorge sat for about two hours and was delighted with his gift. What a welcome it had been!

On Sunday, our last day in the city, our friends wanted to see a bull-fight. One was to take place at 4:00 P.M. in the great bullring in Mexico City. As we walked the streets that day, we saw stretch limousines adorned with beautiful girls lounging across the hoods. They were laughing and talking to people as they drove slowly by, inviting them to come to the bull fight. It was a unique and attractive bit of promotion!

We arrived at the bullring well ahead of time. It was a huge oval area with a dirt floor and two gates, one for the charging bull to enter and the other for him to leave, dead, on a sled. Fifteen minutes before the fight, the *picadors* advanced slowly on horseback toward the judges at the far end, bowed, and then backed slowly away.

The judges and VIPs faced a huge clock. The fight was to start exactly at 4:00 P.M.; a heavy fine was levied for each minute late. The entrance gate swung open exactly at 4:00 P.M., and out rushed a raging bull. The *picadors*, with long prods to anger the bull, waited in the ring. They were mounted on horses, which were protected underneath with boards.

When the bull charged, jerking its horns under the horse's belly, the *picadors* speared it in the shoulders to break the neck muscles, so the head would automatically lower before engaging with the *toreros*, who were on foot. The *toreros'* costumes were ostentatious and grand; a red cape covered the hand holding the dagger. They waved their capes to attract the bulls away from the *picadors*. When in combat, the cape was held to one side, enticing the bull to charge the cape. This long drama readied the bull for the *coup de grace*.

For a good performance, the crowd went wild, throwing valuables as well as clothing into the ring. If the *torero* fails to kill the bull quickly, the crowd becomes angry, booing and shouting obscenities. Good *toreros* are highly praised and honoured; their performance decides the size of the purse. The fight was quite an eye-opener for our friends. York became very excited, hollering "bravo" and "ole" loudly with the crowd.

The next day we were off early for Pátzcuaro and Janitzio Island. The following morning we took the boat for Janitzio Island, seeing dugout canoes and fishermen with butterfly nets en route. As we approached the island, we could see endless lines of fishing nets hung up to dry along the shore. We landed and wandered through the streets that mount the hill, higher and higher. The island is populated with Tarascan Indians, who at that time were very friendly. York did many paintings there; he was impressed with the dignity of the Tarascan women, straight and tall as they mended the nets, including *Tarascans and Nets* (1951), *Butterfly Nets* (1950) and *Dugout Canoes* (1951).

On our return to Pátzcuaro, we drove further around the lake to Erongaricuaro, a weaving village where much excellent work originated and was sold in Mexico City and other centres. We met and talked with Mrs. Gordon, a devoted artisan who started the whole enterprise. After visiting Tzintzuntzan, we returned to San Miguel. Since we had only one extra bedroom, the Grahams stayed with Leonard and Reva. Our guests enjoyed a few days of sightseeing and meeting our friends in San Miguel.

PANTON'S POEM

So many things happened during those early six-month trips to Mexico. York felt he needed at least that much time for a good working session, and Mexican law demanded that foreigners must leave and re-enter after six months.

Soon after we arrived in San Miguel for the first time, we received a letter from our Toronto friend Alec Panton, who penned a memorable Mexican poem in our honour. It seems fitting to end this chapter with his literary effort!

The Rainbow's End—in Mexico

The migrant robin southward bound
Forsakes the North for friendlier ground
Instinctively elects to go
To Mexico.

The rich suspend their vast affairs
To winter in the tropic airs,
And sign a lot of cheques to go
To Mexico.

But one needs not a banker's till
Nor knows the robin's inborn skill,
But only how to sketch to go
To Mexico.

Oh, who shall know the rainbow's end,
What heights the artist's soul ascend?
We damn well hope York gets to know
In Mexico.

And if on Gall'ry walls, you face
His paintings of that fabled place,
I'm sure you'll be the next to go
To Mexico.

And Lela, if his blood once more
Is stirred by some Aztec Squaw,
Protect him from her sexy glow
In Mexico.

When Spring's warm call the robin heeds
Though York's purse fails his homing needs,
We pray our friend collects the dough
In Mexico.

And now, we wait his vow, to end
His exile soon, and thus each friend
On this condition lets him go
To Mexico.

VII

1950-1952

Steady Progress

WE RELUCTANTLY RETURNED from our first Mexican sojourn in March of 1950. As the Mexico trip signified York's absolute abandonment of a commercial career to paint full-time, we now consciously lowered our standard of living. York was busy teaching. Except for summers at Doon, the rest were night classes. He taught one night each at the AGT and the OCA and two nights at the Artists' Workshop in Toronto, run by Barbara Wells, and an evening class for businessmen on Centre Island. He guarded his painting time during the day. Alec Panton was then principal of OCA and asked York to teach there. York said he did not have more time for teaching. But Alec informed York that it was "his duty." York reluctantly agreed to one evening a week. It was too much, however, and he began to feel tired most of the time.

One of Jack Bush's students at the AGT was Jim Gairdner, a stockbroker. Jack felt Jim was a natural "primitive" and wanted to keep him painting in his unique style. This annoyed Jim so he quit Jack's class and joined York's, but York had the same idea. Jim said, "Damn it, I'm paying to be taught and no one will teach me." He then tried Cleeve, with much the same result. They all became good friends, however, and Jim was so determined about painting that he built a studio on his estate near Oakville.

Jim was quite a rough diamond. His first wife had recently died; this was perhaps the reason for his devotion to painting. He told us of her spunky personality and their happy life together. When she died, he planned a big party with all their friends. He had her dressed beautifully for the party and placed her sitting in a chair with a drink nearby, looking as lifelike as possible. He saw no reason why she shouldn't enjoy her own wake!

Jim's studio was perfect and the envy of every artist. He invited his artist friends for a cornerstone ceremony. Cleeve did the honours and was rewarded with a silver trowel. When the building was finished we were invited to celebrate. The studio, set at a distance from the mansion, had a well stocked bar, kitchen and bedroom. Graceful swans swam in the small bay of Lake Ontario.

York exhibited less in 1950, probably because of the drain of teaching. He was presented with an inscribed silver cigarette box at the end of his three-year tenure as president of the OSA; Cleeve Horne followed him as president in 1949. York was still on the council of the OSA and RCA. He was invited to exhibit with the CGP in 1950 at the AGT, and sent *Mexican Pattern* (1950); *Cocktail Party* (1949) went to the CNE that summer. In 1950, the AGT replaced the society exhibitions with an "Exhibition of Contemporary Painting"; York's *The Mill* (1950), inspired by an old mill near the Doon School, was accepted that year. York sent his portrait of *Jack Kent Cooke* to a touring portraiture show organised by Hart House.

A MOVE WEST?

At around this time, York seriously considered an offer from Dean Riddell of Regina College to direct their new Regina College School of Art and the Banff Summer School, and act as curator of the Mackenzie collection. When Riddell came east to discuss his proposal, York maintained he needed summer vacations to paint in order to continue progressing as an artist. The dean agreed that York would only head the art gallery, and asked us to sell our house and move west to start that autumn.

When the contract arrived by mail, however, it clearly stated that York was to take both positions. York thus declined both jobs, in spite of the accompanying salary and honour. He was first a painter and nothing could disturb that. Kenneth Lochhead thus succeeded Gus Kenderdine as curator of the collection, and became the first director of the school.

THE NEW LAING GALLERIES

York had numerous solo exhibitions in 1950. In May he was honoured when Blair Laing chose an exhibition of his work to open the newly built gallery at 194 Bloor Street West; Florence Wyle's "Rivers of America" series was also shown, along with works by other artists. The gallery, designed by local architect Gordon Adamson, was the first building in Toronto designed specifically as a commercial art gallery. Jack and Jean Kent Cooke treated us to a fine dinner before the opening, drove us around in their big convertible sports car, and deposited us in style at the gallery entrance. Cleeve and Jean wired congratulations from England.

The exhibition, which featured thirty-five of York's recent Mexican paintings, received positive reviews in the Toronto papers. Pearl McCarthy of the *Globe and Mail* (May 27, 1950) claimed that, "there is not a superficial picture of mere atmosphere or the spooky emotionalism that overcomes some artists who come up against the folk ways and religious pageantry of Mexico." At the same time, she maintained that his "form is never a merely intellectual exercise, but the framework of warm picture-making." She concluded that York's "brilliance" was "consistently combined with taste."

A DEALER IN MONTREAL

We were pleased when in 1950, William Watson of the prestigious Watson Art Galleries, at 1434 Sherbrooke Street West in Montreal, offered to represent York. The several paintings York sent to test the waters were well received.

A solo exhibition of forty-one works followed in the spring of 1951. This show included Mexican subjects, Québec landscapes inspired by our 1945 sketching trip, and ballet scenes. The glowing reception he received was very encouraging. The artist and writer Michael Forster declared in the *Montreal Standard* (April 21, 1951) that York's Montreal exhibition was long overdue, and that he had fine command of duco and oil. Robert Ayre, well-known art critic for the *Montreal Star* (April 28, 1951), said that York had, "a great appetite for the colour and rhythm of life," and that he was "an extremely accomplished painter, healthily enjoying the exercise of his faculties as much as he enjoys what he sees in Canada and in Mexico." That exhibition marked the beginning of a happy relationship with the Watson Galleries, the Montreal public and critics.

DUCO — AN EXCITING NEW MEDIUM

During our first trip to Mexico in 1949-50, York was surprised to find serious artists using automobile paint in their paintings. Since the mid-1930s, Mexican artists had been experimenting with synthetic, fast-drying materials in an effort to extend the life of their murals. David Alfaro Siqueiros was the leading advocate of synthetic paints. While spending time in prison, Siquieros had apparently worked with anything he could get his hands on, including pyroxylin. Pyroxylin is a cellulose nitrate that forms the basis of automobile paint. In Canada, pyroxylin-based paints were distributed by Canadian Industries Limited (C.I.L.), so the paints were nicknamed "Cilco"; the American version, retailed by E.I. DuPont de Nemours, was called "Duco."

York experimented with duco and found it had to be applied to a rigid surface such as wood or masonite. Although some artists prized duco for its smooth high gloss, York tried to achieve a textured matt effect by adding sand, celite (ground sea shells), or marble dust. Duco dried very quickly, eliminating the need when painting with oils to wait for one colour to dry before applying another. With oils, there was the potential of bad reactions between certain colours, or of cracking caused by over-painting when the layer beneath was not sufficiently dry. York returned to Toronto in 1950, enthusiastic about duco, and began introducing it to his peers.

York's experimentation was rewarded when the AGT purchased their first duco painting, his *Peons* (1949) in 1950. Lotta Dempsey of the *Toronto Daily Star* (November 9, 1950) wrote that York had "gone right out on a limb" with his opinion that duco would one day "replace oils to a large extent," and commented on that, "the rough, thick, heavy effect it is possible to get is fresh and exciting." During York's third summer as an art instructor at Doon everyone was anxious to know about this new medium. A number of his Mexican duco canvases were hung in their annual summer exhibition and in his solo show there in November of 1950.

OTHER ART-RELATED EVENTS

In late 1950 the CBC made a film, "Canadian Artists in San Miguel," which featured York, Fred Taylor and Leonard Brooks. The NFB film "Social Workers in Vancouver," which included York's *Welfare Worker*, was also released that year. *Western Home Monthly* ran York's Siqueiros interview.

York took great pleasure in doing works of art for special occasions. He completed a book of humorous paintings as a retirement gift for AGT president Harold Walker. This book was filled with York's paintings in the distinctive styles of many artists, including Picasso, Degas, Cleeve Horne, Gauguin, Tom Thomson, Renoir, Kandinsky, and David Milne. Thomson's painting, for example, was signed "Thomas Thomson" and titled *East Wind*. Beneath the "Milne" painting, York wrote, "Sorry I didn't ever get to the gallery." When Harold first opened the book at his farewell dinner, he was momentarily fooled into thinking the paintings were genuine works by the various artists. I hope this book ends up in the AGO collection.

On March 5, 1951 York gave a painting demonstration for the AGT at the Leaside Public Library. He employed a ballet model, commenting as he painted. In the latter half he became so engrossed in the painting that he completely forgot the audience. Everyone seemed pleased enough for the opportunity of watching an artist in action. Later he confided that he no longer believed in demonstrations, as he was compelled to do things for effect that he would not ordinarily do. Being such a strong supporter of the AGT, however, he did another demonstration in the sculpture court in December, trying to be completely honest with his painting and answering questions later.

A MEMORABLE OSA EXHIBITION

The 79th OSA exhibition in the spring of 1951 was rather controversial. Four of the society's more conservative members—Archibald Barnes, Manly MacDonald, Kenneth Forbes and Angus MacDonald—resigned in protest over the high number of 'modern' works in the show. It was a most unfortunate event, as there should be room for all directions of art in any group.

It was reminiscent of the early struggle of the Group of Seven, some of whose members were accused of painting things like "the inside of a drunkard's stomach." The modern paintings at the OSA were called "monstrosities" and "meaningless doodlings." The exhibition jury was composed of serious artists: Syd Hallam, Yvonne McKague Housser, Jock Macdonald, Bobs Cogill Haworth, York, and Cleeve. The controversy generated considerable press coverage, including a front-page article in the *Toronto Daily Star* (March 8, 1951) and another article in the *Telegram* (March 9, 1951).

The exhibition was opened by Viscount Alexander, Canada's Governor General. Like when he opened the RCA show at the Art Gallery of Toronto in 1946, Viscount Alexander engaged in serious art discussions with York and other artists. York won the J.W.L. Forster award for the "best picture" for his duco painting *Toluca Market* (1950). Viscount Alexander took special pleasure in presenting the award to York, and a photo was taken of them discussing the painting. The *American Art Digest* of April 1951 mentioned York's prize, and his recent experiments with duco. When the OSA show toured to London, the large variety of media employed by the painters attracted the public and press. The reviewer for the *London Free Press* (April 23, 1951) commented on the particular popularity of tempera, but also gesso, beeswax, collage, and York's duco.

Canadian Art (October 1951) ran a photo of York interviewing artists during the OSA opening. Gallery staff believed the attendance, at well over two thousand, to be the largest in the gallery's fifty-one-year history. During these years, art was really reaching the people, largely through the art societies, with the support of the galleries. But credit must be given to a particularly lively and talented group of artists who brought the societies to life.

MAJOR ARTICLES BY AND ABOUT YORK

"At Home In Sun or Studio," an article in *Saturday Night* (July 31, 1951) by Paul Duval, focused on York's everyday life. The photographs accompanying the article included a picture of York painting a landscape, a picture of him relaxing with Alec Panton and Cleeve Horne in our uniquely painted recreation room, and a picture of York playing his flute with Virginia seated at the piano. Duval highlighted various facets of York's career and personality, including his interest in figure and landscape painting, his musical talents and love of the ridiculous, and his growing attraction to Mexico.

Canadian Industries Limited, Canadian suppliers of the American product duco, were delighted that York had found a new use for their product. They ran an article in *Oval* (December 1951), their company magazine, titled "Colours Beautiful." The article, accompanied by a colour reproduction of *Toluca Market*, featured a remarkable account of how paints and colours have been used in fine art from prehistoric times to today. The writer also mentioned York's encounter with duco in Mexico, and his sharing of information about the new medium upon his return to Toronto. The photograph of Viscount Alexander and York discussing the prize-winning *Toluca Market* was also included. C.I.L. then offered to keep York supplied with as much duco as he would need for the duration of his career.

York sent two more duco paintings to the RCA exhibition at the AGT in late 1951: *White Figures of Acambay* (1951), later purchased by the AGT, and *Guanajuato* (1951), a painting depicting an interesting university town a good hour distant from San Miguel. Both paintings were inspired by our second visit to Mexico, from May to September of 1951. Guanajuato was huddled in a steep valley, with only one main street, which ran the length of the city. Many of the streets were very narrow, allowing only foot traffic. The streets, which rose gradually from below, highlighted the buildings up the hills, making it a great visual attraction for artists. The colours of the houses were carefully chosen by a committee, and one had to have building plans approved, and obtain permission to change colours.

Guanajuato featured a well-arranged food and crafts market. Another big attraction, although not for the queasy, was an underground crypt lined with ancient corpses removed from their graves. The dry, sandy soil preserved the bodies, and though shrunken with parchment-like skin they were quite lifelike. The bodies were apparently exhumed when payment for upkeep ceases.

In 1955, the National Gallery invited the Mexican artist José Gutiérrez, director of the experimental workshop in plastics and paintings at the National Polytechnic of Mexico, to deliver a series of lectures on new materials in Canadian cities from Vancouver to Montreal. The next year, the National Gallery published a book by Gutiérrez, *From Fresco to Plastics: New Materials for Easel and Mural Paintings*. Donald Buchanan, editor of *Canadian Art*, asked York to review this book. York was pleased to do this, but it was a time-consuming task finding English equivalents for the Spanish names for ingredients and locating the actual ingredients, and he was already giving information to many interested artists. His brief review was published in *Canadian Art* (Summer 1956). When Donald later asked York to do a book on the new media, York pleaded lack of time. Donald never forgave him, and became an unjustified enemy.

In 1950 York was invited by the Royal Architectural Institute of Canada to write his opinions on the state of Canadian art. The resulting article, "From Ontario's Eastern Border to the Rockies," was published in the Institute's journal in December of 1951. In his text, York contemplated the highly individualistic nature of contemporary painting in various regions of the country, and wondered how to promote a uniquely Canadian school of painting not based on realistic landscape studies. He spoke of his interview with David Alfaro Siqueiros and the Mexican painters' development of international recognition. York also clearly stated that a "very sincere effort to advance the quality of Canadian painting" was evident in 1950.

When looking back at 1950s' art, he hoped it could be said that an increasing number of artists were "developing in a more modern direction," and that the momentum generated decades before by the Group of Seven had been "relayed to the creative work of the Fifties."

York was able to write such a comprehensive article because of his years of jurying many exhibitions, and his resulting familiarity with thousands of works of art. He thus gained much perspicacity and knowledge from an often-thankless job. The fact that he was consistently chosen by his peers as a juror is evidence of his ability and fairness of judgement.

RETREAT IN MEXICO

York started the new year with a solo exhibition entitled "Recent Paintings" at Laing Galleries in January. The bulk of the canvases were subjects inspired by our first trip to Mexico in 1949-50 and our second trip there in 1951.

Paul Duval's review in *Saturday Night* (January 12, 1952), which included a reproduction of *Patscuaro* (1951), stated that the show included "a number of his most important works to date." He also argued that York's new duco works "reveal a new richness in the artist's handling of this relatively new addition to materials for making pictures." The newspaper advertisements for the Laing show featured pictures of the duco companion pieces, *Indias in White* (1950), and the AGT's *White Figures of Acambay*.

L.A.C. Panton's article, "Retreat in Mexico—A Canadian Painter Abroad," a thoughtful piece on York's recent Mexican sojourns and paintings, was published in *Canadian Art* (Spring 1952). Panton lauded York's decision to give up a relatively lucrative career in commercial art in order to devote himself to painting full-time. Mexico, "remote from the complexities and excitements of life at home in Canada," was a cheap, accessible, relaxing place where "the landscape and native life have a romantic attraction for the artist." Indeed, the many artists who were attracted to Mexico in the 1940s and 1950s included Dorothy Stevens, Stanley Cosgrove, Roy Kiyooka, Yvonne McKague Housser, Fred Ross, Ron Spickett, Toni Onley and Walter Yarwood.

More important than the landscape, however, was York's need to free himself from the pressure in Toronto to paint in a particular style. Panton quoted York as saying it was difficult, "even hazardous, to paint Canada in terms which are not those adopted by others, and almost impossible to remain independent of current modes, their sponsors and supporters." Panton concluded by noting York's recent emphasis on painting as design, and asserted that in all of his later works, "there is a thoughtful, even scholarly and sensitive, employment of plastic design as a subtle and expressive language, supported but not submerged by delicate or robust, but always rich, colour and refined drawing."

York and I continued to travel to Mexico regularly for many decades. As Paul Duval was to write of York in *York Wilson* (1978), however, the impact of those first two trips "was truly pivotal to his entire career as an artist. They left him with a creative drive that he was not to relinquish."

York receiving the J.W.L Forster Award from Viscount Alexander at the Art Gallery of Toronto. Toronto, 1951. Photograph by the Toronto Star.

York in his first studio in Mexico, in the house on Calle Recreo. San Miguel de Allende, 1949. Photograph by Lela Wilson.

VIII

1952-1953

New York, Europe and the Canary Islands

YORK'S ENQUIRING NATURE AND INBORN DESIRE to prove himself in other places led us to book passage for a February trip on the *Rhinedam*, sailing from New York for Le Havre en route to the Canary Islands. It was to be our first trip to Europe. Toronto friends gave us a great send-off and we stopped over in New York to see old friends, Charles and Christine Hutchings and Todd and Edna Russell.

NEW YORK

Todd, star of New York's "Howdy Doody Show," took us to the famous Henri's, a favourite restaurant of people in show business. This particular evening, we were joined by Ralph Bellamy, the American stage and screen actor. York had a psychic sense and often interpreted handwriting. Henri, the proprietor, asked him to read the handwriting of his girlfriend.

York didn't read the actual words, but used his intuition to "read" form, weight, distance between letters, and their position on the page. York told Henri many surprising things about his girlfriend that only Henri knew. Henri gave York another letter to read. The writing was very different, but York realised it was written by the same person, now very upset. Henri told York that he was right in every regard, the second letter having been written after they had broken their engagement.

A group that had gathered was listening in amazement. Ralph Bellamy asked if York would read his handwriting. York again gave an astounding reading, saying that Ralph's previous marriage had broken up and that he was about to marry the same sort of person, and would face the same problems. Ralph was shaken. Ralph's friends later told York that his words were absolutely true. One of the onlookers was John Reid King, host of a popular New York television show. He immediately offered York a spot on the program but York turned it down.

PARIS, SEVILLE AND MADRID

We boarded the *Rhinedam*, which we later learned was called a "tub" because of its constant rolling motion. We had trouble staying in our bunks the first night! We were good sailors though and didn't miss a meal. On-board entertainment included afternoon tea, an orchestra, dancing, films, bars, swimming pool, library, and long walks on deck. We also spent time with our new friends Chuck and Bobbie MacIntosh, who had driven from California in three days in order to catch the boat. Chuck was an engineer and Bobbie an architect.

We arrived at Le Havre and caught the train to Paris, where we were surprised to see snow and slush. Chuck and Bobbie appeared immediately thereafter and we went everywhere, enjoying our first glimpse of Paris, especially the Louvre. York did many quick sketches there, including *Kiosks* (1952) and *Paris in the Rain* (1952) and others depicting tree-lined avenues and nuns with enormous, starched white hats. The MacIntoshes then left to ski and climb in Switzerland.

Our voyage to the Spanish border on a dirty train, sitting in long rows of facing seats, kept us up all night. Our legs ached from holding close, and trying not to disturb the opposite person. On board we met A.T.S. McGhee, a businessman from London who was also going to Madrid and the Prado. In the morning we boarded the Talgo, a clean and fast train, for the quick trip to Madrid. We agreed to meet McGhee the next morning to visit the Prado. He turned out to be a good companion and profoundly interested in art.

The Prado contained countless treasures, including works by Piero della Francesca. York was interested by the space and abstract quality of his works, and could never spend enough time looking at them. We also enjoyed Hieronymus Bosch, Velázquez and other great Spanish and Italian masters. We discovered drawings by Goya under the eaves, and the Prado became a must-see museum for us.

In Seville we were astounded with the Moorish decoration in the palace and the beautiful gardens with orange and lemon trees. When the guard retreated, York jumped and grabbed two oranges. As he landed, the guard had turned, but did not see us. I tried one right away and never tasted anything so bitter. I convinced York to try the orange, but he was suspicious and tested it gingerly. We laughed over our stolen fruit and remembered that Seville oranges make the best marmalade precisely because of their bitterness.

THE CANARY ISLANDS

A few days later, we boarded the ship for the Canary Islands. We hurried to explore the vessel and found horses and bulls in crates on the lower deck, being shipped to the Canaries for bullfights. We sailed into the Mediterranean, past Cadiz and Gibraltar and out into the ocean. The boat was so full that one could hardly move. By the second day many had disappeared and there were fewer passengers each day out on deck. We could only surmise that many weren't good sailors.

It took three days to reach the town of Las Palmas on the island of Gran Canaria; from there we were to travel overnight to the island of Tenerife, our destination. York was worried that he would not be able to find masonite in Tenerife to use as a support for duco. He approached a well-dressed man near the dock, using the French word *isorel* or masonite. It turned out that this Mr. Alcovera spoke a little English, knew exactly what we wanted, and even accompanied us to purchase it. We later visited him and his wife at their home in Las Palmas.

Landing in Santa Cruz de Tenerife, a city on the island of Tenerife, we went directly to the Hotel Pino de Oro with its lovely gardens, owned by an Englishman, Jack Lewis. He showed us a room, which cost $1 per day, all meals included. York discovered an unused billiard room, and was able to use it as a studio. A few days later Mr. Lewis gave us a second-storey corner room with a balcony facing the mountains.

The hotel was at the head of *Las Ramblas*, the main tree-lined boulevard that featured a walkway with benches and sculptures. Large herds of goats wandered down the boulevard; it was amusing to see a goat or the occasional camel with huge red tree blossoms sticking out of its mouth. We could see people who lived in caves going up the hills, where they cooked their meals over a small fire at the cave entrance. The women carried the loads, which sometimes included a sizeable piece of furniture. We learned that the cave dwellers were the indigenous *Guanches*, the native Canary Islanders living on the island of Tenerife. Few of the *Guanches* had survived the massacre by the Spaniards, who hunted them out with killer dogs or canines, thus giving rise to *Canarias*, the Spanish name for the islands.

The *lecheras*, or milkmaids, on the streets each morning with their milk cans, long skirts and white sun bonnets, were a subject for York's brush. His duco painting *Lecheras* (1956) was the result.

MEETING THE PINTO GROTE FAMILY

On returning to our hotel one evening, we stopped to listen to music outside a house. A young man came down the street and paused to talk with us in Spanish, enquiring why we were waiting there. He said it was his younger brother's birthday and invited us to join the party. The young man's name was Eduardo Pinto Grote, and his younger brother was José Manuel. We found ourselves in the midst of a group of young people, including Eduardo's older brother Dr. Carlos Pinto Grote. We all had a great time, singing and laughing until it came time to leave. Carlos then said we must visit his family for tea every day at 6:00 P.M. We thanked him, left, and returned for tea three days later.

Presiding over the heavily laden table was their mother Laura, a very beautiful woman dressed in black. Teatime was a lively gathering as it was the first time each day when the family gathered to exchange the day's news. A psychiatrist by profession, Carlos was also a writer of poetry and prose and one of two art critics on the islands. He visited York's hotel studio and was deeply interested in York's work. People living in Franco's Spain had seen little art from the outside and they were curious.

MEETING EDUARDO WESTERDAHL

I started Spanish lessons with Hilda Comacho and during our conversation we talked about art. Hilda told me of her boyfriend, the art critic Eduardo Westerdahl, whom she brought to the studio. This was a case of love at first sight on all sides and we became lifelong friends. Westerdahl was the manager of a bank and one of the foremost art critics in Spain and South America. Among his friends were Picasso, Tenerife painter Oscar Dominguez, Juan Gris, Joan Miró, Ben Nicholson and many others about whom he had written extensively.

Eduardo talked about art regularly on the radio, and wrote articles for newspapers. Under Franco, Westerdahl felt Spain's art lagged fifty years behind the times. Eduardo and Hilda welcomed artists from other countries, often giving them studio space in the home that he shared with his mother. His mother was a dear woman with a pure *Guanchen* name who had married a Swede. The walls of Eduardo's home were covered from floor to ceiling with paintings by the world's most advanced painters. His efforts to introduce contemporary art to

Spain during the isolation of the Franco regime were like a breath of fresh air to his fellow artists.

Westerdahl was instrumental in bringing the first exhibition of Cubist art to Spain. York's work reflected some Cubist influences and Westerdahl was entranced. He would bring young artists to York's studio, including Hilda's son Fredy, who was a deaf-mute. Fredy had many opportunities to observe people and was an accomplished mimic. At parties he would pantomime people, causing much hilarity, as he highlighted all the idiosyncrasies they tried to hide. York's paintings and his ability to laugh endeared him to Fredy. A sort of mental telepathy seemed to develop between them. One day when York expected Fredy he hid a painting with which he was displeased. Fredy came in, walked directly to the hiding place, found the painting, and motioned toward it for an explanation.

A SIX-WEEK STAY IN A LUXURIOUS HOUSE

After a few weeks at our Tenerife hotel, Peggy Phillips, an English guest of the hotel, told us her friend Dyllis Davies would like to lend us her home for six weeks while she was away. It was illegal for Dyllis to charge rent, so we agreed to pay the servants' wages. The beautiful home, previously the French Consulate, had many rooms and a suitable studio space on the second floor. We happily accepted as it would help us stretch our precious dollars.

Our street was called *Las Mimosas* because of its many lovely yellow mimosa trees. Often it was a little frightening walking home at night, as fierce dogs barked from the banks of the steep roads, keeping abreast as we passed. There was no protective barrier, only a prohibitive high jump. A friend warned us never to come unannounced, as we were only safe if they were present.

While we were at Dyllis' house, her cat gave birth to kittens. One day, the maid was holding kittens on her lap when the mother cat came to investigate. York did a drawing of this scene, which he gave to Dyllis on her return. The resulting painting *Una Familia* (1952) was purchased by the National Gallery of Canada from York's exhibition at William Watson's Montreal gallery in November of 1952.

York painted steadily and completed quite a number of canvases by the time Dyllis returned. Carlos came to say he had a studio for York, and invited us to move in with them as part of the family, not visitors. We joined them in late March and stayed until July.

LIVING WITH THE PINTO FAMILY

The Pintos had a cook and breakfast was served to each person whenever they appeared. Lunch was the main meal of the day at 2:00 P.M.; afternoon tea occurred four hours later. A light supper brought us together again at 10:00 P.M. We often went to the local yacht club with the Pintos before supper. We swam, played tennis, or sat on the veranda, enjoying the yachts and expansive sea view.

Laura, the family matriarch, appeared each day for tea. Her husband, a poet, had died during the struggle against Franco. Laura's beauty was famous all over Spain, because the King had singled her out when she was young and invited her to the palace. Now she only emerged from her darkened room at tea and busied herself all night while others slept. The sun never touched her—she had a beautiful white complexion, perfect makeup, long painted fingernails, always dressed in black and smoked with a long cigarette holder. Conversation was lively. As none of the five adults spoke a word of English, our Spanish improved quickly.

Often Laura invited us to her room, where we had many private conversations. She stayed in her darkened room all day. She had had an operation in the past, and the doctor kept her on morphine for too long. Now she was unable to break the habit. A doctor on another island told her there was only one person who could help her, Dr. Carlos Pinto. She said that it was impossible for her to go to her own son for help. She wanted so much to free herself of the habit.

Laura had a German father and a Spanish mother. After her father died, her mother married Don Pedro Cabrera, a fine Spanish gentleman. He had a beautiful estate in La Laguna, Tenerife that we visited many times with our new friends. The Pintos made us honorary members of their small drama group, *Vino Poco*. The extroverted York was a welcome addition. The beautiful gardens of Don Pedro's estate were the usual locale for the plays. Don Pedro had travelled considerably and had a great interest in art and literature. Imagine our surprise on finding in his home a Leonardo drawing and a painting by the Flemish artist David Teniers the Younger. His large library, separate from the main house, had many first and rare editions. He unfortunately died before our return in 1957.

Carlos mentioned an important book that had been published in Canada, Hans Selye's *Stress* (1950). There was only one English copy in the islands, which the doctors took turns reading. We thought of our Montreal friends Maxwell and Bea Henderson, and asked them to mail a copy to us. Within a short time along came the huge volume and we were pleased to present it to Carlos. My Spanish was given another boost when I translated the tome for him.

Franco's revolution had been planned on the island of Tenerife, in the forest near the Teide volcano. Carlos' father and many of his friends had died in the ensuing civil war. The *coup* was unpopular around the world and put Spain's progress well behind other countries in so many ways. Carlos would tell us stories about it, but only inside his own home and never on the street or in the club. He worried that Franco had spies everywhere and because his father had been against Franco, he would never be able to hold an important position in medicine.

TOURING THE ISLAND OF TENERIFE

About midway in our sojourn Carlos drove us around the island. We were anxious to see the fishing villages and the different aspects of Tenerife. It rose from sea level to 6400 feet, where pine trees grew. As always, York stopped to sketch as we travelled.

The first night's stop was in a spartan inn in a small fishing village. We washed for dinner at an outside basin under a tree, had a drink and a nice simple meal. The entire bill for the three of us, with breakfast, was about $1. After starting at dawn the second day we reached a special place in the afternoon where Carlos wished to buy goat's milk cheese. He said, "From this point, we could make Santa Cruz tonight if you wished." Sensing that he would like to return, we agreed and thereby missed seeing the last part of the island. We saw this rugged, mountainous region only upon our return in 1957.

Eduardo Westerdahl would rent a car on Sundays and we, along with Hilda, would tour different parts of Tenerife. We stopped for lunch at various outdoor restaurants, sometimes located in an open field, where the fare was usually seafood. While Eduardo spoke only Spanish he was accustomed to talking with foreigners and had a way of choosing easily comprehensible words. Whenever an artist from afar came to town Eduardo would give a little party at his home and always invited us. This is how we met the Belgian artist Luc Peire. Luc was on his way to the Belgian Congo with his wife Jenny. During the Peires' short visit, Luc made a film called "Night Fishing," which included the work of local artists. When they left, we saw them off at the dock, where muscular black men were loading huge stalks of bananas on the boat. York got so excited thinking about the Belgian Congo that I could hardly get him off the boat before the gangplank was lifted.

While living in Santa Cruz de Tenerife, a letter arrived from the US government asking us if we were still in the USA, as we had failed to turn in an obligatory notice that we had left the country. We found Mr. Snidow, the US consul, and filled out the necessary papers. Mr. Snidow later invited us to his home, where we were amazed to see many paintings by Edvard Munch, which he had acquired on a posting in Sweden. One portrait reminded me of Fred Varley's work. It was a profile, facing left, with colour and composition similar to Varley's.

One Sunday Eduardo invited York to go on a wine-tasting tour at Arafo, a place famous for its vineyards. York actually did settle down to sketch while his friends went into the first cellar. When they brought wine for him to taste, he joined them. They visited many famous cellars. The wine was stored in large, wooden barrels and the first pitcher of wine drawn was thrown out. York had a keen sense of taste and surprised the others by selecting the best. Eduardo and York returned to Santa Cruz late for Hilda's dinner. In they came, feeling no pain, to regale us with tales of their experiences.

We travelled to many places in search of painting subjects, including Puerto de la Cruz, Bajamar, and La Orotava. At Easter we went to La Orotava to see the magnificent carpets of flowers. Millions of fresh petals held in place with wet sand covered the main thoroughfare, creating intricate designs like Persian carpets. People avoided stepping on them all day; the priests were the first to walk on them en route to church in the early evening.

Our daughter Virginia, then living in Toronto, was to be married. She had designed her wedding dress and sent the design to me with her own measurements, and those of her two grandmothers. They all liked the idea of having their dresses made in the Canaries by my newly discovered Norwegian dressmaker, who had designed my dress for the wedding. All the dresses fitted beautifully.

YORK'S EXHIBITION IN SANTA CRUZ DE TENERIFE

Near the end of our sojourn in the Canaries, Eduardo Westerdahl asked York if he would show his paintings in the municipal gallery, *Círculo de Bellas Artes de Tenerife*. York explained that he couldn't afford to frame them, and it would be difficult to transport the framed works back to Canada. Eduardo was anxious that they be shown so the artists and public could see what was happening in art elsewhere. He talked it over with his committee and returned to tell York they would pay for the frames, which they would keep for future use. York was unable to offer anything for sale, as the new paintings were needed for an exhibition to be held at Toronto's Laing Galleries upon our return to Canada.

The exhibition, which featured thirty-one paintings and six drawings, opened in June of 1952 to a crowded gallery. Eduardo wrote a fine appreciation of York's work for the catalogue; he, Carlos Pinto and others discussed the show on the radio and in the local press. The exhibition was a rewarding and successful conclusion to a wonderful stay in the Canary Islands.

York and myself aboard the Rhinedam, *en route from New York City to Le Havre, France, 1952.*

York with the Pinto family during our second visit to the Canary Islands. Carlos' wife Delia stands behind him on the left with their child. Eduardo's wife stands behind him in the centre. La Laguna, Canary Islands, 1957.

IX

1953

A Glimpse of Morocco and Our Return Home

WE COULDN'T LEAVE THE CANARY ISLANDS without a glimpse of Morocco, just a short distance by plane. It was then July. We had three weeks before sailing home and so we decided on a two-week visit. We were warned that the heat would be intense but York was determined to go.

CASABLANCA

York's instincts didn't let him down; the very different culture fired his imagination. The women were veiled and very mysterious; York felt their eyes said more than words. Their long, straight caftans were always spotless. The men dressed in pristine white, with yellow leather slip-ons inside their shoes. There were camels, lots of bicycles, and mysterious supposedly dangerous *medinas* (old walled areas of shops) with pocketsize stores. We wandered alone all over the city while York filled sketchbooks with fast drawings.

FEZ

The only foreigners on the bus to Fez, we marvelled at Moroccan men wrapped in wool from head to toe in the unbearable heat! It was even hotter in Fez. We found it necessary to be back in our fan-cooled hotel room by 11:00 A.M. We just lay there nude, flat out under the ceiling fan and took occasional cold showers.

We ventured out at midnight looking for dinner at a sidewalk café. The temperature was still 95°F. On emerging in the morning we were surrounded by a group of guides and York asked them, "If one would like to take us by streetcar to the *medina*, wait while I sketch, and then accompany us back on the streetcar." They all disappeared quickly, except a man named Abdullah. He had just finished his milk route in the medina, he knew everyone and would be happy to return with us while York sketched.

We boarded a streetcar and Abdullah paid the fare for us, before York could even get his hand in his pocket. York laughingly told Abdullah that he didn't have to go that far! The medina had huge piles of melons and other produce piled outside the gates. Burros were entering with loads, and narrow alleyways were jammed with people. York sketched furiously. Abdullah stood near, while I examined the hole-in-the-wall shops. Children gathered to watch York work. Suddenly Abdullah walloped a young boy and sent him flying. Astounded, York said, "Why did you do that?" Abdullah explained, "He was going to rob you, he was at your back pocket." It was unbelievable to us that these little children had to be watched.

It was a remarkable morning, nearing 11:00 A.M. and the heat was unbearable. So back we went to the dubious comfort of our hotel room. I imagine Abdullah received a nice tip, and it was good instruction for the future. We followed the same routine the following day, but without a guide. We ran into some American soldiers posted outside of town, who said they were there in case of trouble. They didn't explain but said the temperature during the day was 135°F and even the natives were suffering.

RABAT

After a few days we took a bus for Rabat, the capital, which seemed cooler. We got in touch with a Canadian friend married to a titled Moroccan, and were invited for lunch. She knew about York and his work. She did a lot of riding and kept her horse in King Hassan's stable. She took us there to see her horse and those of the King. She seemed to have freedom to wander at the Palace—the guards all greeted her and stepped aside. We also viewed the harem full of women and children.

RETURN TO SANTA CRUZ DE TENERIFE

On the return trip to Tenerife the plane took us to the island of Gran Canaria, where we took an overnight boat to Tenerife. It was a lovely voyage and the water was calm and placid.

Our final week with the Pintos was a busy one, packing and saying our goodbyes. When the time neared for our departure Eduardo Westerdahl said they would name a street after York, as he had brought so much to their islands! York gave a painting to Eduardo, one to Carlos and a watercolour to Carlos' mother Laura. Laura begged to return with us, thinking she could get help with her morphine problem in Canada. We had to refuse, much as we loved her, for it would have been a major responsibility.

Shortly before our departure Maud Dominguez, a French woman and former wife of Tenerife painter Oscar Dominguez, began to appear with Eduardo, while his girlfriend Hilda became less visible. Maud excelled in jewellery design, usually enamel on copper. Maud's own marriage with Oscar had broken up because he had a wandering eye. Oscar was then living with a French countess in her castle atop a mountain in France. Maud was an interesting, intelligent and cosmopolitan woman, and good to Eduardo. A short time later Maud and Eduardo were married. It was a terrible blow to Hilda, and she soon died.

York had two crates custom-made for his paintings and a crane lifted them on board our ship bound for London, England. Many friends were at dockside to see us off. We of course said we would be back, but no one believed us. We proved them all wrong when we visited again in 1957.

VISITING LONDON

We were anxious to see the galleries and museums of London on our first visit to this fascinating city. In a few days we would take the train to Southampton, board the Rhinedam for New York, and then take the train to Toronto. We had carried a bank draft in case there was need for more money, thinking it would be simple presenting it to a bank in London.

Upon our arrival at the bank, the teller asked, "Do you have an account here?" We replied no. "Well, who do you know in London?" "Gilbert Harding of the BBC," we answered. "Oh really, he's quite a character, speaks his mind, stirs up lots of mischief, but is no good as a bank reference. Who else do you know?" We thought of Bernie Braden. "Oh, you don't know Bernie Braden, do you? He's so popular here, we all feel part of his family, he's marvellous but of course is no good as a bank reference." He then asked, "Who do you know at Canada House?" We did not know who was at Canada House then, but was sure they would know of York's work. The teller left and eventually returned to say the bank would cash our draft.

We visited the Tate Gallery, the National Gallery, the theatre and the Tower of London, where the two princes smothered in the tower had the same surname as York's mother, Maude York. We enjoyed lunches in pubs and tasted our first bangers and mash, rode the double-decker buses and marvelled at the cockney accents spoken by the women conductors who called everyone "dearie." We met A.T.S. McGhee, who took us to the London Festival Hall and to see the swans on the Thames.

THE VOYAGE HOME

Soon we were off to Southampton to board the *Rhinedam*. The sight of seeing the fragile Tenerife crates lifted by the crane unnerved York. He immediately found the ship's carpenter and had new crates made on board.

After a good crossing we arrived in New York and faced the difficult New York Customs officers, who demanded we ship the paintings separately to Toronto. We argued and pleaded to no avail and were sent from one person to another. Finally I was sent to make arrangements, leaving York talking, when he soon signalled me to wait. He caught up and said, "Keep going before someone stops us, I've just received clearance." We arrived in Toronto and all was well.

AN ARTIST'S CONTRACT

Upon our return to Toronto in mid-August, York went to the Laing Galleries to discuss his contract, signed the previous year. The custom whereby art gallery dealers gave contracts to artists was rare in 1952. The Laing Galleries of Toronto had offered York a guaranteed annual income of $10,000. York would be given more from sales exceeding this amount, and if less was sold, the gallery would purchase paintings up to this value. This was a very fair deal, and a dream for most artists. York signed the contract without much thought because he enjoyed working with his friend Blair Laing, who had plans to show York's work in other countries. York was conscious of the fact that Arthur Laing, Blair's father, controlled the gallery.

The contract took the form of a monthly cheque, which we received throughout our stay in the Canary Islands. The cheque would arrive in Tenerife without any information about the works sold. York began feeling that it was a cold commercial deal that lacked the excitement of knowing which paintings had sold to whom. York was a strong individualist for whom the love and excitement of painting outweighed the economic benefits. Toward the end of our stay in Tenerife York decided to end the contract upon our return home.

The year of York's contract with the Laing Gallery was coming to an end. He visited Arthur Laing, suggested they return to the old consignment system and tried to explain his position. Laing was taken aback, feeling that he had done something special in giving York the contract. They had sold more than agreed and Laing was willing to raise the guaranteed amount substantially. York tried to explain that money had nothing to do with it, he just wanted to be free. It had to do with his spirit and reason for painting. This made no sense to the elderly Arthur, who lost his temper and screamed, "Get your things out of here, I will have nothing more to do with you."

So York bundled up the remainder of his work and drove directly to Roberts Gallery, owned by Jack Wildridge, who welcomed York and represented him for the rest of his career. Blair Laing soon visited to assure York that all would quiet down and that he should return to their gallery. Blair was a good friend and tried many times over the next few years to persuade York to return.

BACK IN THE SWING OF THINGS

Upon our return we were pleased to learn that Paul Duval's important book, *Canadian Drawings and Prints* (1952) included York's drawing *Mexican Girl* (1951). Claire Wallace interviewed York about our extended stay in the Canary Islands and broadcast a program mentioning the Islands' history, social customs, scenery and daily life.

In November York had a highly successful solo exhibition—his first ever sell-out—at the Watson Art Galleries in Montreal. The exhibition was comprised of thirty-one works in duco from the Canary Islands trip. The show was reviewed in the Montreal Gazette (November 8, 1952), the *Montreal Star* (November 15, 1952), *La Vie* (November 15, 1952) and *Canadian Art* (Spring 1952). Two of York's duco pieces from the show were purchased by the National Gallery of Canada, *Una Familia* and the cityscape *Santa Cruz de Tenerife* (1952).

York's recent work was celebrated by Paul Duval in a full-page article, "At Home Abroad," in *Saturday Night* (December 20, 1952). "Ballerinas, burros, businessmen and race track habitués are a few of the varied sources for this artist's catholic approach to nature," wrote Duval. York's solo show at the Watson Galleries revealed that the artist had "developed from a spirited and competent reporter of the passing scene into one of Canada's most original and vigorous creative painters." Duval concluded with the observation that York's biggest advances were in his use of colour. "Today, he is one of the country's outstanding colourists."

One of the most important things for an artist is to have his or her work invited to one of the prestigious international exhibitions. While we were still in Tenerife, Gordon Washburn, curator of the 1952 Carnegie International, to be held at the Carnegie Institute in Pittsburgh, visited Canada and selected work by York and five other artists—B.C. Binning, Paul-Émile Borduas, Stanley Cosgrove, Marthe Rakine and Goodridge Roberts—to represent Canada. Mr. Washburn personally selected *Margaritones* (1952), one of York's Mexican paintings, from the walls of Laing Galleries.

1953

Lotta Dempsey opened the year on a positive note with her observation in the *Globe and Mail* (January 9, 1953) that York's paintings were "reaching even new heights of expression," and that his "strong, sensitive creativeness is helping to bring us fresh praise from abroad for Canadian art and themes."

A rather bizarre incident occurred at the AGT at about this time when the artist W.J.B. Newcombe declared that Communist ideology had supposedly influenced the jury's choice of some of the works in the current exhibition of the Canadian Society of Graphic Arts at the AGT. The CSGA selected a panel of five prominent individuals—York, Paul Duval, William Winter, Alec Panton and Syd Watson—to examine the exhibition for signs of Communist influence. As a report in the *Telegram* (March 31, 1953) indicated, after careful consideration of the works and the issue, the panel found no evidence of such influence. An article in the *Globe and Mail* (April 2, 1953), however, reported that Newcombe was still not satisfied. The accusation unfortunately generated extensive press coverage.

The six-person jury in charge of selecting the work of Canadian artists for the CNE Art Gallery in the summer of 1953 consisted of Lionel Thomas (Vancouver), LeMoine FitzGerald (Winnipeg), Paul Duval, and three Toronto painters, York, Cleeve and Syd Watson; a group photograph was published in the *Globe and Mail* (July 27, 1953). They assembled in Toronto a month prior to the CNE's opening in mid-August. The jury took their job very seriously; Pearl McCarthy remarked in the *Globe and Mail* that they "had done a wonderful job of selecting 'Sound Canadian Work.'" As the *Telegram* (May 19, 1953) reported, York had earlier served on a three-person jury with Charles Comfort and Eric Aldwinckle that adjudicated a competition to find a muralist suitable to decorate the new offices of the *Telegram*.

Our 1952 trip was reflected in the titles of the paintings York sent to the art society exhibitions in 1953. *Moroccan Conversation Piece* (1952) and *Women of Casablanca* (1952) went to the OSA show at the AGT, while *Fez, Morocco* (1952) went to the RCA exhibition at the AGT in late 1953. York's portrait of Oscar de Lall was also included in the RCA show. This unusual portrait was the result of our early arrival for RCA jury duty. Oscar wanted to do a portrait of me, and York returned the favour by doing a portrait of him. Both were included in the exhibition; the wet oils were handled carefully through the jurying and installation process.

The numerous works York contributed to the OSA Little Pictures Exhibition at Eaton's College Street Galleries were reviewed in the *Telegram* (January 17, 1953) as "easily the tours de force in the admiral OSA annual exhibition." York sent *The Medina at Fez* (1952) to the National Gallery's "Annual Exhibition of Canadian Painting" in March.

Wilson was well represented at the AGT in November of 1953. Ten works in a three-person exhibition with Yvonne McKague Housser and Alec Panton, including *Cactus Forms* (1954), *Sun and Nets* (1953), and *Indian Dance* (1954) represented him. His *Moroccan Group* (1953), *Floristas* (1952) and *Moroccan Types* (1953) were included in the Women's Committee exhibition, also held at the AGT that month.

York was selected to do a portrait of David Walker, a Conservative candidate running in the Rosedale riding and later a Senator. The finished portrait, published in the *Globe and Mail* (November 24, 1953) and presented to Walker by Arthur Meighen, now hangs in Toronto's Albany Club.

THE "CITIES OF CANADA" PAINTING COLLECTION

York was honoured to be involved in one of the most ambitious painting programs ever to take place in Canada, when the House of Seagram commissioned some twenty artists to paint images of twenty-nine Canadian cities. Some of the other artists selected were A.C. Leighton, Franklin Arbuckle, W.J. Phillips, Robert Pilot, Harold Beament, Goodridge Roberts and Albert Cloutier. York was chosen to do pictures of Regina and Sarnia.

When Seagram's sent the collection on an international tour in 1953, York had completed *Regina* (1953). It was reproduced in the catalogue, along with a brief biography of York and his description of the city. York chose an aerial view in order to convey the idea that Regina is literally an island set in a desert of wheat. He painted from the roof of the Saskatchewan Hotel, which enabled him to show the strange effect of the Parliament Buildings "rising" up out of the wheat fields on the edge of the city.

New Liberty magazine (May 1953) reproduced fourteen of the city paintings in full colour, including York's *Regina*. When York finished *Sarnia* later that year, Rose Macdonald of the *Telegram* declared it "one of the most outstanding paintings in the collection, and also, in its interpretative quality, nearest of any in the show to abstract painting."

York and Alec Panton in York's studio, in our home at 8 Apsley Road. Toronto, early 1950s.

X

1953-1956

The McGill and Salvation Army Murals; Meeting Rico Lebrun

YORK AND I NEEDED SOME NEW TABLES for our living room. A framed, well-supported piece of masonite seemed ideal. He completed a magnificent work which served as our coffee table, and later did two more on drawing boards, as he was too impatient to wait for other materials. He roughed the surface of our circular metal patio table and proceeded to paint it in great style; it unfortunately chipped and did not last.

On special occasions he did tables for friends, the first for Jean and Cleeve Horne for their new Claremont farmhouse. The table he did for Jack Wildridge's cottage was unfortunately stolen. One of his best tables was later done for our Tenerife friend, Carlos Pinto.

NEW FRIENDS

We hosted mad, creative costume parties at our home, and sometimes at the Hornes'. The early group consisted of Syd and Ethel Hallam, A.J. and Margaret Casson, Alec and Marian Panton, Cleeve and Jean Horne, Eric Aldwinckle, Syd and Helen Watson, Paul Duval, Wally and Kay Graham, and Jack and Mabel Bush. Some fell by the wayside over the years, while others were added: Ettore (Mazz) and Joanne Mazzoleni, Herman and Violet Voaden, Yvonne McKague Housser, Isabel McLaughlin, and Bobs and Peter Haworth. Other later additions and visitors were Elsie and Mac Samples, Barbara and Peter Ivey, Ayala and Sam Zacks, Corinne McLuhan and Beryl and Dick Ivey. Ayala thought we were a bunch of children who had never grown up.

"The Gang" spent many long, crazy weekends at the Mazzolenis' summer home at Grand Bend on Lake Erie. York painted a table for Joanne and Mazz in appreciation. They had a metal table on hand, which, like our patio table, chipped and had deteriorated when I last saw it.

THE MCGILL MURAL

The *Globe and Mail* of June 11, 1953 and the *Telegram* (June 13, 1953) both announced that York had won a national competition for the design of a mural for the extension of the Redpath Library at McGill University in Montreal. The competition was administered by the RCA.

The mural had to feature images of various university buildings, past and present, and portraits of six men who had played critical roles in the university's development: the founder James McGill, the first principal Bishop George Mountain, former principals Sir William Dawson and Edwin Meredith, first chancellor Dewey Day and William Molson, builder of McGill's first library. York tackled this challenging project with relish. His winning sketch was published in the *Montreal Star* on December 4, 1953 and featured in the 74th annual RCA exhibition in Toronto.

The cartoon was painted in the rented Toronto studio of the famed Canadian artist C.W. Jefferys. York felt honoured to use Jefferys' small mural steps and eventually acquired them. Virginia, who assisted York throughout the McGill project, vividly recalls LeMoine FitzGerald's visit to the hallowed studio. York took the large cartoon, painted in duco on masonite, by train to Montreal for presentation. It was accepted.

York purchased the paints used in the McGill mural at a Toronto auto repair shop. He mixed the colours with sand to reduce gloss and lend texture, and applied them to large masonite panels prepared with a white ground. The mural was to be situated on the upper mezzanine level of the main reading room. Scaffolding was installed and York went to work. The work progressed well; university professors including Hugh MacLennan sometimes stopped by for a chat.

The 12' x 18' mural painting, like the final sketch, features half-length images of the six luminaries posed in a stately frieze above the facades of university buildings including Redpath Hall, Dawson Hall and the Redpath Museum. Burnside, James McGill's tiny house, occupies the centre foreground. The mural took four months to complete and was unveiled on October 6, 1953. The *Montreal Gazette* (September 23, 1953) reported the mural's completion in a major article accompanied by photographs of the new reading room and mural in progress. The writer noted the mural's unique medium, and quoted York's statement that "it is the only one so painted in Canada." The new mural was also featured in an article in the *Globe and Mail* (November 7, 1953).

The McGill mural proved to be the only commission of York's career secured through competition. As Paul Duval reported in *York Wilson* (1978), York later declared that it was "a mistake to enter competitions. When you attempt to create with someone dangling a material incentive in front of you...it is impossible to be relaxed and be yourself."

McGill celebrated its 100th anniversary in 1955 with a commemorative exhibition in the Redpath Museum of the work of Sir William Dawson, principal of McGill from 1855 to 1893. The booklet produced for the occasion showed York's mural on the cover, with a caption pointing out Dawson's portrait.

OUR RETURN TO SAN MIGUEL TO MEET RICO LEBRUN

York learned in the autumn of 1953 that Rico Lebrun was living in San Miguel. York had been aware of Lebrun's work since the Italian artist emigrated from Naples to New York in 1925. His accomplished work, with its superb draughtsmanship, began to appear in American publications including *Vogue*, *The New Yorker* and *Harper's Bazaar*. We thus left for San Miguel in September of 1953 with the express purpose of meeting Lebrun, who was fully conscious of York's work as well. Although we didn't know it at the time, Rico had served on the jury for the 1952 Pittsburgh International Exhibition, in which York's *Margaritones* was included. Both men were anxious to meet.

Upon our arrival, our friend Dr. Francisco Olsina held a dinner party in our honour, with Leonard and Reva Brooks and Rico Lebrun and his wife Constance. After the introductions, Rico and York were so self-conscious they didn't talk to each other for the rest of the evening. The next morning I met Constance, daughter of the California architect Reginald Johnson, in the market and invited her and Rico for drinks. They came and it was love at first sight for all of us. Rico and York talked until long past dinnertime. It turned out to be Rico's birthday, so we celebrated with an impromptu party.

York's studio was at Hospicio No. 8. Its windows faced north onto the street; a seldom-used door inside the street door opened into the studio. The day after Rico's birthday he turned up at York's studio, tapping on the window. York let him in by this "secret" door. I had standing instructions that York was never to be disturbed before five o'clock in the afternoon. York and Rico had been chatting quietly for some time when I appeared shortly after 5:00 P.M. On hearing my approach Rico hid behind some plants. He invited us for dinner that night. This was the pattern for most of the winter.

Rico was an early bird, starting in his studio at daybreak and working until 2:00 P.M. He saw all of York's works, discussing them in detail, and then invited York to his studio. They exchanged ideas and talked endlessly; Constance and I were fortunately just as interested. Constance usually sat at Rico's feet and gazed adoringly at her husband while he spoke, seeming to hang on every word. It's possible they hadn't been married very long!

RICO'S FASCINATING LECTURES

Rico worked quickly and on a very large scale. He had great sheets of brown paper all over the studio floor, apart from endless small studies. He was a great draughtsman but not much of a colourist. His work was often based on the idea of man's inhumanity to man. He was well versed in art history and his lectures at the *Instituto Allende* were something that even seasoned painters did not want to miss. One morning Rico said to York, "You are giving the lecture this morning." York pleaded his lack of preparation, to which Rico replied, "Just tell them what you are trying to do in your work."

York felt somewhat more at ease, and proceeded to deliver a most interesting lecture. He knew he had to, with Rico sitting in the front row! After Rico's first two lectures he asked York for any criticism. York replied, "Well, if I have to think of something, it might be that you always seem to be talking directly to me." Rico said, "I am, because if I start to talk bullshit, I know that you will know and no one else here knows enough."

Rico always placed York front and centre and delivered the whole lecture to him. He was so relaxed, walking back and forth as he talked, because he knew his subject well. In one lecture he gave the history of the era, what was happening politically and in every direction, showing how it affected painting and why particular events had happened. He covered many periods this way, noting them with dates on the blackboard.

OTHERS MEET RICO

John Crown, a visiting concert pianist and professor of music at the University College of Los Angeles, happened to attend this particularly expansive lecture. John proposed that he tackle the history of music in a similar manner, but with a smaller, select group around his piano. A day was set, and John and Sally Crown invited a few friends. John outlined the eras in the same way and played music befitting each era, explaining why it had progressed in certain directions. It was a wonderful evening. The Crowns had become our friends almost on arrival, and joined our small group.

That autumn York's former student, the stockbroker Jim Gairdner and his new wife Kay turned up in San Miguel. Kay was a lovely gentle person, so different to the sporty, hale Jim. We had them to dinner and served duck, freshly shot and brought over by Stirling Dickinson.

York talked about Rico's work. Jim was anxious to meet Rico and see his work, a difficult proposition since Rico rarely allowed anyone in his studio. York talked to Rico of this wealthy philanthropist who had funded so many good causes and was devoted to painting. Rico agreed that we could bring them the next morning. Jim stood quietly looking as Rico showed his large abstract sketches. Rico eventually showed Jim some small studies; a picture of a fish skeleton on a plate caught Jim's eye. Jim asked if he could purchase it, but Rico replied, "It belongs to York; if he says you can have it, it's a gift." York was taken aback, wondering what Rico's motive could be, but quickly agreed.

Later Rico explained that if he did a favour for Jim, Jim might be moved to do something for art in Canada. Jim and Kay were pleased with their acquisition, but I think Jim was a little uncomfortable, as he was accustomed to being the generous one. Back in Toronto, Jim framed the Lebrun sketch and installed it on his office wall, where it stayed until shortly before his death. He then sent the sketch to York, saying it was his turn to enjoy it.

RICO'S ADVICE TO YORK

One afternoon when Rico sneaked into York's studio, he found York working on a painting, which apparently included a few "hot licks." Rico gave him hell, punching every word through gritted teeth, while pantomiming slapping his face from side to side, saying, "Don't ever let me catch you doing that sort of thing again." It really shook York up, as it was a facility that he had to fight from his days as a commercial artist. Since Rico had also evolved from commercial to fine art, he spotted the problems immediately.

As York's three-year tenure as OSA president had been so successful, the RCA had him in mind as its next president. Rico convinced York that his life should be dedicated to painting and not carried away with administrative tasks, however illustrious. York was still young then and in his prime, and accepting these prestigious positions was a temptation. He was fortunate to have a few older friends who understood these traps.

SAYING FAREWELL TO RICO

When it came time for us to return to Toronto, Rico and Constance proposed that we go with them to Los Angeles. There were many people Rico wanted York to meet and perhaps collaborate with. Rico felt that York shouldn't waste his time on murals, but York maintained that murals were right for him. He liked working on a large scale, and had the gift of being able to visualise proportions accordingly. Rico had never done a mural. Nothing could have pleased York more than spending time with Rico, but fate may have been kind. Rico was a very strong personality, and too much time with him could be damaging.

This proved true in the case of our friend Jimmy Pinto. Jim and Rico had become close friends in San Miguel, and referred to themselves as brothers. Rico returned to Italy in 1959 to become artist-in-residence at the American Academy in Rome, and invited Jim to accompany him to Italy. We later noticed how a year with Rico changed Jimmy noticeably, he became moody and testy as though something deep-rooted was bothering him. His paintings were less interesting, and his amazing colour sense seemed diminished.

Rico was offered a mural commission at Pomona College in Claremont, California in 1959. He asked York to assist but York refused, saying he was a muralist and not an assistant. Jim Pinto and the California artist William Ptaszynski assisted Rico. When complete, the small mural was very much Rico's, with practically no colour. Jimmy was not given proper credit.

Jimmy continued to teach advanced painting at the *Instituto Allende*, winding up as dean of painters there. He seemed to go into a sort of a decline for a while. Jim and Rushka had a serious motor accident, which left Rushka lame. At the time there was speculation that it may not have been accidental. Many years later, his work became more interesting. Jimmy died in 1990, and Rushka was so distraught that she didn't wish to live and took her own life. It was goodbye to two dear friends.

York was on the Exhibition Committee at the AGT, and was instrumental in arranging an exhibition of Rico's work there in March of 1958. Rico's arrival caused much excitement. The Mazelow Gallery organised a concurrent Lebrun exhibition, and Rico gave a workshop at the Ontario College of Art. The AGT purchased *Descent from the Cross* (1950) from the exhibition. As we were then away on a painting trip in the West Indies, Rico had dinner with our neighbours, Wallace and Kay Graham. Rico said it felt strange looking over at our empty house next door.

OUR DREAM HOME AT 41 ALCINA AVENUE

York had been using the master bedroom as his studio in our home at 8 Apsley Road since 1943. We finally decided to do something about it and started looking at houses but it seemed impossible to find a ready-made studio, so we switched to looking for building lots.

We first asked Gordon Adamson to be our architect, and then John Parkin. Both replied that the job was too small to put through their respective practices. They were in agreement, however, when we asked John Layng. John was delighted to take on the project. He visualised a small piece of property with a house that required little upkeep, thus giving us the freedom of an apartment. At this point we happened to be spending the weekend with Wallace and Kay Graham at the Hornes' farm near Claremont. Finding property taxes very high, Wally was thinking of selling some of his property in Wychwood Park. We agreed on a price of $7,000.

York's only instructions to John Layng were that the house must be interesting and that it must include a two-storey, north-facing studio of specific dimensions. We had by then travelled to numerous countries where we had enjoyed flagstone floors. John Layng and Gordon Adamson both advised against it, saying the stone surfaces were dirty and would shale. John Goba, the builder, supported us and we finally got our stone floors, which were finished with silicone to harden the surface.

Radiant heating was in vogue as it was very space-efficient and did not create drafts. A six-inch block of cement covered in flagstones contained the hot water pipes in the ground floor. The bedrooms on the second floor had an extra layer of plaster wrapped around the ceiling pipes. We found it amusing that Gordon rushed to use flagstone floors in another house completed before ours.

While living in an apartment on Yonge Street in 1954 waiting for our house to be built, the musical "Guys and Dolls" came to the Royal Alexander Theatre. Our new friend Graeme Wilson brought the lovely star Margo Moser to visit. Margo gave us two tickets for the show; this was the beginning of a lifelong friendship.

We were finally able to move in to our new home in June of 1955. It was very exciting for us as York at long last had a studio especially designed for his needs and I had the pleasure of arranging the rest of the house and garden.

Our old friends Wally and Kay, now next-door neighbours, said their children missed their tree house, which had been uprooted for our home, and Kay missed her asparagus bed. Kay was very keen on the poetry of Emily Dickinson and early Canadian pottery, among other things. She became more and more interested in the visual arts and loved to visit York's studio on any pretence just to watch him work, which didn't exactly please him. Wally often wandered over to our back patio on a Sunday morning. One such morning he turned up to find York complaining about a painful toe. Wally examined it and decided it was gout. Although he had done his thesis on gout, he hadn't seen a case in years, so he became quite excited and suggested York have a couple of beers (which worsens the pain) to see what would happen. Gout is very painful, and York told him to go to hell. The problem soon cleared up. We had many pleasant times together, often playing croquet on their spacious lawn.

1954 ART ACTIVITIES

The OSA held a memorial exhibition in early 1954 of the work of Syd Hallam, who died in November of 1953. York was invited to write a tribute for the catalogue in honour of his close friend. Syd's great humour and quick wit will always be remembered.

An illustrated article on two recent murals, York's at McGill and Stanley Cosgrove's at the *Collège de Saint-Laurent*, near Montreal, was featured in *Canadian Art* (Winter 1954). A photograph of the McGill mural accompanied the article. *Welfare Worker* came back to haunt us when it was reproduced in *Saturday Night* (April 10, 1954) along with scenes of a beer parlour and a trolley car by Franklin Arbuckle and a painting of a midnight snack at a greasy spoon by William Winter. The article was ironically titled "How Canadians Behave Themselves."

The Williams Memorial Art Museum in London mounted a two-person exhibition of the work of York and the Ottawa-born painter Roger Larivière in March. An article in the London *Free Press* (March 20, 1954) entitled "Canadian in Mexico, Canadian in Canada" reproduced both artists' works. York was invited to have a solo exhibition at Hart House in September. Complimentary reviews appeared in *The Varsity* (September 23, 1954) and the *Globe and Mail* (September 25, 1954), in which Pearl McCarthy said that York's "semi-abstracts have grown in stature beyond what could have been foretold." York was still teaching three evenings each week at that time.

While Rico Lebrun was in San Miguel, one of his students was Toronto artist Bob Hedrick. Rico felt that York could help Bob stay on the right course, so he gave Bob a letter of introduction to deliver to York. York invited Bob to visit, doing his best to get Bob's trust and interest in an effort to discover how he could assist him. Bob seemed sullen and difficult, so York simply invited Bob to contact him if needed. Bob went on to become a well-known painter and sculptor.

It was time again for the RCA exhibition in Montreal; York sent a large canvas, *Seated Figure* (1954), which was reproduced in the catalogue. A solo exhibition of York's work opened at Montreal's Watson Galleries in late October. The show was reviewed in *La Presse* (October 30, 1954). The *Gazette* (October 30, 1954) thought the show a success, and Robert Ayre of the *Montreal Star* (November 6, 1954) decided that, "This is a show that calls for serious attention. You should take your time with it. Its quality comes out in contemplation."

In November, York's paintings were placed in a historical context in an article in *Maclean's* (November 15, 1954) entitled "A Gallery of Northern Painting." The work of York, billed as "one of the most talented members of the generation that followed the Group" of Seven was discussed with paintings by A.Y. Jackson, Fred Varley, Lawren Harris and Sir Frederick Banting, who had accompanied Jackson to the Arctic in 1927. The writer mentioned that the sketch for York's *Mile 804, Alaska Highway*, reproduced in colour, was inspired by a scene York saw through the inch-thick frost covering his taxi window!

1955

The year opened with York's solo exhibition at the Roberts Gallery, a show that featured mostly his Mexican paintings. Rose Macdonald of the

Telegram (January 21, 1955) remarked on York's "markedly heightened" stature and focused on his successful use of "subtle tonalities of color: color frequently used transparently and, though this is not emphasised, with reference to the purposes of the cubists." Of his figure works, Macdonald cited *Mexican Madonnas* (1955) and *Market by Day* (1955).

As the *Telegram* (January 8, 1955) reported, the 83rd annual OSA exhibition opened at the AGT in early January to an audience of 1700, its second-largest attendance ever. The growing interest in art and the success of art-related social events were due to many factors: the Women's Committee, the hard-working members of the art societies and the dedicated gallery members, touring exhibitions, lectures, demonstrations, York's live broadcasts from the gallery during openings, and stringent jurying. The jury that year, composed of York, Jack Bush, A.J. Casson, Syd Watson and Oscar Cahén, selected only eighty-five of four hundred works submitted. In the *Telegram* (January 8, 1955) Rose Macdonald reported the unique "light panel" method of voting, first devised by Cleeve Horne in 1949. York's *Growing Forms* (1955) included in the show, was mentioned in *Canadian Art* (Spring 1955) as creating "an upward feeling with flame shapes unfurling and casting dark shadows in a light, earthy texture" and in the *Telegram* (January 8, 1955) as a "distinguished, unusual and subtly expressed, albeit almost sculptural concept of the Canadian landscape."

Charlotte Whitton, mayor of Ottawa, opened the exhibition. Syd Watson, then OSA president, invited a few of us back to his and Helen's home for a reception that evening. We drove Mayor Whitton there and arrived to find chaos. The Watson home had been robbed and all the liquor, among other things, had been stolen. The police arrived in minutes. Cleeve and Jean went home to get more liquor. Meanwhile Mayor Whitton declared, "I'm in charge here!" and began instructing the police. As people arrived they sat down in the rows of chairs facing a policeman standing guard at the door. As everyone looked at the policeman on guard and he stared back, someone called out, "Do you know who that is giving orders? She is Mayor Whitton of Ottawa." The policeman was shaken and he cried, "Jesus Christ, I thought I had seen that puss before."

The Agent General for Ontario, J.S.P. Armstrong, sponsored a program for Canadian artists to show their work in England. Almost all of the 142 works included in the exhibition were drawn from Canadian collections, assembled by Blair Laing and shipped to London. The show was opened on

January 19, 1955 by Field Marshal The Earl of Alexander and The Countess Alexander of Tunis at the galleries of Fortnum and Mason, owned by Canadian business magnate Garfield Weston. Sir Gerald Kelly, president of the Royal Academy, gave York's duco painting *Mexican Women* (1955) an honourable mention. The *Illustrated London News* (February 5, 1955) reproduced the work of seven Canadians, including York.

The medium of drawing, often neglected in public exhibitions, was brought to the fore by members of the OSA, who decided to stage a drawing exhibition at Eaton's College Street Galleries in February of 1955. York's contributions to the show included the fine, sensitive *Ballerina* (1954) and *Today's Religion* (1954), which depicted a row of houses, each adorned with a television aerial.

Some of Toronto's interior decorators designed special rooms at the CNE that summer; one room displaying the furniture of the American designer Edward Womley included York's *Moroccan Conversation Piece* over the fireplace. York showed *Montmartre at Night* (1954) at the Montreal Museum of Fine Art's spring exhibition, and sent *Echo* (1954) to the touring CGP exhibition. The AGT purchased York's duco painting *Janitzio Island* (1954) in 1955.

THE SALVATION ARMY MURAL, 1955

The new Salvation Army headquarters, at Albert and James behind Toronto's old city hall, was designed by John B. Parkin Associates and completed in late 1955. John Parkin chose York to do a mural for the prayer room and Jack Nichols for a mural at the building's entrance. York agreed to the commission in late 1954 and set to work on his design.

York had some difficulty with the Salvation Army Property Board over his first proposal. He felt that nothing in the prayer room should distract the supplicants from their communion with God. He thus proposed an image of Christ, arms outstretched, indicating "Come Unto Me." In a letter to John Parkin on January 7, 1955, Brigadier A.G. Cameron informed the architect that this concept "would not be readily appreciated by the general Salvation Army following," and instead proposed the "idea of 'Mercy Seat', Shekinah Glory or Heavenly Light penetrating to earth and a semblance of upraised hands."

York decided he wished to withdraw from the commission. He soon received a call from W. Wycliffe Booth, the Salvation Army's new territorial commander who arrived in Toronto to take up his post in 1955. General Booth requested a meeting at his home with York to discuss the mural. They had a long conversation, during which General Booth asked York how well he knew the Bible. Although York answered in the negative, he had been a choir boy and had taught Sunday school. The General wanted to get to know York and they talked for two or three hours over tea. General Booth eventually managed to get York's new sketch accepted by the Property Board.

York's design expressed the six verses of the Twenty-third Psalm in six sections of a 9' x 15' mural. He used a new medium with which he had been experimenting, vinyl acetate. He engaged our daughter Virginia as his assistant as she was familiar with the new medium. We had all worked together to find the correct materials for the new formula. Obliging chemists in Canada and the USA helped us to identify ingredients, and they supplied us with enough samples to complete the small mural. With the necessary materials assembled, York attempted to mix the medium for the first time. He added the chemicals to a huge container while I stirred steadily. We noticed a quick build-up of heat, and backed away in fear that an explosion might occur! Luckily this was not the case, and many gallons were later mixed without any worries.

When the mural was nearly complete, York began to experience chest pains. He told no one and made excuses to lunch alone for some respite. He was pretty sure what the problem was and knew Virginia would tell me if she discovered it. He was anxious to finish the mural. The pressures of his teaching and the difficulties with the Property Board did not help.

The day the mural was finished, York confessed his chest pains. It was midnight. I called over Wally Graham, a doctor, who examined York and decided to admit him to the hospital, "just to be on the safe side." As they left, Wally told me he was fairly certain it was a heart attack. York was somewhat surprised when he was escorted to a wheelchair at the hospital. Dr. W.F. Greenwood, a heart specialist and friend of Wally's, examined York and assigned him to bed rest. It wasn't until the second day when York heard the retiring nurse mentioning the term "cardiac arrest." York was then forty-eight years old. After three weeks bed rest, he was allowed home for Christmas.

When the mural was complete, some Board members asked for changes, as they felt it wasn't finished. John Parkin called a meeting. John listened until everyone had their say and York explained his thinking related to the mural. John then turned to York and asked him if the mural was finished. York replied with an unequivocal yes. John then turned to the Board and declared, "The artist says the mural is finished and we must listen to what the artist says." He immediately disbanded the meeting and walked out!

"Modernistic Murals in Salvation Army Building," a front page article in the *Globe and Mail* (January 9, 1956), showed reproductions of the two finished murals. Pearl McCarthy wrote of the "floating idealism" of Jack Nichols' work, and that the colour and form of York's mural "justifies that much-abused word, significant." She concluded that the art and architecture of the new Salvation Army building stood as "Canada's most humanistic expression of modernism, being, as the saying goes, 'of our day.'"

Long after the Salvation Army mural was completed, York published an article in *The Canadian Architect* (May 1957), in which he reflected on the problems inherent to the marriage of art and architecture. If the client expected the mural to "be a decorative embellishment to the architecture and, at the same time, to act as an illustration," which of these functions was to take precedence? In the case of the Salvation Army mural, York had opted for a less literal interpretation of the Twenty-third Psalm so that the painting was consistent with the modern style of the building. York related the difficulties of the Property Board's acceptance of a contemporary idiom. The real success of the mural, he concluded, will be realised, "if people feel persuaded to visit the prayer room more often, and find it conducive to prayer."

York at work on his mural for the Redpath Library, McGill University.
Montreal, 1953. Photograph by the Montreal Gazette.

XI

1954-1957

The Imperial Oil Mural

IN EARLY 1954 YORK RECEIVED ONE OF THE BIGGEST commissions of his creative career, a mural for the entrance of Toronto's new Imperial Oil Building at 111 St. Clair Avenue West. Cleeve Horne had been engaged to direct the art work for the building. He was convinced that York should paint the entrance mural; he simply presented three of York's paintings to the Board and they approved his choice. The contract was signed in November of 1954. Cleeve chose Syd Watson to do a mural in the board room, and Oscar Cahén to do one in the cafeteria.

York's mural was over two years in the planning; he spent nearly a year doing preliminary drawings. During his convalescence from his heart attack in December of 1955, he read extensively on the history and properties of oil. York was given free creative rein in the selection and treatment of his theme. He later worked up his drawings into large cartoons ready for presentation to the Board.

It was arranged for the Board members to visit York's studio to see the cartoons. The dark-suited, Homburg-hatted men filed into our entrance hall at the agreed minute. They removed their hats, folded and stacked their top coats methodically, and filed down the stairs to the studio. After exchanging greetings, York explained his mural. They listened carefully. There were a few words, a few nods of approval, and then the spokesperson informed York to commence work. They then filed out, retrieved their coats and hats and departed. The whole exercise took no longer than twenty minutes!

THE MEDIUM

York had experimented successfully with vinyl acetate on the Salvation Army mural. The Imperial Oil mural, however, was much larger in scale. It was to be composed of two panels, each 21' high by 32' wide. York searched for the purest powdered colours available and found those distributed in Canada lacking, as they were diluted with too much chalk. He then imported the necessary pure pigments from New York in 1956. The dry pigments would be mixed with the liquid vinyl acetate.

Imperial Oil's laboratory further tested all the materials for durability. Each colour was tested with a brush rigged to move repeatedly over the surface for long periods of time, thus simulating hundreds of years of wear. Extremely bright sunlight and artificial light were used over long periods to test fading. The chemists finally approved vinyl acetate, and predicted it would outlast oils. The advantages of vinyl acetate are numerous. It is completely permanent, and can be applied to any surface. As the painted surface is matt in finish, the mural could be viewed from any angle without glare. Furthermore, it dries rapidly, and can be cleaned without damaging the painted surface.

PREPARATION

Work began on the mural in July of 1956. York collaborated with the engineers to design the mural surfaces. They "floated" the two panels at a small distance from the actual wall, so that any vibrations caused by an earthquake, for example, would not crack the mural surface. An intricate air circulation system installed on a grid behind the wall prevented condensation. York preferred a rough ground, and had the plasterer swirl his sack-covered arm over the wet surface of specially prepared plaster. Fourteen gallons of a vinyl undercoat were applied to the plaster to seal it before painting began. The preparation of the wall surface was completed by mid-August.

In July, York took out a one-year insurance policy to cover his two assistants, Bob Paterson and Jack Bechtel. Bob Paterson was an outstanding student from the Ontario College of Art who had been recommended by principal Syd Watson. Jack Bechtel was a former student of York's and fellow instructor at the Doon School of Fine Art. When Bob and Jack arrived to start work at the end of August, York had had his large original sketch photographed in colour, section by section. Each slide, representing a sixteen-foot width of the finished mural, was projected on to the wall in the darkness of night. The shapes were then outlined directly on the wall in India ink. In late September, York made boxes with handles to carry paints and supplies up the scaffolding. The mammoth task of painting the mural had begun.

THE FILM

Imperial Oil engaged Ottawa's Crawley Films to record the execution of the mural. Director Quentin Brown filmed background footage in York's studio, where York displayed the cartoon and explained his concept for the mural to Jack and Bob. The crew was on site for many nights early in the project, filming York, Jack and Bob high up on the scaffolding as they traced the main lines of the design onto the wall with the aid of the projected slides. Paul Duval reported in the *Telegram* (September 8, 1956) that the "vast foyer" of the building had been "transformed into a motion picture studio," where cameras would record "the launching of the largest painting ever to decorate a Canadian building." The finished film was discussed in an article in *Public Relations in Canada* (November-December 1957), along with another Crawley production, "The Legend of the Raven."

As fall approached, the building front, eventually to be clad in glass, was still open. It was a mighty cold operation at times; work ceased in early October due to the winter weather. York enjoyed much camaraderie with the men who were constructing the building. One worker said, "You think you're Michelangelo." York replied, "I am, is there someone else using my name?" One cartoon showed York as Rembrandt, painting by numbers. Imperial Oil's annual report for 1956 featured a colour photograph of the three artists at work on the mural, the left side then partially finished.

OTHER ART ACTIVITY IN 1956

While York's attention was devoted largely to the planning and execution of the Imperial Oil mural for much of 1956, the "fine art" part of his life continued unabated. York sent his duco painting *Nocturne* (1956) to the annual OSA exhibition at the AGT. He was included in a five-person show held at the Bennington Heights Community Centre that same month; the other artists represented were Aba Bayefsky, John Hall, Tom Hodgson, and Charles Wakefield.

Thou Preparest a Table (1955), a study for the Salvation Army mural, was included in the annual spring exhibition at the Montreal Museum of Fine Arts. York sent *Montmartre at Night* to "Canadian Abstract Painting," curated by Jean-René Ostiguy of the National Gallery of Canada in mid-1956 and circulated in the United States. "Canadian Artists Abroad," a show assembled by the London Public Library and Art

Museum in March and toured by the National Gallery through 1956, included four of York's works: *Indian Harbour, Guanajuato* (1951), *Una Familia* and *Dancers* (1955).

In the summer, the CNE planned a special exhibition to celebrate its 75th anniversary. Two thousand entry forms were mailed to professional artists across Canada. Cleeve Horne was chairman of the selection jury, which included Cleeve, York, Lionel Thomas, LeMoine FitzGerald, Syd Watson and Paul Duval. They accepted one hundred works. That year, the CNE for the first time allocated $1,500 to purchase works, which were later given to smaller art galleries.

York also acted as a judge for the Western Art Fair, held in London in September. After the experience, he had a long interview with Lenore Crawford of the *Free Press* in London, during which he suggested numerous major changes to the organisation and structure of the fair. His key suggestions included widening the show's representation, increasing the jury's standards, purchasing two works from the show for the permanent collection of the Williams Memorial Art Museum, eliminating the amateur sections and other displays, and establishing a section for serious art students to show their work.

York's works were included in three shows in November and December of 1956. *New Growth* (1956) was included in the second annual exhibition of the Winnipeg Art Association, and his 'rejected' Salvation Army mural study *Come Unto Me* (1955) was shown at the annual RCA exhibition in Montreal. An exhibition of contemporary Canadian art, sponsored jointly by the *Globe and Mail* and Grand and Toy, and held at 8 Wellington Street West late in the year, featured York's *Fire Devastation* (1956). The purpose of this show, as stated in the catalogue, was to "initiate a project of displaying works of Canadian art in the business district of Toronto."

The Montreal Museum of Fine Arts organised a show of the work of York and Philip Surrey, held in Gallery XII of the museum. York sent numerous, diverse works to this show. Among those mentioned in reviews were: *Quebec Barns* (1946), *Reptile* (1956), *Growing Forms, Bottles* (1956), *Fishing Village* (1955), *Dancers* (1949), *Musician* (1953) and *Melon Market, Fez* (1953).

A great sadness struck at that time, when the brilliant painter Oscar Cahén was killed in a car accident on his way home to Oakville, on 26 November.

COMPLETION OF THE IMPERIAL OIL MURAL

On the 15th of February in 1957, York had a meeting with Imperial Oil's Board of Directors. The finished mural, six months and forty five gallons of paint later, was approved at that meeting. *Time* magazine (April 29, 1957) carried news of the completed work. Front page articles appeared in the *Globe and Mail* (April 19, 1957) and the *Telegram* (June 4, 1957). *The Canadian Architect* (June 1957) carried colour photographs of the completed work. Paul Duval published an extensive article in the *Telegram* (February 15, 1957) which related the mural's story from planning to completion. Duval sang York's praises, saying it was not only York's "masterpiece," but the biggest and best work in Canada, unsurpassed by any other single work of art.

An in-depth review by Michael Jacot was published in the *Imperial Oil Review* (June 1957). The theme of York's mural, the story of oil from its beginnings to its contemporary uses, was described by Jacot. The left panel showed "the early period as a rocky landscape set in a weird prehistoric atmosphere; a flowing oil well symbolises the discovery of oil." A beam of light drew the viewer's eye to the right panel, where a giant hand symbolising humanity, holds the atom. "This symbol of man rearranging molecule clusters," Jacot continued, "is surrounded by the result of his scientific achievements," including the evolution of modern transportation and highways, symbolised by an abstract linear pattern. The right panel thus showed "the effect of oil and its products on our present-day mode of living."

Jacot concluded by quoting some early praise for the mural, including that of Paul Duval, and declared that A.Y. Jackson had said, "I think this is the finest thing of its kind ever done in Canada." The success of the mural, Jacot argued, depended on its expression of Canada's "amazing industrial and cultural growth" in the "language of today."

Imperial Oil published a fine brochure entitled "Mural," which included large colour photographs and a descriptive text by Paul Duval. Thousands of copies of the brochure were handed out during countless public tours of the new building, opened in early 1957. The Imperial Oil mural was a personal and artistic triumph for York. If people thought the mural's style unusual at its completion, York was confident it would be absorbed and understood by passers-by in years to come. As Pearl McCarthy wrote in the *Globe and Mail* (December 7, 1957), "As the months go by, York Wilson's murals in the foyer confirm their place of honour."

FRED FINLEY'S POEM

By the time York completed the Imperial Oil mural, his affinity for and skill with the new painting materials was well known among Toronto artists. Fred Finley decided to pen a poem on this topic, which we received by mail in Mexico.

> While trapped in sheets and pillow slip
> Aboard your antiseptic ship,
> You steer a course through charted ways
> Towards the port of active days;
> Please give a kindly thought or two
> To those whom you persuaded to
> Forsake tradition, make a play
> With AYAF, Flexol, M.I.K.
>
> You draw a picture clear and bright
> A masterpiece in Vinylite;
> You sang the siren song of hope
> To many an unsuspecting dope;
> You won us over one and all
> With Acetone and Butanol.
> Now toiling over masonite
> With Duco, Thinner and Celite,
> We scratch and scrabble, rage and groan,
> And breathe the fumes of Acetone.
>
> Please think of us, benighted souls,
> Bewitched, besotted by the Ols,
> Flex, Alcho, Carbit, Tolu, Xyl,
> Steeped in V.M.C.H. the while
> Reflect on what our fate will be
> With M.I.K. and D.O.P.,
> If you don't quickly reappear
> To put us, once more, in the clear.

XII

1957-1958

Spain, the Canary Islands, Italy and Belgium

WE LEFT TORONTO IN JUNE OF 1957 and stayed abroad for exactly one year. York, exhausted from the Imperial Oil commission, was ready for a holiday and was anxious to return to his painting. We flew to Paris where we bought a Renault car. We had planned a year in Italy but first drove through France, down the beautiful Loire valley and into Spain from Biarritz.

THE ALTAMIRA CAVES

Since we were close to the famous Altamira caves near Santander, we stopped in and had the experience of a lifetime. Only three or four persons were allowed in the caves at one time, in order to keep the temperature constant. We had passed by the Lascaux caves in France but they were already closed because of deterioration due to high temperatures caused by too many visitors.

In the caves there were outgrowths of rock, some just a few feet from the ceiling. The artist who painted the ceiling must have been lying down and studying the rock formations before making the drawings. In other parts of the cave one could stand or crouch to examine other drawings. York climbed up on the rock and lay there studying the drawings. The coloured pigment from charcoal, red or yellow earth had been applied with fat rendered from animals. We felt privileged to be so close to our distant ancestors!

LISBON

We carried on, hugging the coast the length of Portugal and arrived at Lisbon where we joined our friend Ronaldo de Silva, a Brazilian ambassador whom we had met in Toronto. We dined at different restaurants each evening as we drove south to Estoril, the famous playground of deposed royalty. In one restaurant we were quietly having our dinner when a waiter near us suddenly burst into a well-known song from an opera. He was answered by other waiters from various parts of the restaurant. It was very gay, with everyone having a good time.

TOLEDO AND MADRID

We left Lisbon and drove to Toledo, where we spent a few days enjoying the works of El Greco. We saw several of his paintings of saints in a church, and were spellbound by his famous mural, *The Burial of the Count of Orgaz* (1586-1599) at the church of Santo Tomé. York spent a long time in front of this mural. We visited El Greco's supposed studio, as it wasn't known until long after his death that he had even lived there. We particularly enjoyed El Greco's *View of Toledo* (1608-1614) and stood on the very spot where he must have painted it.

Again we visited the Prado in Madrid, going back to our favourites such as Piero della Francesca and Fra Filippo Lippi. York always spent much time looking at paintings by Piero della Francesca. We again viewed the drawings of Goya. They had been moved from the gallery under the eaves and were now seen with the benefit of much better light.

OUR ANNIVERSARY IN TENERIFE

It was very hot in Madrid that July, and as it was nearing our wedding anniversary on July 13th York asked me what I would like to do for our anniversary. Without skipping a beat I replied, "Fly to the Canaries." York thought it a wonderful idea and we phoned the Pintos in Tenerife that evening. Carlos said, "Come, we have moved as you know to La Laguna and have lots of room and a studio for York." We found a safe place to park our car for two or three weeks and boarded the plane for Tenerife the next day.

Carlos was now head of the psychiatric hospital in Tenerife, not far from his newly acquired ancestral home in La Laguna, in hilly country just eight kilometres from Santa Cruz. Carlos' wife Delia made one of her special, rare cakes to celebrate our arrival. We were joined by Eduardo and Maud Westerdahl, and Carlos' two brothers, Eduardo and José Manuel, and their wives.

York discovered that Carlos still had tins of duco, and he decided to make one table for each of the three Pinto brothers. The latter two rushed out to buy some masonite but instead returned with arborite. This was unfortunate, as duco chipped from this hard, shiny type of surface. Carlos did acquire a piece of masonite, which York made into a large, fine table in reds and blacks for him and Delia. They were so pleased with their treasures. Carlos later mentioned that the two arborite tables had chipped. José Manuel had framed and hung his "table" on the wall.

ISLAND HOPPING

We had heard many stories about the island of Lanzarote, north east of Tenerife, and decided to go there for a few days, after which we would move in with Eduardo and Maud. We took a small plane from Tenerife that touched down on the island of Fuerteventura. Landing at Lanzarote was even more scary. The plane bounced twice high in the air and on descending, we found the small airfield to be riddled with deep pot holes. We headed for Arrecife, the capital. Carlos had an old pharmacist friend living there; we found him immediately and gave him a letter from Carlos. He decided he and his wife would join us and hired a taxi to tour the island the following day.

The black sand and clear blue water were an astounding combination. The hilly island, completely built by erupting lava, was covered with fine black sand. All the earth had been brought from elsewhere over the centuries. We explored caves where the *Guanches* had hidden and lived to avoid the Spaniards. When we walked up the side of the volcano the ground became so hot we had to move continually. The taxi driver surprised us when he dug in the sand and pulled out baked potatoes and eggs cooked by the natural heat, and thoughtfully replaced them with others. This constant heat would produce all the energy needed on the island if it could be harnessed, but the cost of such a scheme was prohibitive.

The greatest surprise of all was their vineyards. The young vines and trees were planted in great holes, the roots were covered with earth and then covered with sand to preserve any moisture. The vines and trees were fully-grown, but did not show above the top rim of each hole, as the sandy wind would have cut them off. Their vineyards and orchards had been built up in this way over many centuries.

AT THE HOME OF EDUARDO AND MAUD

Upon our return to Tenerife, we moved to the Westerdahls'. We were surprised to see a pistol on the table, which Maud picked up, pointed at the ceiling and fired. In came the maid. Maud explained that it demeaned the maid to be summoned by a bell, so she used a gun that fired blanks. It seemed that Maud's sense of humour matched Eduardo's! They had been married the year before and Maud was well along in her first pregnancy.

The Westerdahls were close friends of Pablo Picasso and stayed with him when visiting France. They told us many intimate stories about Picasso, such as Picasso's first flush toilet, which had been installed the day before they arrived. Picasso rushed them straight to the bathroom to show them the great wonder which he kept flushing, laughing and saying, it flushes every time! Picasso apparently didn't like his socks to be washed and would hide them. Maud said they could stand up on their own. One of Picasso's goat sculptures was installed at the front of his house; they all had their pictures taken sitting on it and gave us copies.

Eduardo's lovely *Guanchen* mother and his former girlfriend Hilda had both died since our last visit to the Canaries. Hilda's death shocked us, and nothing was ever explained. Hilda's son Fredy was now an architect and painter. Eduardo still watched over Fredy, now able to articulate a few sounds.

During our short sojourn with Eduardo and Maud, York did a portrait drawing of Eduardo, now in the museum dedicated to Westerdahl in Santa Cruz de Tenerife. I don't think Eduardo liked the portrait; it was likely too realistic for a man responsible for the first Cubist exhibition in Tenerife. It was too bad York hadn't done a collage portrait, similar in concept to the ones he later did of Ettore Mazzoleni and Sir John A. Macdonald.

During our trip Eduardo spoke on the radio and in the papers about York, saying he was back for a few weeks to be with his old friends prior to spending a year in Italy. He described York's great mural for Imperial Oil and the Crawley film. His articles on art were so knowledgeable about world painting; he was continually teaching art in the broadest sense possible.

BACK TO SPAIN

We bid our Canary Island friends farewell and flew back to Madrid. It was August and when the plane door opened it was like stepping into a furnace. Our friends Max and Sophie Stewart met us and on reaching our car, we decided to drive into the hills that night in order to escape the unbearable heat. By evening we were on much higher ground to the north, and enjoyed a good night's sleep in the cooler air. En route to

Barcelona we stopped at a huge natural cathedral in the rocks, where one descended some hundred steps to reach the floor of the chasm, and looked up in awe at this towering, grand work of nature.

We reached Barcelona and looked for the work of the great Spanish architect, Antoni Gaudí. We saw the impressive facade of the Church of the Sagrada Familia, left unfinished through lack of funds, and the beautiful Casa Milá. Apart from the buildings' crazy wonderful shapes, the surfaces were encrusted with pieces of broken ceramic and glass. At first no one took Gaudí seriously and when he died, he was buried in an unknown pauper's grave. His genius is now recognised and celebrated.

FRANCE

We then started north toward France along the beautiful Costa Brava, crossing at Perpignan. There wasn't a room in Perpignan for the night, nor in the next one or two towns. It was getting late, we had no dinner and were getting desperate and so we asked a gas station attendant, who recommended a certain lady who rented rooms. It was nearly midnight when we knocked on her door and explained our plight. She had nothing available, but said one of her permanent tenants, a doctor, was away for the weekend. We could spend the night in his bed and no one would be the wiser! We touched nothing, our bags on the floor, and slipped into his bed. Thank goodness for the ingenuity of a French woman!

VENICE

We had trouble getting rooms all along the French Riviera, often going inland to a village. We visited all the museums along the way, and on entering Italy we followed the northern route to Venice, first stopping in Verona. Upon our arrival in September, we headed for the pension Da Cici on the island of Salute, not far from the famous church of Santa Maria della Salute. Eduardo Westerdahl had given us the name of an art critic, Matilda Mamprim; we contacted her and luck was with us. She knew of an available studio on the second floor of a building at 43 Zitelle Giudecca overlooking the Giudecca Canal, where ocean-going ships passed in front of our windows and balcony. We had the tremendous upper-storey studio, which ran from the rear to the front of the building. There was a small bedroom, bathroom and kitchen. We moved in and York went to work.

In Canada we had agreed to meet Ernesto Barbini, the famous Canadian opera conductor and former assistant conductor of the Metropolitan Opera, on the Rialto Bridge at an appointed time a few days after our arrival. He said he wanted to introduce York to Venice; his father had been an artist and he knew all the best sketching spots. Ernesto proceeded to show York some of the sketching places. York didn't admit he had already found some of these spots, including one in the bend of a small canal where other artists had wiped their brushes on the stones.

Life was very pleasant in Venice, with no traffic and clean air. Ernesto took us by gondola to the island of Murano to see the beautiful Venetian glass. En route the gondolier was singing and Ernesto immediately identified the name and composer of the opera. The gondolier disagreed, saying it was a different opera. I spoke up in Italian to say, "He is Maestro Ernesto Barbini, conductor of opera at the Metropolitan in New York and now in Canada." The gondolier scoffed, "If he's a conductor of opera, I'm Giuseppe Verdi." And that was that! At the glass factory Ernesto was recognised. Some of his ancestors had apparently been glass blowers and at one time "Barbini" money had been the currency of the day.

We carried on to Burano, where exquisite lace was made. That evening we had dinner at a restaurant just off the Piazza San Marco where a singer was entertaining the guests and then passing the hat. Ernesto told us later that the singer had started out as a young girl with a very good voice, but had fallen on hard times. It made him very sad, and so he tipped her generously, which dumbfounded her. The next day he took us to see the house where he was born. Ernesto opened the gate and we stepped into the front garden. He then pointed to a window, tears streaming down his face, saying that was the room in which he was born. Oh those wonderful, sentimental Italians!

Ernesto introduced us to the director of the art gallery, near the Rialto Bridge, who took us to dinner that evening. The director spoke English and had a great sense of humour—he and York kept the table in stitches. The gallery had to be visited in daylight as they didn't have electricity.

The night before Ernesto's departure we had dinner at his home, still occupied by his sister Adele, who spoke limited English. The talented family cook had been lured out of retirement for the occasion. We often took long walks with Adele, who told us some of the recent history of Venice. While passing a stand of what seemed like overripe tomatoes, she explained that they were "kaki" or persimmons, a great favourite of ours ever since.

York's colours began to change in Venice. He was gaining confidence using the colour red, with which he had had difficulty in the past. We often went to Café Montin, frequented by many artists. We met the daughter of Peggy Guggenheim, who took us to meet her mother and see her famous art collection, which included the work of Surrealist painters like Max Ernst.

By the middle of October the weather was cold and our tiny pot-bellied stove in the middle of the studio gave little warmth. It was hard to sleep in the cold bedroom unless I first warmed my feet in hot water. Sometimes we would go to a movie just to sit among other bodies to get warm.

TO ROME

We headed for Rome on the first of November. En route we visited the marvellous mosaics at Ravenna. It was a fortuitous visit, as the mosaic panels had been moved down to eye level for cleaning and repairs. York looked up the mosaic factories and learned a great deal about the different kinds of tesserae—glass, marble, ceramic and gold.

We saw Piero della Francesca's magnificent mid-fifteenth century murals at the Church of San Francesco in Arezzo. On crossing the Po River I thought of Giovanni Guareschi's *Mondo Piccolo "Don Camillo"* (1951), one of the first books I had read in Italian and in which the river Po was often mentioned. We stopped briefly in Assisi, the birthplace of St. Francis, who loved and protected animals.

Then we carried on to Rome to visit Chuck and Bobby MacIntosh who lived on Allesandro Fleming, named after the British scientist and discoverer of penicillin. It was a great reunion, with so many tales to tell. Through the MacIntoshes we became friends with many of the American engineers stationed in Rome, loaned by the US to Italy after World War II. We started studio hunting but could not find anything. York's head was brimming with ideas for sketches and by the third day he was ready to take anything so he could get to work. That day we rented an apartment on Via d'Arpino in the Parioli district, a posh residential section near the Borghese Gardens. It had rare central heating, a large living and dining room and a beautiful garden. York made a studio out of the dining room, opening the French doors onto the terrace, and working outside when the weather permitted.

It was an unusually warm winter. The flowers didn't freeze in the garden and it seldom rained. York was at work on large canvases, mostly Venetian subjects, while making notes and sketches in and around Rome. On our many walks exploring Rome we often strolled through the Borghese Gardens.

MEETING FULVIO ARA

While York was working I would wander on my own, later taking him to see anything of interest. One day I looked inside the Banco de Lavoro and discovered murals by Afro, an Italian artist whose work had delighted us when we saw it in New York. It turned out that Fulvio Ara, the manager, had commissioned Afro, but he was disappointed because his co-workers showed so little interest in the finished murals. I took York to see them and he was very impressed. We invited Fulvio to the studio, and he became interested in York's work. Fulvio's wife had recently died, and he was to start his holidays soon.

During his holiday, Fulvio acted as our tour guide. After work each afternoon we joined Fulvio and walked to many famed sites, including the churches, the Spanish Steps, the Appian way, the catacombs, the fountains, the Coliseum and the art galleries. We often sat in the open cafés on Via Veneto watching the crowds go by, later dining in favourite little bistros. On weekends we took sketching trips to the different surrounding towns, where we learned interesting facts about each locale.

At Lake Nemi, for example, we learned that one of the early emperor's pleasure craft had been discovered at the bottom of the lake. It was highly fragile and utmost care had been used to raise it; the lake had been drained and a structure was built around the boat. A museum was built at the lake shore in order not to move it further than necessary. The job finished, the boat was photographed and studied extensively, as they had realised the boat was the pleasure craft of the Roman emperor Hadrian. When the Germans were retreating from Italy during World War II, they burned everything as they went to slow up their pursuers. As they approached Lake Nemi, the Italians pleaded with the Germans to spare the boat, saying it was their history too, but to no avail. The Italians have since built an exact replica, using the metal pieces that survived the fire.

ROME GALLERIES

Sundays often found us visiting Rome's museums, including the Etruscan Museum and the Museum of Contemporary Art. Sometimes our American friends asked York to explain the abstract works in the museum, such as those by Jackson Pollock.

York was very privileged to be invited to share in an exhibition at Galleria Appia Antica in Rome with a group of his artist friends: Casetta, Helani, Meo, Nikos, and Vasghiem. York showed mostly Venice paintings and mountain landscapes. Quite a number of York's choice Venice paintings were sold to our American engineer friends, some of which made their way to the United States. Rosemary Boxer, a Toronto columnist stationed in Rome, interviewed York.

Charles Moses, an American who owned Gallery 83 at Via Margutta 83, showed the work of young Italian painters. We became friendly with Charles and many of his artists. On my return to Canada I imported some of their small works, including paintings on matchbox covers and table place mats, to sell in the AGT gift shop. The lovely items sold readily.

A TRIP SOUTH

After spending the whole winter in Rome, we decided to drive south in mid-May of 1958, eventually crossing to the island of Sicily at Palermo. Just before reaching Naples, at Pozzuoli, we were surprised to see the yellow earth bubbling and apparently steaming with sulphur. We then crossed the Messina Straits to Palermo, seat of the Mafia. Next came Monreale with its beautiful mosaics, the Phoenician medieval city of Trapani, and magnificent Greek ruins at Agrigento.

We climbed a lovely hill to the top and there was beautiful Taormina. We stayed at a fine pension with a view of Mount Etna. The meals were excellent and the owner delightful. York did many sketches from the window and around town, including the ruins of the old Greek theatre. After a few days York had filled all his sketch panels and books so we headed back to Rome.

EXPO 1958 IN BRUSSELS

We bid farewell to our friends in Rome and headed for Belgium and the World Expo of 1958. We had been invited to stay with Glen Bannerman, the Canadian Commissioner General, and would meet our friends Luc and Jenny Peire. They always left their Paris studio in the summer for the cooler air in Knokke on the sea, their home base in Belgium.

We met Jenny and Luc the day after our arrival in Brussels and Luc took us to see the Belgian exhibit at Expo, a fantastic display based on the Belgian Congo. The Peires had been on their way to the Congo when we first met them in the Canaries in 1952. We were struck speechless by the grandeur and interest of this display, which Luc had curated.

We then visited the Canadian pavilion. Outside the pavilion we admired an excellent fence-like structure by the Québec sculptor Louis Archambault. Inside the art gallery were featured works by the usual group chosen by the National Gallery, including Goodridge Roberts, Alfred Pellan, and Jean-Paul Mousseau. Luc examined the paintings carefully but seemed rather perplexed and then asked, "Why would Canada choose dead painters?" We were very embarrassed to explain that the painters were not dead. Here we were at a World Expo where every country was showing its most advanced art and Canada had nothing new to offer. Roberts was a fine artist and a friend, but his type of painting was dated. It was a disappointing exhibition.

After a lovely visit with Luc and Jenny we headed back to Paris in mid June, and flew home to Toronto soon after. We had been gone exactly one year.

XIII

1958-1959

At Home and in the Caribbean

OUR RETURN TO TORONTO IN JUNE of 1958 was reported in two articles in the *Globe and Mail*. In the first article on July 11, Lotta Dempsey noted York's return to Toronto "after long wandering," and recorded his opinions of international abstract art. After visiting numerous pavilions at the Brussels exposition, York had concluded that "painters in the world today are painting alike," and that it was difficult to distinguish the works seen in the various exhibitions without consulting the catalogue.

Pearl McCarthy wrote on July 19 that York believed "painting matter without subject matter has had it," and that the "international style, as it is called, seems to me to be at an end." York was cautious in expressing such opinions, as he did not want to be seen as a conservative reactionary. When Lotta Dempsey asked York what pleased him most at that point in his career, he replied, "That I can spend my time painting."

OTHER ARTISTS' MURALS

While we were still abroad, York was one of several artists invited to join a competition for a mural at the new airport in Gander, Newfoundland. The National Gallery of Canada announced on March 5, 1958 that Kenneth Lochhead, a well-known abstractionist then living and working in Regina, had submitted the winning painting and that York had come in second. Lochhead's proposed design and a detail of York's submission were reproduced in *Canadian Art* (Spring 1958).

In the summer of 1958, Harold Town finished a mural for the lobby of the administration building at the Robert H. Saunders St. Lawrence Generating Station near Cornwall, Ontario. Cleeve Horne, liaison for Ontario Hydro, had chosen Town for the 37' x 10' mural project. The night prior to the mural's unveiling, Cleeve received word that it was going to be reviewed viciously by the local media. Cleeve phoned York in great agitation and asked him to try and avert the attack by making a favourable statement to the press. York was happy to comply, and the attack was avoided. York's positive comments appear in the brochure distributed by Ontario Hydro.

1958 ART ACTIVITIES

1958 brought the usual opportunities for York to exhibit his recent work. He sent *Cathedral* (1958) to the OSA show at the AGT in March; *Bull Fight* (1958) and *Winter Beginning* (1958) to the CNE in summer; *Pizzicato* (1957) to the Vancouver Art Gallery in October, and *Venice* (1958) to the RCA in Montreal in November.

York's work was included in a unique group show held at Toronto's Park Gallery in March. The show featured twelve paintings by twelve Canadian artists commissioned by the beauty expert Helena Rubinstein. She had become interested in contemporary art after meeting Pablo Picasso. The artists, who included Riopelle, Ghitta Caiserman, Kazuo Nakamura, Ray Mead and Jacques de Tonnancour, were asked to portray either spring, summer, autumn or winter. Ms. Rubinstein wrote in the catalogue that, "In these pictures, I find the same spirit of adventure and daring which has made Canada a great northern nation." After the show, the collection went to Rubinstein in New York. On her death she bequeathed the paintings to her Toronto niece, Meta Kolin. York and I were invited to the Kolin home to see the paintings as well as their marvellous collection of vivid blue glass.

One of York's earlier works, *The March Past*, entered the new Beaverbrook Gallery in Fredericton, established by Lord Beaverbrook in 1959. Paul Duval assisted in selecting the gallery's purchases. At this time, he parted with *The March Past*, which he had borrowed since its inclusion in the 1948 OSA and RCA exhibitions.

TWO SOLO SHOWS

In the fall of 1958 York was honoured with two solo exhibitions. Hart House opened its fall season with a show of York's work. We were disappointed when following the show, the student newspaper *The Varsity* (November 6, 1958) published a long satirical review of York's work. What we didn't know at the time was that resentment and envy of York's success were beginning to grow.

A solo exhibition of York's recent work, mainly Italian painting, opened at the Roberts Gallery in October. Jack Wildridge was so excited about York's new paintings that he threw us a party prior to the opening, with friends, collectors and fellow artists invited. The exhibition was well received and sold out completely. Reg Bradley, director of the Sarnia Public Library and Art Gallery, hurried to Toronto before the opening and purchased *Corner of Venice* (1958) for the Sarnia collection. What pleased York most was that the exhibition put the Roberts Gallery in the black. Jack Wildridge had inherited tremendous debt from his father.

Lotta Dempsey raved about the show in the *Toronto Daily Star* (October 30, 1958). "No recent event in Canadian art circles," she declared, "has had such impact as the York Wilson show at the Roberts Gallery." She wrote that the exhibition was considered by many to signify as important a new chapter in Canadian painting, "as the occasion on which the Group of Seven burst upon the scene." Paul Duval, who usually supported York's work, did not agree with Dempsey. In his review in the *Telegram* (November 1, 1958) he described York's paintings in a manner which serious painters hate to hear, saying "but we believe that much of the power of Wilson's best earlier work has given way here to charm and prettiness, especially in color."

A MEMORY OF SKETCHING IN SAN MIGUEL

In his book, *Watercolour, A Challenge* (1957), Leonard Brooks related an interesting story about a sketching experiment in San Miguel which arose out of a conversation with York and Jack Baldwin, an instructor at the *Instituto Allende*. Jack often took his students afield in search of sketching spots. York argued that paintings were everywhere and that one didn't have to go great distances to find something, but Jack disagreed. York suggested the three of them test his proposition the next morning by deciding to stop at a predetermined distance and paint whatever was available.

The painters agreed, and they started out the following morning, stopping at the agreed distance. Leonard and York immediately got to work, producing studies of cacti, some so small they had to get down on the ground to distinguish shapes. Jack wandered, unable to find anything. On returning to their studios York and Leonard worked up larger pictures from their sketches. Jack later confided that he was so upset he hadn't slept since and had decided to give up painting. He later became well-known as a sculptor in his native Ohio. This experiment started York's whole series of cactus studies, including his *Cactus Forms* (1950) and *Cactus Abstraction* (1954).

A 1959 PAINTING TRIP TO THE CARIBBEAN

When our friends Dick and Evelyn van Valkenburg and Cleeve and Jean Horne talked about renting a yacht and sailing in the West Indies, we quickly agreed to join them. Cleeve was born in Jamaica of English parents and had inherited a small island off Grenada, where he and Jean vacationed. The van Valkenburgs and ourselves booked our flight to Puerto Rico in February of 1959. We were to pick up the yacht at Grenada, where we would meet Cleeve and Jean.

On arrival we took a taxi heading for a lovely hotel by the sea, which Evelyn had seen in a tourist folder. After about a week of sightseeing and sketching, we arranged a flight to Barbados, where we met our old friend Jim Gairdner. We then flew to the Virgin Islands, where York sketched at various places including St. Croix. Our next stop was beautiful Tobago and the hustle and bustle of Trinidad.

Next was Grenada, where the Hornes took us immediately to the harbour to see our yacht, the *Harebell*. Our English captain told us the *Harebell* had recently arrived from Germany, where it had been stored since World War II. The Hornes then toured us around Grenada, where York made some quick sketches, and we went to see the island Cleeve had inherited. Once a whaling base, the island was long since deserted. Only derelict boats and cabins remained. Cleeve had no idea what to do with the island! After a few days we boarded our yacht, stocked with provisions and ready to sail.

We had a crew of seven, a congenial lot. The cook often prepared a picnic lunch and we would go ashore to any island, inhabited or not, to eat. Our first stop was St. Vincent and the Grenadines. We always slept aboard the yacht, but if near an interesting place we anchored for the night and went ashore for dinner.

One day when lunching on the Windward Islands, we picked up large interesting shells, long tropical pods with huge seeds and the large fans of a sea plant, which I managed to bring home. We would take as much time as possible exploring the islands while York sketched. He especially liked harbours and fishing boats. Among our stops were the Windward Islands of St. Lucia, Martinique and Dominica and the Leeward Islands of Guadalupe and Antigua. There was a small sailing boat aboard and often during stops for swimming, Jean and I would take it out for a sail.

When we said goodbye to the *Harebell* and its crew at Antigua, it was a relief to be on *terra firma* again. In a few days we flew back to Puerto Rico to board our plane for New York. It was one of the most frightening flights I have experienced. We seemed to be in the eye of a developing hurricane and the plane was tossed about, quite helpless against the elements.

ART ACTIVITIES IN 1959

At the 87th annual OSA exhibition in March at the AGT, York's painting *Queen of the Adriatic* (1959) was one of three paintings awarded a $1,000 prize by the Baxter Art Foundation, founded by William Baxter, publisher of *Canadian Teacher, Theatre Canada* and *Canadian Commentator*. Gordon Smith and Ron Spickett were the other winners. The jury for the Baxter awards consisted of Martin Baldwin, OCA instructor Fred Finley and Cleeve Horne. Pearl McCarthy, writing in the *Globe and Mail* (March 12, 1959), asserted that York was, "outstanding as a man working for a synthesis of realist and abstract qualities. In that he may be more ahead of his time than the people now considered avant-garde."

The Baxter Art Foundation had two projects: awarding fellowships to senior Canadian artists, and giving three annual awards, which were in effect purchases of works of art for the Foundation's collection. The first Canadian artist given a fellowship was Herbert S. Palmer. Unfortunately the foundation did not last long. I don't know what brought about its demise.

York rarely enlarged sketches. Instead he placed several around him, reliving the experience and abstracting from several, aiming for the essence of the place. The Caribbean trip kept him busy over the following several months. York sent *Grenada Harbour* (1959) and four Italian canvases to the annual Stratford Art Festival. The festival organisers had invited ten painters to each exhibit five works for the theatre season. Apart from York, the artists were: Jack Shadbolt, Gordon Smith, Harold Town, Jack Nichols, Jacques de Tonnancour, Goodridge Roberts, Jean-Paul Lemieux, Alex Colville and Jean-Paul Riopelle. *Rome* (1959), included in this show, was purchased by Sam and Ayala Zacks. When this painting did not turn up in the catalogue of the Zacks' bequest to the Art Gallery of Ontario in 1970, I asked Ayala as to its whereabouts. She replied, "Do you think I'm crazy, I took two paintings to Israel, *Rome* and a Riopelle!" She says the painting will eventually go to an Israeli museum.

Back in his studio in Toronto, York gathered a few of his sketches and placed them around him for atmosphere. Many interesting semi-abstract canvases resulted from that trip. The AGT's 13th annual exhibition included York's *St. Lucia Harbour* (1959), *Beach at Bequia* (1959) and *Medieval Figure* (1958). He sent *Caribbean Port* (1959) to the RCA exhibition at the *Musée de la Province de Québec* and *Red Abstraction* (1959), to the Canadian Group of Painters' show at the AGT, both in late 1959. *Caribbean Town* (1959) and *West Indian Scene* (1959) went to the Art Gallery of Hamilton's annual exhibition. The Halifax Picture Loan Society showed *Mexican Landscape* in their second annual exhibition at the Citadel Museum in Halifax.

Reinhold Publishing of New York invited Leonard Brooks to write a book on art. His first book *Watercolour, a Challenge* was so successful that he was asked to write another. *Oil Painting Traditional and New* (1959) was the result. The second book included reproductions of York's works *Portofino, Italy* (1958) and *Puerto de la Cruz* (1956). Leonard hadn't previously thought of including the work of other artists, but in discussion with Mr. Reinhold he happened to mention, "I wish you could see York Wilson's painting of the subject." Reinhold replied, "Why can't we?" Leonard thus started illustrating his book with works by a few artists.

DEFENDING ABSTRACT ART

A big showdown had been brewing against abstract painting, more and more of which was shown in Toronto exhibitions. In 1959, seven artists, including Kenneth Forbes, resigned from the OSA in protest. Their criticisms focused on the current exhibition of French art at the AGT, which Forbes labelled as "trash." York was selected as the defender of abstract painting, and the debate, complete with photographs and reproductions of abstract paintings, took a whole page of the *Toronto Daily Star* on August 5, 1959.

York's most memorable statement from his written defence was that, "Paintings are like stocks. The good ones get more valuable and the bad ones fade away. It appears to me these paintings are good enough to stay valuable." York then proceeded to defend the works of Picasso, Cezanne, van Gogh and Matisse on an individual basis. He concluded that the four painters were innovators who were "completely essential to this particular era of painting and I'm sure their work will never be forgotten."

A LOVELY LETTER

That summer, we were surprised to receive a letter from Lawren Harris, once of the Group of Seven and then living in Vancouver. Lawren had stopped in Toronto specifically to look at the Imperial Oil mural, and felt compelled to write to York. His letter of July 14, 1959 said this:

Dear Mr. Wilson:

Although it is certainly not my customary habit to write so-called "fan" letters to my colleagues, in this singular instance I feel moved to do so. The reason being that on my way here, I made a point of stopping over in Toronto with the express purpose of seeing your Imperial Oil Building murals. I am happily convinced that this break in my journey was completely justified and rewarded, for said murals proved to be beyond my fondest expectations, which were based upon previously-seen small colour reproductions.

You have succeeded in a gigantic undertaking, the very thought of which would undoubtedly terrify the great majority of your contemporaries in our profession. I found that your vision and interpretation of the theme was equally matched by its exciting and excellent execution. To me, it is a most stimulating and compelling major creative effort, and one which very well could prove to be a milestone in Canadian Art. I look forward to spending further time in its presence when opportunity presents itself.

Belatedly, I offer and add my sincerest heartfelt congratulations to the many such sentiments you must surely have received on behalf this work of such aesthetical and material magnitude.

York, Jean Horne, myself, and Dick van Valkenburg aboard the Harebell. West Indies, 1959.

XIV

1958-1960

The O'Keefe Centre Mural

IT WAS ANNOUNCED IN THE NOVEMBER 21, 1958 edition of the *Globe and Mail* that York had been commissioned to complete "what is believed will be the largest mural in Canada" for the lobby of the new O'Keefe Centre, then under construction. York signed the contract with the O'Keefe Centre that month. In a press release issued by the Centre on November 20, York said, "I am delighted to have the opportunity to undertake this major work. It presents many unusual challenges never before encountered by a Canadian artist. In addition to the tremendous length, the rendering will be influenced by a slight elliptical curve of the lobby wall."

York had been informed of the commission in 1957. During our year in Europe, he spent considerable studio time in Italy working on his proposal. His theme for the 100' x 15' mural, *The Seven Lively Arts*, would include references to music, dance, painting, sculpture, architecture, literature and theatre. York worked on the preliminary drawings and sketches for over a year. In the autumn of 1959, the final mural sketch was ready for presentation to the Board, which included, among others, Centre architect Earle Morgan, Charles Comfort, AGT director Martin Baldwin, A.J. Casson and Syd Watson.

The unveiling and approval of York's final sketch was reported in many newspapers, including the *Oshawa Times* on September 28, the *Toronto Daily Star* and Hamilton *Spectator* on September 29, the *Globe and Mail* the following day, and the *Sudbury Daily Star* on October 1. In the Sudbury paper, Herbert Whittaker wrote that to illustrate his theme, York "ranged from cave painting to skyscrapers, from opera to Chinese proverbs. The symbols he selected are cleverly linked together to sweep across the O'Keefe lobby." Other symbols employed by York, wrote Lotta Dempsey in the *Toronto Daily Star*, included the Parthenon and a Gothic arch for architecture; a totem pole, the Sphinx and the Venus de Milo for sculpture, and drums, wind and string instruments and a scene from a Wagnerian opera for music.

Like many journalists, Dempsey was impressed by the massive size of the planned mural. She wrote that painting the mural "would be like preparing to brush-stroke your way in a five-yard swathe across the ice at Maple Leaf Gardens; a good third of the way down a football field; or along more than half a New York city block." To execute such a large project, York hired Bob Paterson and John Labonte-Smith as assistants. York and Bob had of course worked together on the Imperial Oil mural; John Labonte-Smith was a Toronto artist and graduate of the OCA.

York used the same medium and working method at the O'Keefe Centre as he had at the Imperial Oil building in 1956. Dry pigments were mixed with liquid vinyl acetate, which were applied to the wall's plaster surface. As before, the final colour sketches, each about four feet square, were photographed in colour and projected onto the north wall of the foyer. Herbert Irvine, the building's interior decorator, had worked with York early in 1959 to assure the carpet colours harmonised with the colours of the mural and the Carrara marble walls.

THE UNION DEBACLE

Work on the mural began in December of 1959. York was under great pressure to complete the mural for the planned opening of the O'Keefe Centre the following October. Soon after York, Bob and John started work, however, they became embroiled in a heated labour dispute which threatened to stop work on the mural and the building. The Union had lain in wait to pressure York to become a member since their discovery of his non-union status on the Imperial Oil project.

York was approached by representatives of the International Brotherhood of Painters, Decorators and Paperhangers of America, who had discovered the artists were the only non-union workers on the O'Keefe project. Labour reporter Wilfred List reported York's opinion in the *Globe and Mail* (January 18, 1960) that Harry Colnett, Canadian vice-president of the union, wanted the mural "finished by persons carrying a union card." Before the issue hit the papers, York had already met with the union officials numerous times, informing them in no uncertain terms that he had no intention of joining their union. List also quoted York's opinion that, "Fine art is an individual and creative form of expression. I don't see how you can possibly unionize people who work as individuals. This is a serious matter as far as artists are concerned."

The struggle continued day after day. Many articles appeared in newspapers in Toronto and across Canada. The radio and television news programs carried daily coverage. The papers published letters to the editor and others were written directly to York. Some writers said they agreed with York but could not do so publicly. We received many telephone calls at the house from people on both sides of the issue. Some callers used disgusting language and threatened bodily harm.

The battle escalated. The union insisted that any member of their scenic division could finish painting York's mural. As Maggie Grant reported in the *Globe and Mail* (January 26, 1960), the union argument rested on the assumption that if its members "could paint houses they could assuredly paint a mere mural." Frank Tumpane had published an article in the *Telegram* (January 19, 1960) declaring that Glenn Gould's and Elvis Presley's union membership had not destroyed their individuality, and wondered why an artist's case was different from a musician's. The next day, the *Globe and Mail* (January 20, 1960) published a letter from Al Collier, a well-known painter and OSA president, who explained that a musician often played someone else's composition, whereas a painter was a work's sole creator.

The cartoonists for the local newspapers fortunately found some humour in the situation. Reidford of the *Globe and Mail* (January 19, 1960) published a cartoon showing two house painters at work in beret and smock, with one saying to the other, "OK, Clancy, So You're a Muralist." Lewis Parker of the *Toronto Daily Star* (January 19, 1960) showed Rembrandt perched on a ladder painting *The Night Watch* "by numbers," with a shop steward providing instructions. The caption read, "Rembrandt! Thou Shouldst Be Living At This Hour: O'Keefe's Hath Need Of Thee." In the *Telegram*, Grassick showed York being pursued by members of the International Brotherhood of Painters, Decorators and Paperhangers, using his palette to fend off the brushes and paint cans they were throwing at him.

O'Keefe Centre officials, meanwhile, became concerned that the situation might develop into a work stoppage that would threaten the building's completion. York, John and Bob had already stopped working on the mural. The Brotherhood were quietly lobbying Bob and John, promising them higher wages and shorter hours if they joined the union. Their efforts met with vehement refusals. The union's final tactic was to offer York an honorary union membership, which he politely refused, saying "I don't wish to be so honoured."

The art societies finally banded together to help York. The RCA, OSA, SSC and CGP began to issue public statements in his support. The painter Doris McCarthy advised York to obtain legal advice from Bora Laskin, a law professor at the University of Toronto and later Chief Justice of the Supreme Court of Canada. Laskin wondered why York and the societies hadn't approached him sooner. The Toronto lawyer George Ferguson was eventually chosen to represent York.

Laskin and Ferguson began working quietly undercover. In early February, Laskin told York they were close to a settlement, and asked us not to appear to gloat, as it might undo everything. He also asked that we disappear for a few days, and not let anyone know where we were. We holed up in our own house, with the lights off and the phone ringing constantly. It was hard to get any sleep! After a few days Bora informed us that the matter was settled. He did not tell us how the settlement was achieved, in order to assure our silence.

This lack of information caused York many difficulties, as in the case when he was interviewed by June Callwood on television. June invited both the union representatives and York on her program. The union didn't turn up so June took their side, asking some leading and difficult questions. York was almost tongue-tied not being allowed to answer sensibly because of Bora Laskin's directive. June was unaware of the stress that York was under. The interview was a disaster, and York was embarrassed. June and her husband Trent Frayne had been our friends for many years but this incident strained our relationship with them.

York was pleased that he was able to preserve artists' individuality and freedom. The four art societies shared the legal fees with York. An official statement on the union incident was prepared by a labour authority and made available from the societies.

BACK TO WORK AT LAST

The artists were now happily back at work. Some newspapers claimed that York was required by the terms of settlement to work alone, but that was not true. Lotta Dempsey of the *Toronto Daily Star* (April 1, 1960) donned a hard hat and came to interview York at the work site. York told Lotta that he was pleased that so many of the men working on the Centre's construction had stopped to ask him about the mural's symbolic content. Some were even interested in purchasing the 'small pictures' he was working from. As with the Imperial Oil project, York enjoyed an excellent rapport with the workers.

The Seven Lively Arts mural was completed in May of 1960. The finished work was covered for protection from dust and damage while the building neared completion. Reproductions of the mural began to appear in many newspapers, including the *Toronto Daily Star* (August 22, 1960). The full mural was photographed in colour for use in promotional brochures distributed by the O'Keefe Centre. In his brochure text, Paul Duval wrote that the seven arts "have been immortalised by painters and sculptors for many centuries. York Wilson's mural lends them an original and contemporary dress." Duval concluded that the purpose of a mural is to "humanise a building, to identify its purpose and activities. York Wilson's painting does this ideally for the O'Keefe Centre. It is high drama in pictorial form."

On October 1, the day of the centre's grand opening, Pearl McCarthy reviewed the mural in the *Globe* magazine in glowing terms. She listed the mural's "ingredients" as "hours of thought and study, more than 50 gallons of painting medium, weeks of preliminary work on sketches, [and] six months with two helpers in construction helmets painting on the specially treated cement wall." She asserted that the mural was a "unified work" which the public could understand, and be attracted by "picking out such symbols as a quotation from Confucius, a cave painting and a modern skyscraper. It may make many think for the first time of the fact that art is long and life is short."

THE CENTRE OPENS ON OCTOBER I

The great day of the opening of the O'Keefe Centre had finally arrived. It was just like a Hollywood gala, with bright lights, beautifully-gowned women and handsome men, and journalists stopping important people for interviews as they entered the building. Excitement ran high. On entering the main lobby, everyone instinctively stopped to examine York's magnificent mural.

The colours were rich, and the mural was realistic enough to encourage extended study. York hoped that visitors would keep discovering new things in the mural, thus keeping it forever interesting. With the help of our friend Ettore Mazzoleni, an opera conductor and principal of the Royal Conservatory of Music, York used an obscure bar of music in the mural, hoping to pique viewers' interest. Apparently they schemed too well, as the excerpt still has not been recognised! Today only Joanne Mazzoleni and I know the answer. Let's hope it will be discovered while we're around.

The Centre's opening performance was the new musical, "Camelot," starring Richard Burton, Julie Andrews and Robert Goulet. The musical was being premiered in Toronto before its opening in New York. The director Moss Hart planned to rework the production after the reaction from Toronto audiences. The elaborate program included a page showing a photograph of York's near-finished mural.

The Centre's programming also included regular art shows, installed in a lounge on the lower level. A committee whose members over the years included York, Ayala Zacks, Royal Ontario Museum director Theodore Allen (Ted) Heinrich, A.J. Casson and Paul Duval directed the exhibition program. The opening exhibition featured the work of 25 Ontario painters, ranging from Dennis Burton, Jack Bush and Richard Gorman to Yvonne McKague Housser, Tony Urquhart, Michael Snow and York. In the first fifteen years of its operation, ninety-five exhibitions were held at the centre. Since the Centre's audiences came from near and far, the shows proved to be a great boon to Canadian visual arts.

After the reception, performance of "Camelot" and a celebrity party on the opening night, we headed home at about 3:30 A.M. The social columns were filled with names. We came home and realised someone had broken into our house. We found my opened purses strewn along the hall corridor, and discovered that some cash, a fur coat and jacket, my new typewriter and a small suitcase were missing. Six months later, the police called to say they had found my typewriter in a pawn shop!

In spite of everything it was a grand and exciting evening. Centre manager Hugh Walker and his wife Shirley were fine and thoughtful hosts. Even the friendly doorman always said to York, "It's your theatre," and gave us special service. York's mural was completely cleaned and restored in 1986. As Hugh Walker wrote in his book *The O'Keefe Centre: Thirty Years of Theatre History* (1991), "the mural now looks as good as new."

The 1960 edition of the *World Book Encyclopaedia* included a reproduction of York's Imperial Oil mural in progress under the subject of "Mural Painting." He thus joined some of the world's great muralists featured in the encyclopaedia, including Michelangelo and Thomas Hart Benton.

XV

1960-1963

Our First Three Years in Paris

SINCE THERE WAS A LENGTHY BREAK between York's completion of the mural in May and the opening of the O'Keefe Centre in October, we decided to spend the intervening four months in San Miguel. It was a much-needed rest for York, and provided him with the opportunity to get back to easel painting. We returned in time for the opening, and left for Paris soon after. Pierre Dupuy, former Canadian ambassador to Italy and now posted in France, invited us to join him there.

OUR PARIS STUDIO

After a few days at the Hotel Solferino on Paris' Left Bank, we picked up the Renault car we had ordered in Canada and started to look for a studio. The first studio we saw, at 12 Boulevard Pereire, was perfect. The enormous two-storey studio had a balcony at one end and a toilet and washroom at the other. The entrance hall, with stairs and a coal bin, led to the studio. There was a small dining room and kitchen; upstairs was a large bedroom, bathroom and a balcony which overlooked the studio. It was sparsely furnished and the kitchen was tiny, but with such excellent space and lighting, little else mattered.

BROWN PAPER PACKAGES

Luc Peire took York around the city to buy supplies. I went to one of the big department stores and purchased a small washing machine and vacuum cleaner. When my purchases were delivered wrapped in brown paper, York began to eye the big sheets of paper. He always found it difficult to get started in a new studio. He had been going to the Louvre daily, making drawings of early sculptures.

Now he started transferring these drawings on to the large sheets of brown paper and newspaper, using India ink and black gouache, and collaging newspaper fragments onto the brown paper. He hung these works from the balcony and began to relax and feel at home. He was planning to destroy the collages, not recognising he had just embarked on a new phase. He saw the works as a trick to loosen him up and get started. He did begin some painted canvases, much larger than usual and with a freer and looser style.

About this time we had a visit from Jean Cassou, director of the *Musée National d'Art Moderne.* He immediately inquired about the large banners hanging from the balcony. York explained they had helped him break in his new studio, and that he would destroy them eventually. Jean Cassou exploded, "Under no circumstances must you destroy them, they are unique and have their own authority. They would make marvellous tapestries!" After this praise York began to wonder how to preserve them. He sealed the front and back with a clear plastic medium. A Toronto art restorer later mounted them on good quality linen for extra strength. *The Lion Hunt* (1960) was invited to the 1965 Cardiff Commonwealth Arts Festival in England and the AGT purchased *Le Figaro* (1961) in 1965.

SOCIAL LIFE

In Paris one seems to live 'art' all the time. The artist works in his or her studio all day, goes to openings most evenings and gathers with other artists for dinner or drinks to talk about art. Artists generally haven't much money so they instinctively gather wherever a little food is available, at celebrations, openings and embassy parties, or at inexpensive restaurants. Luc and Jenny introduced us to *La Petite Hostellerie*, which served a glass of wine, a small main course and a dessert for about $1 Canadian. We were fortunate in having influential friends visiting Paris who took us to some famous places.

The wildest few days we ever had were when Blair Laing made one of his frequent visits to Paris. Blair searched us out, still hopeful he could woo York back to his gallery. York did not change dealers, even though he liked Blair and knew he would increase his international exposure. Blair took us to the *Café de la Pays* for breakfast, the *Tour d'Argent* with its numbered ducks for dinner, the *Folies Bergère* and the *Théâtre du Absurde.* On our first visit to the Lido on the Champs Elysées, Blair slipped a large bill to the *maitre d'* and we were escorted to a front-and-centre table. I could scarcely believe it when a whole skating rink was rolled out on stage, full of skaters. Thank goodness Blair left after two or three days and life got back to normal.

I decided to invite Luc and Jenny, and the Sbindens, owners of the Hotel Solferino, as our first dinner guests. I was naive and decided to serve a Canadian dinner of roast beef and Yorkshire pudding. I didn't understand French cuts of meat and tried to explain to the butcher how to cut a rolled rib roast. I had a tiny kitchen with a two-burner stove and a small oven. I cooked everything carefully and proudly brought the roast to our round oak table in the studio. I placed the roast in front of York with the carving knife and fork. The table was very shaky, wobbling back and forth with each thrust of the knife. York sawed away without making much of an impression; all eyes were on him and one pair of hands after another surreptitiously held the table steady. The plate kept bouncing around and the roast suddenly took off and landed on the floor. No one said a word. Someone grabbed the roast and put it back on the plate, and York carried on. Somehow we got through that dinner! Never again did I try to tell a French butcher how to cut a roast.

My friend Shelagh Wainman-Wood gave me a French cookbook, whose husband Tom was a minister at the Canadian embassy. One easy pitfall when using the cookbook was mixing up French and English. I once decided to serve *poulet suprème*, which required raisins to be added at the last minute. I forgot the recipe was written in French, and read "raisins" as "grapes." The green seedless grapes proved to be an excellent addition and when our French guests asked the name of the recipe, I replied, "Oh, it's a French recipe, *poulet suprème*, don't you know it?" They had never heard of it. I was puzzled until I realised my translation errors had resulted in the birth of a new dish.

I began exchanging language lessons with Lylianne Schreiber, the eighteen-year-old daughter of a couturière on Rue de Toqueville. Lylianne became interested in York's painting and offered to give him French lessons. As always, he learned a few catch phrases and peeled them off at the right moments in an over-emphasised accent, which impressed some people. I told him not to worry about the language, as it was more important if all his energy went into his work. This succeeded for the most part, except during social events conducted in French. This was frustrating, as he would miss nuances, often presenting his point of view in English. Some kidded that he would soon have all Paris speaking English.

NEW FORMS OF POETRY AND MUSIC

The art critic Henri Chopin was a prominent member of the *Poésie Concrète* group. Luc took us to Henri's Sunday afternoon gatherings of poets, artists and writers. Apart from readings, much of the poetry was taped. This was our introduction to *Poésie Concrète*. A spoken word or two would be followed by silence, heavy breathing, more silence, a whistle, silence, a loud crash, and so on. Often the silences would be long and people got sleepy, only to be jolted awake by the next loud bang. Everyone raved about this new art form, even Luc and Jenny. We went along with it for a while, thinking we must be missing something.

We subscribed to Chopin's poetry magazine, which contained more of the same confusing work. A pocket at the back of each magazine contained a small recording of the same monotonous nonsense. After having given it a fair trial, we found we were busy Sunday afternoons. It was difficult as the Chopins were popular among our friends and we met constantly. They were intelligent and great fun, but we couldn't help feeling we were missing something.

Another experience was the *Musique Concrète* concerts at the conservatory. At the appointed hour the lights would dim but no one came on stage. A great silence was followed by a loud indecipherable bang. We jumped, looked around and saw nothing. Another silence was ended by a second ungodly noise from another direction, and so on. We soon gave that up.

Returning home from the conservatory one night by the subway, we decided to move our car to the now-vacant space in front of the studio. Near where we left it a policeman was directing traffic around an obvious wreck. Taking a closer look, we realised it was our precious car, now unrecognisably foreshortened against a tree with another damaged car behind and a large Chrysler rammed into it in front. We asked the gendarme what had happened and what to do. He told us to report the accident at the police station the next morning.

Our phone started ringing early in the morning as neighbours on their way to work had recognised our car. One caller was the couturière Madame Schreiber, who told us Lylianne would accompany us to the station. As we entered the building there was a hubbub of conversation between policemen lolling around. As the gorgeous Lylianne came into view all conversation stopped and every eye followed her. When we reported the accident, she had immediate attention and all particulars were quickly noted. We had a new car in a few days, with the slightest deduction. Never underestimate the power of a beautiful woman on a French man, or any man for that matter!

MEETING OTHER CANADIAN ARTISTS

While in Paris we met Marcelle Ferron, a painter from Québec who had a knack for getting government grants. Marcelle had left a husband and daughter in Québec, and lived with Guy Trédez, a doctor and artist. They had a house in Clamart on the outskirts of Paris. Our first visit was an eye-opener. Marcelle, like Riopelle a student of Borduas, had a studio in the garage and painted with the doors open for light. It wasn't easy to move around, as large canvases were stacked everywhere. She had such a commanding presence, slashing away with her brush in a flamboyant fashion, that one scarcely noticed the dirt and heavy layers of paint caked everywhere.

We were invited to lunch at Marcelle's one day with Leonard and Reva Brooks, and Lionel Roy, the Canadian ambassador to UNESCO. After hours of talking and looking at paintings, we wondered if we were mistaken about lunch. Marcelle talked on and on in the manner of a *grande dame*, though her fingernails were clogged with paint. She made no move to go to the kitchen or clear the cluttered coffee table. We had forgotten that Paquerette Villeneuve, a Canadian Press correspondent living in Paris, had made a brief appearance and then had disappeared. She reappeared, cleared the coffee table and brought in a delicious lunch which she had been preparing all the while. Marcelle didn't miss a beat, appearing not to notice the transition, and didn't lift a finger while the rest of us scurried around. Guy was busy pouring drinks and being a congenial host. His paintings were quite refined, as was he. Sam Zacks later took paintings by Guy and Marcelle back to Canada.

Many years later Marcelle arranged an exhibition with Roberts Gallery in Toronto. She did as well as could be expected for a first exhibition. The following year she doubled her prices. Roberts felt they wouldn't be able to sell them at the new prices and she left in a huff for another gallery. There is too little rapport now between artists in Québec and the rest of Canada. It was much better when the art society annuals moved between Québec and Ontario, creating a feeling of unity.

We used to visit with Ulysse Comtois and Rita Letendre in Paris. Rita came to the city in 1962 on a Canada Council grant. I liked Ulysse's work, which was more refined than Rita's at the time. She was then involved with a profusion of colours with lots of black but today is known more for her geometric works, some of which have been effective on building exteriors, especially the one at Long Beach State College in California. Rita's mixed Québecois/Iroquoian descent enchanted Italians when she exhibited there.

CANADIAN EXHIBITIONS

While in Paris we went to see an African dance performance, and as usual took seats close to the stage so York could sketch. The exciting fast movements inspired York's large black and white drawing *African Tempo* (1960) which was shown in a solo drawing exhibition at Roberts Gallery in mid-October of 1960. In "From (Almost) Realism to Abstraction," his review for the *Telegram* (October 29, 1960), Paul Duval wrote that York's drawings showed a "restless experimentation." He chose *Dreamer* (1960) and *Bianca* (1959) as York's superior nude studies. "For larger, more rhythmic essays in design," Duval wrote, "he is liable to break sharply with subject matter and create loose, almost pure patterns. *Masqued Figure* (1959), *Dark Construction* (1959) and the sparkling *African Tempo* fit into this category." *Nymph* (1955) and *Orpheus* (1960), also featured in that exhibition, are now in the collection of the Art Gallery of Ontario.

York maintained an active exhibition schedule in 1960. The OSA and AIO circulated an exhibition of York's O'Keefe Centre mural studies to high schools, colleges and art centres. *Gondola Mobile* (1958) was included in the 1960 MMFA's spring exhibition, and a black and white gouache titled *Drawing* (1960) went to the CGP exhibition, also at the MMFA. The 81st annual RCA show at the AGT included York's *Landscape* (1960) and *Ontario Abstraction* (1959), while Sam and Ayala Zacks loaned *Venus* (1959), to the "Tribute to Women" show at the CNE that summer. "Contemporary Canadian Painting" at the AGT near the year's end included *Mexicana* (1960) and *Sculptural Forms* (1960). *Mexicana* is now in the collection of the National Gallery of Canada.

Volume three of Bob Hubbard's book, *Paintings and Sculptures*, published by the National Gallery in 1960, included reproductions of York's *Una Familia* and *Santa Cruz de Tenerife* (both of 1952). *Venetian*

Vista (1958) entered the AGO collection as a gift from the J.S. McLean foundation.

A POETIC TRIBUTE FROM GRAEME WILSON

While in Paris, York was continuing with large works on brown paper and small gouaches. His old friend, the British poet Graeme Wilson, then serving with the British Foreign Service, had started making regular trips to Paris for NATO meetings. He spent all his spare time in York's studio, completely absorbed in York's painting. He once said he could slip into York's skin and feel perfectly at home. They discussed art by the hour, first the brown paper drawings and newspaper collages, then the gouaches, which Graeme and I helped York to name. Graeme's poetic bent influenced York's titles.

Graeme was a great historian. He became very caught up with one of York's recent collages, a large oval called *A Propos de Shaka* (1962). York was a member of the French salon *L'Oeil de Boeuf*, where all the works in their exhibitions were either round or oval. While coming over on the plane for his next NATO meeting Graeme wrote a poem especially for this work, related to the Zulu tribe in Africa.

Shaka Zulu

Here in a shieldshape. Ishilangu,
Of mirror-grass and marker stones
The sorcerers of Shaka Zulu
Cursed and cast their lucking-bones.

Here are the days with Dingiswayo,
The IziCwe, their Queasy eyes;
And here the swaying vulture-shadow
Over the shields and assegais;

Scarred cattle-hide; M'zilikazi
Hidden cattle; muscle-gloss;
And sorghum stains like blackened daisies
Starred on the orgy-hard kaross;

And here, the blood already gnarling
Sunblack in the ochre light,
Are Dingaan's dirk and Shaka snarling
Boneshapes in the kraals of night.

OTHER FRIENDS

Among our friends was an English painter Derek Middleton. He lived with Verity Russell, daughter of a British diplomat, who was working in Paris and waiting for her divorce to be finalised. Derek was a good painter but never had any money, even though his dealer was London's prestigious Redfern Gallery.

When in London Derek had lived in a houseboat on the Thames, next to the boat where the film version of Joyce Cary's novel *The Horse's Mouth* (1944) was made. Derek was very much like the novel's protagonist Gulley Jimson; he would phone his dealer, disguise his voice and rave about the work of Derek Middleton in the hope of sparking a few sales. When he heard one of his paintings had sold and he didn't receive a cheque, he would buy a new suit, look as prosperous as possible and call on his dealer. He would be told that his clothes indicated he didn't need any money, and that the funds went for framing. Later he dressed in rags but then he couldn't get past the secretary; if he did he would be told a similar story.

Derek and Verity had a small two-room apartment on the Rue de Patay, where the studio doubled as a living room with a counter separating a narrow space used as a kitchen. They constantly fought and sometimes Verity would awaken with all the paintings gone from their bedroom walls. Derek had removed them in anger; when confronted he would explain the paintings were much too good for her.

Derek and Verity were great entertainers. Verity was a good cook and dinner, though late, was always worth the wait. Artists usually brought a bottle of wine, the quality of which depended on their particular financial state, and in the early 1960s, the Parisian art market was depressed. It was a great day when the Middletons met Lionel Roy, who always brought a bottle of Scotch and was made a permanent member of the guest list. Sometimes Derek would announce that the party couldn't start because Lionel was late.

When Verity's divorce was finalised, she and Derek decided to get married and they went around holding hands, no more fighting. They purchased new clothes and went to England for the great event. They departed talking about having to drive on the wrong side of the road in England, and were warned not to forget to change on returning to France. We all awaited the happily-married couple's return. In about three weeks, back they came in a battered car, looking as irritated as ever. Something had gone wrong and they didn't get married, so they were back to the usual bickering. On returning to France they drove off the boat and went sailing down the wrong side of the road right into another car.

Lionel Roy was an old friend and former Canadian ambassador to Mexico. We met again when he invited us for New Year's dinner at his apartment on Avenue Monceau. We gradually moved into the habit of frequent dinners at each other's places; he was a bachelor and a good cook, even though he had a cook.

Lionel never tired of talking about York's paintings. If there were other visitors he often took it upon himself to explain the abstractions, and with his vivid imagination it was usually hilarious. York formed the habit of going to small towns to sketch on weekends. Lionel had a large car and diplomatic licence, and escorted us on many of these trips. Lionel and I would leave York at his desired spot to sketch and go off exploring churches, art galleries, or local tourist spots. When Leonard and Reva Brooks visited us in 1961, they joined us on a cold, windy day trip. We left York and Leonard on a bridge to sketch, saying we would be back in an hour. Lionel, Reva and I sped away and got busy looking at churches. Being near Lisieux, famous for its cheeses, we decided to go the extra distance and didn't return for two hours. We found them cold and huddled on their sketching stools, long since finished and mad as hops. Reva jumped out and took pictures of the two forlorn men.

MANY VISITORS

Maestro Ernesto Barbini came to Paris to conduct the Paris Television Orchestra. We held a reception in the studio after the concert; among the guests were Pierre Dupuy and Lionel Roy, who brought René Garneau, the newly-arrived cultural attaché. M. Queille, our landlord, and Madame Queille, a violinist in the orchestra, also attended. There were other Canadians and artist friends. M. Dupuy congratulated us, saying that as we entertained more Canadians than the embassy, we should have some recompense. Since René Garneau had just come from Switzerland but hadn't had time to check with the Embassy as to his new posting, Lionel Roy brought him to our studio to meet his new colleagues. Mr. Dupuy remarked that he had to come to our place to meet his new ministers! During our stay in Paris many Canadians came to our home, including over one hundred from Toronto's Arts & Letters Club.

Our Toronto visitors included William and June Withrow. Bill, the new director of the Art Gallery of Toronto, was under intense strain at the gallery. Apparently Martin Baldwin, the retiring director, was loath to relinquish the reins of power. He would come into the gallery daily and create a scene with Bill in the privacy of his office. During openings, Martin was accustomed to gathering with his small group over coffee in the sculpture court and continued to do so, always excluding the Withrows. In the past we had often been invited to join Martin's group. We made a mental note to try and correct the situation on our return.

Early in our sojourn J. Russell Harper, then curator at the National Gallery of Canada, turned up to see what was going on in our Paris studio. He was very impressed with what he saw and chose three large canvases to send to Ottawa. When an artist is hot, strong support at home can make him a world figure. York never received a government grant. We did everything on his sales earnings and learned how to accomplish unbelievable dreams on the cheap. Fortunately other people and other countries recognised York's talent, which made so many things possible. It was thus a shock to receive a letter from Jack Wildridge, saying the National Gallery had sent the three large canvases to his gallery without any explanation. What should he do with them? It must have been a blow to the enthusiastic Harper to have his judgement questioned. Harper never mentioned York in his later books, nor did Bob Hubbard, except to list him in the index of the permanent collection.

AN IMPORTANT LUNCHEON

Our new friend René Garneau brought Jean Cassou to the studio. Jean was again delighted with what he saw and invited York to a luncheon with the mayors of Paris. This was just before Christmas in 1960 and the luncheon was planned for January. René mentioned that York should have a book of samples to present to the City Fathers. As all York's samples were back in Toronto and York was deeply involved in his work, it was decided that I should return to retrieve the necessary items. I would be gone for two weeks over Christmas and took the first plane out.

I robbed our files for examples of York's work, knowing it was an irrevocable mistake to let an only copy be removed. However when York had the book of samples ready for presentation, René assured him he would accept personal responsibility for its safe return.

The luncheon was a great success. Jean Cassou offered York a retrospective exhibition at the gallery of his choice, mentioning the *Musée National d'Art Moderne*, the *Petit Palais* and the *Musée Galliera*. The French government would pay for everything. Their only request was that the National Gallery of Canada gather some of York's earlier works to round out the retrospective. York and René were in seventh heaven. York was the first English-speaking Canadian to whom France had made such an offer. Alfred Pellan's 1955 retrospective at the *Musée National d'Art Moderne* happened after many years spent in France (1926-1940 and 1952-1955). York's exhibition was slated for late 1963, allowing nearly three years for him and the National Gallery to bring together a cohesive body of work. René was in charge of the arrangements with the National Gallery.

York was pleased and worked happily away in his huge studio. We had dinners back and forth with René and his wife Jacqueline. Pierre Dupuy invited us to many receptions and dinners given by the Embassy, where we met many Paris-based diplomats. We first met Jules Léger, then Canada's representative to NATO, and his wife Gabrielle at a dinner given by Lionel. I remember Gabrielle's first remark after the introduction, "Well, would you like to have a lesson in French, or enjoy the evening?" That endeared us to her and we became great friends.

George and Alison Ignatieff were also in Paris at that time. They held a luncheon for Donald Buchanan, editor of *Canadian Art*, who was hard of hearing. When Donald was passed a large a platter of individually sectioned fish, he slid the whole fish onto his plate, not realising there were portions for others. Alison excused herself and took the platter to the kitchen, hastily looking for something else. Conversation was at its peak and Buchanan was totally unaware of his faux pas.

Robert Elie, director of Québec House, often invited us to special occasions, which helped us to get to know our Québec peers, including Marcelle Ferron, Ulysse Comtois, Rita Letendre, Léon and Rita Bellefleur, Edmund Alleyn and Riopelle, among others.

THE CANADIAN ART SCENE

Meanwhile the art world back in Canada was struggling along as usual on a pittance, trying its best to show Canadian art across Canada but running into more and more opposition from the art galleries. The government was cutting its small grants for operating costs to art societies. The artists did all the work—lending their work without charge, producing catalogues and circulating the exhibitions. One wonders what art galleries are for if not to support the art of the country! With the annual struggle and perseverance of the artists, exhibitions were still squeaking through.

During our stay in Paris, the Roberts Gallery did a good job of keeping York represented at many exhibitions. In 1961 *Mexicana* was shown at the 89th OSA exhibition at the AGT. The National Gallery of Canada's fourth biennial included *Shades of Tlalpujahua* (1959). York was one of "Four Canadian Painters" featured in a show of that name at the O'Keefe Centre, and the AIO continued to circulate the O'Keefe mural studies exhibition. Four of York's oil paintings went to a show at the Winnipeg Art Gallery in late 1961; the Winnipeg critic Jan Kamienski commented that, "From among all pictures in this exhibition, I would give preference to the work of York Wilson. It stands out in the crowd by virtue of its maturity and utmost economy of means."

In mid-1961, York's work was included in "Eight Ontario Painters," held at the Fine Arts Gallery of the University of British Columbia. Ian McNairn wrote in the exhibition catalogue that the show represented a "new group of painters" in Ontario whose work reflected the emergence of a new spirit. McNairn noted that although some of the painters represented in the show—Kazuo Nakamura, William Ronald and Harold Town—belonged to Toronto's Painters Eleven, the Vancouver show did not represent them specifically. In the case of York, who had no group affiliation, McNairn concluded that, "Wilson reflects the direction these artists are taking." The show toured to various centres in Alberta and Saskatchewan through 1961.

News of our activities in Paris began to reach Canadian publications. Nora Harper, Paris representative for the *Toronto Daily Star*, and Helen Palmer, also a *Star* writer, visited us on different occasions. Helen compared our Toronto and Paris studios and homes in her full-page illustrated article in the *Star* on February 18, 1961. Roderick Goodman published a review of York's work in the *Globe and Mail* on July 29, 1961. Paquerette Villeneuve reported York's comment in the *Ottawa Journal* (December 8, 1961) that, "I can't live permanently in Toronto because life would be too easy. I have too many friends and I'm afraid it would decrease my output."

EUROPEAN TRAVEL

Leonard and Reva Brooks arrived in Paris in 1961. They stayed in a hotel right across the street from our studio. We decided to go on a sketching trip with them, through France, Switzerland and Italy. We both took cars, driving in tandem.

We had agreed to meet the German painter Francis Bott and his wife Mania for the opening of his exhibition at the Susan Feigel Gallery in Basel a month later. We drove through Switzerland to Milan and on to Verona and Venice, stopping frequently for York and Leonard to sketch and Reva to take photographs.

Venice as usual was an island of peace, with no traffic, but it was flood time and San Marco was under water. On the way to Rome we stopped again at the Church of San Francesco in Arezzo to see Piero della Francesca's murals. There was no one about when we entered. Scaffolding was in place for the murals to be cleaned and the restorers had gone to lunch. York lamented, "I sure would like to see those murals up close," and Leonard replied, "Why don't you?" York was up in a flash, examining them closely when all hell broke loose. Priests came running from all directions, shouting in Italian. We tried to explain but they wouldn't listen and they just wanted us to leave.

It was delightful renewing our acquaintance with all the points of interest on the way to Rome, and to introduce Leonard and Reva to some of our favourite haunts. We then headed to Florence and enjoyed its many artistic and architectural wonders. Time was running short for Francis' exhibition in Basel so we headed for Bologna and parted with the Brooks, arranging to meet them in Basel or Paris.

We went in search of friends, the Count and Countess de Regi. Elizabeth de Regi had inherited her family's castle which had been vacant during the war and hadn't had a roof for many a year. Francisco de Regi was serving in Italy's foreign service. A few years ago they had started restoring the castle during their holidays and were now living there. We were interested in some of the castle's murals, which included portraits of Elizabeth's ancestors.

AN UNNERVING JOURNEY TO SWITZERLAND

We then headed for Turin and the Simplonpass, close to the Switzerland border. We were surprised how easily we were waved across the border. We went into a restaurant for lunch and enquired as to the driving time to Basel. Although we were in hot summer weather at present, we were told it could be cold ahead, and that there was no way we could make Basel in two days. Our hosts advised us to put ourselves and our car on the train, which travelled directly through the tunnels in the mountains. We hurried to the station and did just that.

We went along nicely for some time, going through tunnels while climbing gradually. We were alone in the car and in our thin summer clothes we became colder and colder on the metal seats. We looked long-ingly at our car on the flatcar behind us, thinking of the warm sweaters locked inside. Suddenly a conductor came in, talking a mile a minute in German but we couldn't understand a word. He kept repeating himself, getting more and more excited, finally leaving in disgust.

The train soon came to a stop and we could see we were on a very high trestle bridge over a ravine. We heard what sounded like an uncoupling noise and sure enough, the train pulled away, leaving us and the flatcar all alone. We couldn't step out, as there was nothing but open rails over a great ravine. We must have sat for nearly an hour, feeling cold and frightened, when we heard a train approaching slowly. We realised we had been dropped off to be picked up by another train going to Basel. We went on and on into the middle of the night, not having eaten since early morning. Suddenly the train stopped. We drove our car onto the nearby road. The station was barely visible in the darkness, but we saw a figure moving in the yard and hailed him.

We were told to continue down the road and we would come to an inn. After some distance we reached the inn and stayed there. After much pleading they found us a bite to eat. In the morning, we were shocked to find our car deep in snow! The snow storm was heavy, and visibility was limited. It was slow going along the excessively winding mountain road, but we finally pulled into our Basel hotel at about 5:00 P.M. While en route to Basel, York had told me he had dreamt the previous night that we were in the Botts' house and Mania was ill in bed upstairs. She asked York if he would tell Francis to come up as she had something important to tell him.

York suggested I enter the hotel and make enquiries while he waited in the car. Strangely, most of the hotel staff were standing together in the hallway, looking very concerned. As I opened the door and identified myself, they told me that Mania had died the night before of a "quick flu" and that Francis had cancelled his exhibition and taken her body to Paris. Thunderstruck, I returned to the car to tell York, and he said, " I know, she died in my dream but I didn't want to tell you." He was always very psychic. We decided to head for Paris without delay. It turned out Mania Bott had died from cortisone poisoning. She had been on cortisone for a long time because of her crippling arthritis.

BACK IN PARIS

During the Brooks' temporary residence in Paris, we noticed how Leonard studied York's paintings. Sometimes while we were visiting with them, he unconsciously turned his back to us to look at York's works. York knew that Leonard had been suffering from depression, as abstraction was becoming more and more dominant in the art world, and Leonard had no feeling for abstraction. During the Paris trip he began gathering all sorts of materials to make collages. This progressed nicely and he did many good things. Later when we were back in Canada, we were some-times amused when we mistook Leonard's work for York's. York was pleased that Leonard had got over his depression, and was painting his own fine abstractions.

Sam Zacks kept us informed about the art scene in Canada with reg-ular letters. In one letter he said, "Whatever did you do to Harold Town? He spends all his time denouncing you!" Sam knew that York had done nothing but support Harold Town; he had arranged his first show at Laing Galleries, had defended his Cornwall mural against the press, and had tried to transfer to Harold a mural commission he was unable to accept. Someone sent us an unidentified newspaper clipping quoting Harold's remark that, "He didn't have to leave Canada to find things to paint. There was enough in his own back yard to keep him busy for the rest of his life!" There was little doubt as to whom he was referring.

We were very excited when in 1962 one of York's new canvases, *Reflexion, Paris* (1962) was invited to the exhibition, "L'Art au Canada," at the *Galerie des Beaux Arts* in Bordeaux, France. York's supporters were Sam Zacks and Ted Heinrich in Toronto. Unbeknownst to us other factions were working against York. Much later we discovered an item in *Canadian Art* by David Silcox, a friend of Harold's, which clearly questioned why York had been included in the Bordeaux show.

There had been other cases of jealousy. One evening on entering the Art Gallery of Toronto, the sculptor Gerald Gladstone came running towards York saying, "I didn't mean it, it's just that someone had to bring you down." York had no idea what he was talking about but later learned that Gerald had said something against him on a radio program. Gerald liked York and hastened to square it with him immediately.

It was interesting how quickly France's main art connoisseurs became conscious of York's work. Michel Seuphor, a world-renowned expert on abstract art, was about to go to press with his new book *La Peinture Abstraite* (1962) when he saw York's work and decided to include an ink drawing titled *Abstraction* (1960). Thus it was that York was the only Canadian artist honoured in a book published in five languages.

We were sitting at a sidewalk café one day while York was sketching the facade of Notre Dame Cathedral when suddenly a familiar voice cried "York!" It was Michael Foytenyi, who had come to Paris to finish "Profile of York Wilson," a CBC film he had started shooting for the CBC series, "The Lively Arts." He set to work immediately in our Paris studio, updating the film with shots of York's new work. We were unfortunately still abroad when it was first aired on February 26, 1963. Susan Macdougall, energetic owner of the Montreal gallery La Collection Tudor, tracked it down through her cousin, who worked at the CBC. He found it stored in a building at the Toronto Airport. The film was somewhat damaged, and the narrator's voice was lost. We first saw the film in 1983 at the AGO, who had purchased a video copy.

Sam and Ayala Zacks gave more than one hundred works of Canadian art to the Agnes Etherington Art Centre at Queen's University in 1962. The gift included three of York's works: *Venus* (1959), a large drawing study for the O'Keefe Centre mural; *African Totem* (1962), a gouache; and *Reflexion, Paris*, an oil on canvas which had represented Canada in "L'Art au Canada," at Bordeaux.

TRAVEL SOUTH

In September we flew to Vienna, where we visited the opera house and the art gallery, with its many wonderful Hieronymus Bosch paintings.

Next we flew to Istanbul, where we settled in a hotel with a view of the Bosporus. York did many paintings from an upper veranda. We crossed into Asia Minor for lunch one day. We saw the great mosques, palaces and the bazaar. Another day we took the boat in the opposite direction to the Princess Islands, where York sketched all day.

Our next stop was Athens. We noticed the ship *Semiramus* was about to sail to various islands, so we impulsively decided on a one-week trip. On board each night after dinner we listened to a lecture about the islands we would visit the following day. It was often mentioned that Lord Elgin should return the famous Elgin Marbles to Greece. I don't suppose there would be any Elgin Marbles if Lord Elgin hadn't rescued them!

We toured Rhodes, Crete and Patmos, where all the buildings are pristine white, a fact common to a lesser degree on other islands and shown in York's paintings. We spent a little time on Mikonos, where York did some sketching inland. We ended by spending a week of painting on the delightful island of Idhra, returned to Athens for a tour of archaeological sites, and then travelled back to Paris. York brought back about twenty-four sketches from this trip.

A QUICK TRIP HOME

We decided to fly home for two weeks in October of 1962 for the opening of York's solo gouache show at the Roberts Gallery. York was welcomed as a favourite son upon our return. As our house was then rented, we stayed with Sam and Ayala Zacks. Lotta Dempsey wrote in the *Toronto Daily Star* (October 13, 1962) that "an air of mounting excitement hovers over the Roberts Gallery, as hours tick away for the opening of York Wilson's new show." Dempsey reproduced part of a letter I had written to her, in which I said, "We are making the trip because we feel the gouaches are an important step in York's work... They are a little more abstract than his former work, but in most cases are based on an idea or feeling."

A photograph of us installing the exhibition, which featured thirty gouache paintings, was published in the *Telegram* on October 18. The Sarnia Public Library and Art Gallery directors Reg Bradley purchased *Grand Oracle* (1962) three days before the opening. Paul Duval wrote in the *Telegram* (October 27, 1962) that York's "semi-abstract fantasies will reveal a wit and humour which is hidden in the large wall paintings." Elizabeth Kilbourn, the reviewer for the *Toronto Daily Star* (November 3, 1962) claimed that "Wilson's very real abilities are no longer sacrificed to a fashionable and mannered style but have been explored for their own sake."

While in Toronto I was interviewed by Mary Jukes of the *Globe and Mail* (October 23,1962) for an article she called, "In Paris Artist's Wife Studies." I spoke mainly of our daily life, and of my study of French language and the Civilisation Course at the Sorbonne. As Mary put it, "Married to an artist who spends six hours a day before his easel, what does she do with herself during cold, rainy, grey days? 'Study,' she confessed, 'six days a week.'"

BACK TO PARIS

The season of exhibitions opened in 1963 with the 83rd annual RCA exhibition, held at the AGT, to which York sent *Bragozzi* (1962). *Queen of the Adriatic* went to the OSA show, also held at the AGT. *Night Images* (1962) was included in the Canadian Group of Painters exhibition at the MMFA. "Master Canadian Painters & Sculptors," organised by the London Public Library and Art Museum, featured York's *Night Abstraction (1961)*.

In Paris, a *L'Oeil de Boeuf* exhibition at Galerie 7 included York's *A Propos de Shaka*, with twenty-seven other works by *L'Oeil de Boeuf* artists. The same work was sent to the VII Bienal in Sao Paolo in 1963, where it was installed with works by School of Paris artists. Francois Thépot, a great colourist and disciple of Mondrian, introduced York to his La Galerie Jacques Casanova in Paris; York's paintings were later exhibited there in a seven-person show. York was also included in an eleven-person exhibition opening in December at La Galerie Orient-Occident.

1963 also saw York's participation in one of the most unique exhibitions of his career. Over one hundred painters and sculptors from around the world were invited to create portraits of "The-Bird-Who-Doesn't-Exist" (*L'Oiseau-Qui-N'Existe-Pas*), the name of a 1956 poem by the French writer Claude Aveline. York and Sorel Etrog were the two Canadian artists invited to do portraits. Other distinguished participants included Marc Chagall, Jean Cocteau, Rufino Tamayo and André Masson. Aveline presented the collection to the *Musée National d'Art Moderne*; the exhibition opened there in October of 1963 and has since gone on tour, including a stop at the *Musée des Beaux Arts* in Le Havre in 1970. When the *Musée National d'Art Moderne* was incorporated within the Pompidou Centre, Aveline's collection went along. It was the object of a large exhibition, "108 Portraits de L'Oiseau-Qui-N'Existe-Pas," which opened there in April of 1978.

Myself and York with Guy Trédez, Leonard Brooks, and Marcelle Ferron at Marcelle's home. Paris, 1961. Photograph by Reva Brooks.

York and I at the Parthenon. Athens, Greece, 1962.

XVI

1963-1964

Our Final Year in Paris

WE CONTINUED TOURING WEEKENDS with Lionel Roy so that York could sketch in the small French towns. Lionel's interest in art was so intense that York presented him with a sketching box, brushes and paints. Lionel was in seventh heaven and jumped right in without inhibition, using wonderful, vibrant colours. He became so caught up in painting that he couldn't wait for weekends and began painting at home as well.

TO MOROCCO

In February of 1963 we headed for Morocco, stopping off to visit Max and Sophie Stewart and the Prado in Madrid, where we awakened the next morning to slush and snow. We left for Tangier, Fez and Casablanca the following day. Finding it still raining, we continued on to Marrakech and the first sun we had seen in weeks.

We were nicely settled in our hotel, with York busy painting, when Dorothy Osborne, a minister from the Canadian embassy in Paris, tracked us down. We went for a walk with Dorothy and ran into Max and Sophie, who were looking for our hotel. They were already settled in the Mamounia hotel so we had a dinner party at our hotel that evening and another at the Mamounia Hotel the next evening. York was anxious to concentrate on his painting, and so the next day we flew with Dorothy to Agadir, on the west coast of Morocco. There wasn't much left of Agadir after a recent tidal wave—tents had been thrown up everywhere—but we found accommodation that night and made arrangements for a taxi trip for Tafraoute in the Atlas mountains the following morning.

The next day we found the road had been washed away in many places, so we helped the driver carry stones to build it up so the car could pass through. Many lost their lives as a result of the tidal wave and in Agadir, whole streets of buildings had disappeared. We finally reached Tafraoute and a nice hotel run by a French couple. They welcomed us, as they had had no guests for days.

During daylight we walked along roads where veiled women dressed in black silk, tilled the fields. They wore unusual red shoes with a high piece at the back to keep sand out. The hotel owner sent a cobbler to make some for us. He just looked at our feet and said he would bring them in a couple of days. I said, "Don't you wish to take measurements?" He replied that it wasn't necessary, as he knew our sizes by looking at our feet. He returned as promised and they fitted nicely, though mine were a little snug. These shoes are now in the collection of the new Bata Shoe Museum in Toronto.

We walked up and down the hills wondering what lay beyond the next rise, discovering the village of Tafraoute and great rocks with prehistoric markings. York made many drawings and sketches there. After a couple of weeks the three of us returned to Agadir. The road had been repaired and a great building program was underway. Dorothy left Agadir for Paris. We decided to make our way along the coast by bus, sketching at towns including Mogador (now Essaouira), Safi, Mazagan (now El Jadida), Rabat and Fez, where we spent the remainder of our time before returning to Paris.

FRENCH CANADIAN INCIDENTS IN PARIS

Near the end of 1962 we became conscious of a few things which we only understood in retrospect. We did not know that feelings had deteriorated so badly with Québec back home. We were astounded by newspaper reports of bombings in Québec. This was Canada, our native country, where such things were unknown. So many French Canadians in Paris were our good friends. A cleaning establishment with several French Canadian clients began to snub us. Marcelle Ferron, long a close friend, declared to us one day that, "We're going to war on you one day," despite the fact she had just requested a painting from York to raise funds to help get the church out of Québec schools.

Everyone now knew about York's retrospective exhibition scheduled for late 1963. Unbeknownst to us, the exhibition was being sabotaged. We no longer heard from Robert Elie, director of Québec House. The most serious thing was that we hadn't heard a word from René Garneau, who was solely responsible for making arrangements with the National Gallery to collect York's early works. York called René repeatedly, but his calls were never returned. It was then almost 1963, and only a year until the show.

York became so upset he found it difficult to paint. It never occurred to him to mention it to our many other close friends at the Canadian embassy, although a number of them must have been under duress.

In the summer of 1963 York finally managed to contact René, who asked, "Well have you been in touch with your friend, Charles Comfort to arrange the collection of works in Canada?" York was speechless and finally said, "Of course not, that was your job." René said that he would write Comfort immediately. The National Gallery's "Fifth Biennial of Canadian Painting" was to be opened by Queen Elizabeth II at the Commonwealth Institute in London on September 19. York was invited to participate, so he sent a large painting titled *Egyptian Dimension* (1962). We decided to attend the opening and René said that we should speak to Charles Comfort in London, as he had not yet heard from him.

The exhibition looked fine. Charles spoke and invited any visiting artists to stand by their paintings. The Queen opened and toured the exhibition, discussing the work with each artist in attendance. Charles then suggested that we join him for dinner, during which York broached the subject of his Paris retrospective. Charles had never heard a word about it! York described the arrangements and Charles said he would do what he could in the little time remaining. We later saw a letter Comfort had written to William Withrow asking for assistance. No funds were forthcoming from anywhere and that was that. It seemed unbelievable to us, as the retrospective was an honour for Canada as well as York!

Canada doesn't handle her talented people well. One has to get outside in order to get strong support that encourages artistic excellence. Lionel Roy was aware of the situation at the embassy and at Québec House. We realised later that he may have been instrumental in the exhibition happening at all. Being a diplomat and close friend, however, he only hinted at what might be going on.

POLITICS TAKE OVER

The shock was tremendous for York. It was hard to believe that his country wouldn't support him in this rare international honour. He changed his plan, and decided to show his recent Paris work in a smaller gallery, the *Musée Galliera*. He immediately wrote to Imperial Oil and the O'Keefe Centre, asking if they would send his large mural studies. They both replied that they would be pleased to do so at their expense.

York suggested another Canadian working in Paris, Jack Nichols; his fine prints would look well in the four smaller salons. Jack, however, decided there was not enough time to prepare an exhibit. René Garneau was pressing for Québec House to fill the remaining four salons at the *Galliera*, but it was decided that the Vancouver artist Joe Plaskett, who lived in Paris, should have one of the small salons and Québec House was invited to exhibit in the other three. They jumped at the idea and decided to fly over the paintings of five Québec artists.

This new arrangement astounded the gallery's committee. Gallery director Madame Dane was at a loss to understand why York was allowing the other artists to exhibit when the whole gallery had been offered to him. York was at a disadvantage as he could not reveal that Canada would not support him. The committee stipulated that it was York's show and he must have the main salon, and that the four small surrounding salons would only fit the works of three other artists. York could have filled the small salons with drawings, sketches and gouaches, but he was depressed. When politics entered the situation, the joy was gone.

René asked York to design the catalogue and posters—large ones for key positions throughout Paris and small ones for shop windows and foyers. York's heart wasn't in the task. He also found it hard to foreground his own work, and had to be reminded that his name should come first.

The Parisian art critics Jacques Lassaigne and Frédéric Mégret contributed essays to the catalogue. Jacques Lassaigne was often among our group of artists and we got to know him a little. He wrote books biased in favour of Québec and one evening showed us a letter from President de Gaulle thanking him for the good work he was doing for Québec. This work of course was to encourage a sovereign Québec. It's puzzling why Garneau would have chosen Lassaigne for the catalogue essay, unless pressure on the Canadian embassy staff was so great that no other choice was possible. In his preface he predictably focused on the Francophone painters, reserving a slight mention of York and Joe for the final paragraph. Frédéric Mégret contributed a brief but complimentary text about York. Frédéric later acquired York's *Gouache Rouge* (1963).

INSTALLING THE EXHIBITION

The day came to hang the exhibition. York's works were mostly large, including the triptych, *A Propos d'Afrique* (1961), titled by Michel

Seuphor. We centred it on the large wall opposite the entrance. There were about twenty-six major canvases in the main salon. The cartoons for the Imperial Oil and O'Keefe Centre murals were installed in a separate area. York had studied the space earlier and being a pro at hanging exhibitions, it was quick work. The exhibition looked magnificent.

We then noticed Joe Plaskett had completed his small section but Robert Elie and his assistants had accomplished little, still trying to decide which galleries to use for the three Québec painters, Alfred Pellan, Jean-Paul Lemieux and Jean McEwen. Elie was inexperienced and the small salons were long and narrow, making it difficult to hang larger paintings. York and I offered to help. Robert looked confused and uncomfortable. I'm sure he thought of us as the enemy, when in fact we thought only of having the exhibition look its best and be a credit to Canada. These painters were also our friends and we naturally wanted to do our best for them in their absence.

York looked over all the works and the spaces and then recommended where he thought the works would look best. Pellan had many small works, so York suggested a longer space; the extra length allowed better spacing. Pellan's colours were strong and two parallel walls had to be hung. I'm sure Robert thought it to be a lesser space and that Pellan was the more important painter. We agreed but thought the longer space would compliment his paintings more. Jean McEwen's larger works were hung in the centre of the three galleries, with its wide door opening on to the main salon, thus making it possible to stand back for viewing. Lemieux had fewer and smaller paintings, which fit nicely in the smaller end gallery. York clearly explained his thinking to Robert, so he would understand we were working with him for everyone's advantage.

We were very fond of Alfred Pellan and would only do our best for him, so we were saddened when he later told us that he had heard the show was poorly installed, to the detriment of his work. It's too bad so much sniping goes on; we have seen it over and over again. Québec artists who were good friends eventually shied away because of the false propaganda against Anglophones. Rita and Léon Bellefleur had been such good friends in Paris, and we discussed many intimate family affairs in a very relaxed atmosphere. When Léon came to Toronto years later for his exhibitions at Roberts Gallery, he always came alone. When I asked why Rita hadn't come, he confided she felt the English didn't like her and she would be uncomfortable. With so much political pressure in Québec, it became hard for Francophone artists to speak English, or to be seen with English-speaking people.

Plans had been made for a grand reception, but it too had become political. Paul Martin, Senior, Minister of External Affairs, came from Ottawa to open the show, called "Cinq Peintres Canadiens." André Malraux, his French counterpart, would attend, as would other important politicians. We were overjoyed and had invited many friends, especially artists. At the last minute René Garneau told us there was such a large guest list that he had to limit our friends to no more than six. I think they would have been happier not to include us at all.

A buffet fit for a king was set up in the main salon. The guests were glittering in evening attire. The speakers talked mostly about the two participating countries, and only incidentally about art. After the opening ceremonies, Pierre Dupuy brought André Malraux over and presented York. No sooner had the introduction been made when Robert Elie interrupted and manoeuvred York away. Much to our delight, Malraux later told Ambassador Dupuy, "This is one of the finest exhibitions I've seen in a long time." That approval mattered; let them play games and jockey for position! We were pleased to see reviews in *Les Nouvelles Littéraires* (December 28, 1963), *Le Figaro* (December 26, 1963) and *Le Monde* (December 26, 1963).

Garneau arranged another opening for the following evening for our friends and gave York a number of photocopied invitations. There were no refreshments and no one from the embassy showed up. I don't suppose they even knew about it. It was a sparse group in that large salon but at least they were interested viewers.

AN EXHIBITION IN DIJON

A group of artists came from Dijon to view the exhibition and were so excited that they requested three of York's paintings to include in their annual "Confrontation" exhibition at the *Musée de Dijon* in January of 1964. York's work was included with that of Picasso, Miró and others.

Lionel Roy was also invited to the show's opening and we went down on the train together. Lionel was rather quiet and formal which was surprising to us, as we had been family for such a long time. He had purchased the odd small painting at a thirty percent discount and we had given him the occasional sketch. Before the *Musée Galliera* exhibition came down, Lionel had York meet him there, as he wished to purchase a major canvas. He chose what York considered his major work, and asked for a fifty percent discount. York was a little concerned as his prices were already far too low. We considered the matter and said that a thirty percent discount was fair. Lionel said, "But this is me, not just any friend, you will never know how I have fought for this exhibition!"

What we didn't realise at the time, but later learned, was that Lionel had known the whole score and had worked very hard behind the scenes on York's behalf. He was not at liberty to tell us during the difficult period of the show's organisation. The whole situation ended badly. Lionel didn't get the painting and I was unable to straighten out the situation that weekend. Lionel was deeply hurt but I really didn't know the extent of his involvement on York's behalf until long after we had left Paris. We didn't hear from him again.

The Dijon weekend was busy. Apart from many little receptions the artists were so enthusiastic about York's painting, they cornered him every spare moment, and invited him to be a member of their salon. *Galeasse* (1963) was purchased for the Dijon Museum. When the cheque signed by André Malraux arrived we considered framing it, but eventually had to cash it. What a pity!

LEAVING PARIS FOR GOOD

In January, a few months before our departure, President and Madame de Gaulle invited us to a reception held in honour of Canadian Prime Minister Lester B. Pearson. We were received by the de Gaulles. Madame de Gaulle was a friendly, cheerful lady but the President gave the impression that he would rather be fishing! Lester was amused by a story I told him which had been told to me by my mother. When Lester's father, the Reverend Pearson was minister of the United Church at Aurora, Ontario, the toddler Lester would busy himself by dusting the pews during the services.

Our departure from Paris was marked by Derek Middleton in a highly humorous fashion. Derek prepared and presented York with a hand-made book painted in watercolour with the help of Luc Peire and Lionel Roy, titled: "York Wilson In Art for Art's Sake, or How to Succeed Without Really Trying. Directed by Lela Wilson; Producer, Luc Peire; Artistic Adviser, Lionel Roy; Sound Effects, Verity. From the Worstselling Novel by Derek Middleton. York Wilson's beard courtesy of the Toronto Mop Co.

Inc." The book included clever scripts followed by witty watercolours depicting York's life from childhood to the present.

Shortly before leaving France we went to Belgium with Michel and Suzanne Seuphor for the great honour our friend Luc Peire was receiving from his native country. The Museum of Bruges was celebrating its purchase of Luc's work, thus opening its doors to contemporary art. Luc was also being honoured in his hometown of Knokke, where we were invited as platform guests along with Luc and Jenny, and then wined and dined in several homes. We visited the Peires' very modern home and studio; the soundproof bathroom was so discreet that one had to push a hidden button to move its sliding entrance door. It was furnished with the latest designs, including a white pedestal table and chairs by Eero Saarinen, and the first vertical venetian blinds I had seen. The garden boasted sculptures by his friends, including the Spanish master José Maria Subirachs.

While in Belgium York had colour plates made of three of his paintings: *La Seine* (1962), *Parc Montsouris* (1962) and *Gouache Bleue* (1962). Luc introduced York and his work to Galerie 123, his Brussels dealer, who asked to handle York's work. The Galerie had an immediate sale when Graeme Wilson heard that *Green Red Black* (1964) was in the Brussels gallery. He asked them to send it to him in Hong Kong.

We were fortunate to be in Belgium during the great festival at Damme. Viewers walked along the canal in the evening to watch the performances in the fine old castles on the opposite side. The lights would go on in each building in turn, revealing glamorous people dancing in period costumes. The lights would go out and one walked along to the next building and the lights would come on revealing something else. It was a spectacular end to our European sojourn.

LUC PEIRE'S TRIBUTE

In April of 1982, many years after our return from Paris, we received a letter from Luc Peire. I think Luc's letter summarises perfectly the impact of Paris on York's painting. Luc wrote in French; the English translation below is my own:

> Painting in his blood, York Wilson is one of the most gifted artists
> I have ever had the opportunity to meet. An extraordinary
> colourist, a lyrical poet who succeeded in imposing rules of order,

purely plastic in forms and colour, combined with a feeling of great liberty. His stay in Paris and his contacts with the little "clique" of artists gathered there from the whole world, forming the "School of Paris," gave birth, for York, to works which in my opinion belong to the very best of his production. Paris was able to see, at the time of his exhibition at the Galliera Museum, a series of pictures of rare quality, adding a page from Canada to universal painting.

Since our meeting in 1952 at Santa Cruz de Tenerife, respect, friendship and humour have remained faithfully present between York, Lela and us.

York's paintings, always new, delight and make one happy.

Leonard Brooks, myself, Lionel Roy, Reva Brooks and York, in the studio at 12 Boulevard Pereire. A portion of York's A Propos d'Afrique *(1961) is visible. Paris, 1961.*

Luc Peire with York and I in the studio at 12 Boulevard Pereire.
Paris, 1962.

XVII

1964-1965

Two Solo Shows, a Retrospective and Two Murals

WE WERE WELCOMED BACK TO CANADA in the spring of 1964, after nearly four years abroad, mainly in Paris. Lotta Dempsey reported our return in the *Globe and Mail,* recalling York's important Paris exhibition, and noting that many of York's recent works would be featured in upcoming solo exhibitions. Indeed, preparations were already underway for these shows, at Roberts Gallery and at Galerie Agnès Lefort, on 1504 Sherbrooke Street West in Montreal and operated by Mira Godard. York divided his Paris paintings between the two shows, which opened within days of each other.

A beautiful bilingual catalogue was produced for use at both venues; the French critics Michel Seuphor and Frédéric Mégret contributed brief but complimentary texts. Seuphor concluded that York was a "man and painter before being Canadian" and that his paintings were a "direct expression of the pre-eminence of both man and painter over ethnic or national allegiance." Seuphor also wrote:

> I would readily call York Wilson a disciplined lyric. All of him is a combination of energy and direction. The muted harmonies lead to an awareness of a sort of peaceful struggle, to the quiet affection of an enthusiastic temperament governed by sensitivity. The rule which guides creativity allows for a margin of liberty which makes it appear that painting creates itself as Nature does. A Nature non-eruptive, which has long since disavowed all excess.
>
> There is, in this painter, a visionary gardener enamored with immensity, but in this gardener is hidden a poet. A poet of intimacy. Only abstract painting permits these propitious harmonies of apparently irreconcilable dimensions.

Frédéric Mégret wrote of York's work at the *Musée Galliera,* and of our Paris sojourn, during which York "'lived' very little of Paris during those four years, preferring to avoid the painting Merry-go-round." He declared that, "When facing York Wilson's lively compositions, warm in colour and refreshing at the same time by subtle glazes, one has the sensation of rediscovering a previous visual experience. Where or Why? Perhaps because the artist from Toronto is painting the free and ever changing image of light."

GALERIE AGNÈS LEFORT

York's exhibition at Galerie Agnès Lefort was a resounding success. Both Dorothy Pfeiffer of the *Montreal Gazette* (April 11, 1964) and Robert Ayre of the *Montreal Star* (April 9, 1964) spoke of York's recent works in glowing terms. Pfeiffer called the show "one of the finest held in this city for some time." Each "colourful panel," she wrote, "filled with friendliness and joie de vivre reaches out to the viewer 'What experience, or mood, or place do I remind you of?' it silently asks. Whatever it is, one recognizes it at once, be it gay, or else nostalgic; the souvenir of a former fact, or of a dream. A sail on a river in France, or Greece? A whiff of the torrid lands of Africa?" Pfeiffer singled out *Roi Christophe* (1961), *Taos* (1964), and *Orage* (1963) for special mention. *Taos* was acquired by the Montreal Museum of Fine Arts from the show.

Robert Ayre wrote that much had happened since York's last solo appearance at the Watson Art Galleries in 1952, and advised his readers that "this exhibition is one pleasure you should not miss." He focused on York's path towards abstraction, noting that, "the deeper he goes in the study of form, color and light, the more he departs from the scene before his eyes in order to distil its essence as he remembers it." *Taos*, wrote Ayre, "is remembered as a dry, desert place in a handsome design of brown stains and shadows without depth," while *Parc Montsouris* was "a fresh greenness." In other canvases, Ayre argued, place had no meaning, for "the painting is the experience. It is not a momentary excitement but an experience that lasts. Color and mood captivate you immediately, but you do not apprehend their full quality, and the subtlety of the form relationships, without long contemplation." Canadian Industries Limited acquired *Parc Montsouris* from the show; it was included in the C.I.L. collection show in Toronto later that year.

ROBERTS GALLERY

The Roberts Gallery show, which featured forty oils and twenty gouaches, was even more successful. Barrie Hale of the *Telegram* (April 18, 1964) reported that the gallery was enjoying sales that exceeded Jack Wildridge's expectations. Hart House purchased *Honfleur* (1964), the London Public Library and Art Museum chose *Lepanto* (1963), and *Ydra* (1964) went to the Winnipeg Art Gallery. An article later that year in the *Financial Post* (December 12, 1964) reported that the art market was on the upswing, and that Roberts' high sales of work by York, A.J. Casson and Jean-Paul Lemieux was a telling indication.

Kay Kritzweiser wrote of York in the *Globe and Mail* (April 11, 1964) that although "Canada may have been denied the results of Wilson's quiet preoccupation with the sweep and color of Italy, Greece and France, French galleries have been very much aware of him—as a painter, not as a Canadian." Elizabeth Kilbourn of the *Toronto Daily Star* (April 18, 1964) regarded York as "a highly accomplished painter who can pull off *Paris* (1962), a handsome atmospheric and finely structured painting," and called his gouaches *Orage* and *Nocturne* exquisite and almost "too seductive to be trusted."

Endymion (1963) was mentioned in the *Globe and Mail* (June 27, 1964) as "outshining everything else" in the exhibition: "the subject of Wilson's painting may escape you but the power can't. The strong blues, blacks, greens and whites merge forcefully over each other, fully suggestive of mythological spirit."

OTHER 1964 ART ACTIVITIES

Endymion was also included in the 85th RCA exhibition, which opened in Montreal in November of 1964. The 84th RCA show, which toured to the National Gallery of Canada in early 1964, included *Sailing Carthage* (1963), which Dr. Franz Meyer, director of Basel's Kunstmuseum, had selected for honorable mention.

In 1964, Painters Eleven artist Alexandra Luke left a collection of art to Oshawa's Robert McLaughlin Art Gallery. York's gouache *Monument* (1962), which Alexandra had purchased at York's gouache exhibition at Roberts Gallery in 1962, was included in her gift. This pleased York, as it was his first work in that collection. Four of York's works of the 1960s and 1970s later joined *Monument* in the Oshawa collection.

VISITING CALIFORNIA

After the opening of York's two solo exhibitions, we flew to Los Angeles to spend the month of May with Virginia, her husband Dr. Edmund Carpenter, an American anthropologist and expert on Inuit culture, and their family. Virginia and Edmund had a house on the campus of California State University at Northridge.

AN IMPULSE PURCHASE

While in Mexico in December of 1964, we met a woman who wished to sell her New York studio at 215 Bowery, corner of Rivington. On our way back from Mexico, we stopped in New York and decided to take it. It was well furnished and although illegal as a residence, the building was full of live-in artists.

It was a large third-floor studio with a kitchen, bathroom, storage room and endless windows. It was heated during working hours and had a small wood burning stove to use at other times. We left a few things there, returned shortly and soon had it in shape. The district was full of winos, who slept on the sidewalk in front of a bar on the opposite side. They were respectful and polite, but always asked for a handout. If successful, they marched right into the bar. The Salvation Army soup kitchen was a few doors down the street.

TWO MURALS AT PORT ARTHUR

The Imperial Oil and O'Keefe Centre projects cemented York's reputation as Canada's leading muralist. When the administrators of the General Hospital in Port Arthur undertook extensive renovations to the building in 1963-64, they commissioned York to execute two murals: a long narrow one (63" x 28') for the main entrance and a smaller one (7' x 12') for a nearby corridor. (The town of Port Arthur amalgamated with Fort William in 1970 to form the city of Thunder Bay). York signed the contract in March 1964 and started conducting in-depth research on medicine, which he continued while we were in Mexico that December.

The Port Arthur project proved to be difficult, as the Board wanted something more figurative than York was wont to do. Having already encountered this difficulty with the Salvation Army mural, York was anxious about the gap between his ideas and the Board's demands. He first proposed a "Garden of Hope" theme, only to be informed in a letter of 24 June by administrator Philip Rickard that the Board desired a subject "that has more identification with the hospital. The phrase 'a little more definitive' cropped up again." Two days later, Rickard wrote that a Port Arthur lawyer felt "strongly on this question of more identification with a hospital." The lawyer pointed to the Imperial Oil mural, which he reasoned had a strong, clear relationship to the oil industry.

York was uneasy presenting his final proposals to the Board. He had decided on a fairly literal topic, *The History of Medicine*, for the large mural, and an abstract *Night and Day* for the smaller one. At the Board meeting, York spent most of his time explaining *The History of Medicine*, and passed quickly over the abstract *Night and Day*. It pleased him that both were accepted. The finished murals, both vinyl acetate on canvas, were installed in April of 1965.

York studied the story of medicine from earliest known times to the present day to prepare for *The History of Medicine* mural. In the text which he wrote for the brochure distributed by the hospital, York asserted that the mural addressed "various ideas, superstitions and treatments related to health, both mental and physical." York adopted a wide-ranging approach to his theme, and incorporated references to many objects, including medicinal plants and herbs, amulets, Aboriginal masks, an Egyptian mummy, a thermometer, the Hippocratic symbol, X-ray technology and bacteria. Like the O'Keefe Centre mural, York integrated these symbols in a dramatic, sweeping fashion.

Night and Day, the smaller abstract mural, was to be situated at the end of an intersection of corridors where people were to turn right. York felt people move in the direction of lighter colours, so he painted the darker tones of night at the left and the brighter yellows and oranges of day at the right. He was later told that the mural did seem to direct people to the right. *Night and Day* was removed from the hospital in 1997 and is now in the collection of the Thunder Bay Art Gallery.

A WONDERFUL RETROSPECTIVE AND A HARSH NEW CRITIC

The Sarnia Public Library and Art Gallery organized the first Canadian retrospective of York's work in 1965. The exhibition included thirty-five of York's works, from *Burlesk No. 2* (1938) and *Cocktail Party* (1948) to

Venice in Red (1957) and *La Seine*. The gallery borrowed the works from York, Roberts Gallery, the National Gallery, the Art Gallery of Ontario and numerous private collectors. The show opened in Sarnia on March 1, and was accompanied by a screening of the 1957 Imperial Oil mural film "Mural." The show then toured to the Agnes Etherington Art Centre in Kingston in April, Charlottetown's Confederation Art Gallery and Museum in May and the Roberts Gallery in June.

While the exhibition was in Sarnia, it received excellent reviews in both Canadian and American newspapers. P.G.S. Large of the *Kingston Whig Standard* (April 17, 1965) wrote that the show there provided an "unusual opportunity" to view the works of an "important Canadian artist" and a "patient composer." In Toronto, Kay Kritzweiser commented in the *Globe and Mail* (June 19, 1965) that the "wonderful bursting vitality of York Wilson's color began its real hold on him in Italy—what a love affair he had for the reds of Italy."

We were not surprised when Harry Malcolmson, new art critic for the *Telegram*, criticized harshly the Toronto leg of York's retrospective. In a review of the art highlights of 1964 published in the *Telegram* on January 2, 1965, Malcolmson had taken a whack at York. He praised Harold Town, Graham Coughtry and Sorel Etrog, but in order to damn York, he reached back to his last Roberts' show in April of 1964. Malcolmson called York's work "inconsequential candy floss" and didn't think "anyone took Wilson seriously anymore." He wrote that he was "therefore saddened to see a presumably impecunious institution like the London Public Gallery laying out nearly $2,000 on a painting that in 15 years they won't want to hang."

Malcolmson published a damning review of York's retrospective in the *Telegram* (June 19, 1965). He opened the review by declaring that the show established "Wilson as a figure of no consequence in Canadian art. The Emperor, it turns out, has no clothes." Malcolmson charged York with "glaring weakness as a draughtsman" and "borrowed themes," and work characterized by an "insipid quality," a "lack of vigor" and "meaningless brightness and gaiety." "The sole merits of these syrupy concoctions," he continued, "are the brilliant colors and the intensity of light." Malcolmson concluded that there was "nothing in the show to suggest Wilson might ever have been significant. I find nothing to recommend Wilson's work. It is tepid in inspiration, wholly without originality, and lacking in technical competence."

Considering Malcolmson's brilliance, it's difficult to understand why he isn't an art critic of international stature. He could then set straight others who had praised York's work, including André Malraux, Jean Cassou, Michel Seuphor and many Canadian curators. The Canadian *Who's Who* hasn't even heard of him! An excerpt from S.N. Behrman's 1960 biography of Max Beerbohm, *Portrait of Max*, comes to mind:

> Turgenev, Max said, appreciated that criticism is a delightful
> pastime for the critics—that, even, it may be delightful for their
> readers, but, he says, it has nothing to do with the artist, nor with
> the process by which art is achieved.

DEVELOPMENTS WITH THE CANADIAN GROUP OF PAINTERS

When we returned to Toronto in early 1964, we learned that York had been elected president of the Canadian Group of Painters in our absence. The CGP executive was desperate, and knew that if they had asked York directly he would have turned them down. The main problem was finding appropriate venues to show their members' work after having been pushed out of the main Canadian art galleries. Without exhibitions, interest in the Group was declining. The CGP executive felt that York was the only one to come up with a solution. Even if the Group was to be dissolved, they wished to leave some sort of record of their accomplishments in furthering Canadian art. The Canadian Group of Painters was a national society; its founding members were the Group of Seven, and artists of merit were added over the years.

York gave much time and thought to the situation, and held many meetings with the executive. He finally came up with a two-part plan to find an established public gallery that would install Group works permanently, and to produce a definitive book on the Group with excellent reproductions of each artist's work. The book's preparation was given to Paul Duval, our most knowledgeable critic. Paul was delighted; his long interest and training in Canadian art had prepared him well. York set out talking to numerous publishers, until Toronto's Clarke-Irwin agreed to produce a high-quality book.

York then tried to find a public gallery who would agree to his exhibition plan. It was hard going but he finally struck an agreement with Bob McMichael of the McMichael Canadian Collection in Kleinburg. Bob agreed to allocate a room permanently to the Canadian Group of Painters. It wasn't large enough to hang all the members' works at one time, so it was agreed that each artist's work would be installed for six months per year. Members were requested to donate paintings that would be juried.

The next task was selecting the illustrations for the CGP book. Since the OSA had a great bank of slides of works and many members belonged to both societies, Syd and Helen Watson and York and myself spent many an evening poring over slides. When the reproduction proofs were ready, York alone would hold out until they were the best possible. The proofing and production process would occupy York intermittently for the next seven years.

Just before York's death in 1984, it was discovered that the CGP Charter was in safe keeping with a lawyer, J. Price Ericksen-Brown. This document should be housed at the McMichael Gallery. Since being taken over by the Ontario government, the McMichael Gallery, has not followed the terms of the contract that York arranged with Bob McMichael. The McMichael's CGP collection is now dispersed and no longer installed as a unit. I have written to two recent directors, including Barbara Tyler, describing York's agreement with Bob. Apparently the museum's staff knows nothing of this agreement, but they promised to look into it. I have also informed them as to the whereabouts of the Charter.

When I happened by chance recently to see the obituary of Mr. Ericksen-Brown, I contacted his widow, Charlotte. She told me that the CGP Charter and related materials are now in the possession of the museum's founders, Robert and Signe McMichael. The McMichaels are pleased about this amazing incident, and I am relieved that this worrying duty has been resolved.

A UNIQUE COMMISSION

William (Bill) Miller, president of Dow Corning in Toronto and a Wychwood Park neighbour, asked York to do a mural that the company could use to demonstrate the quality of their products. York decided to use Dow's silicone caulking as his medium, adding his own pure powdered colours. He would have to work fast as silicone dries very quickly. Dow claimed that silicone was impervious to fire, water and the elements. Dow supplied York with so much silicone that he had enough left over to do the front door of our Alcina Avenue home.

For the Dow mural and for our door, York spread small areas of the pigmented caulking mixture with his hands directly to a fiberglass support. These two works are York's only examples of finger-painting. For the first few years after the door was finished, Bill examined it regularly for any changes. More than thirty years later, the door's colours and condition have not changed at all. The silicone is flexible and rubbery and thus doesn't shrink or crack. When York's mural studies find a permanent home, our front door might be included! Recent developments, however, might prevent this from happening. The Toronto Historical Board is planning to designate our unusual house as "The York Wilson House," and will likely wish to preserve this unique door.

An interesting incident occurred when we were in Athens near the end of May in 1966. We were having dinner with Arthur Blanchette, the Canadian cultural attaché. He asked if we knew William Miller of Dow Corning, and explained that Bill had made an offer to Greece to coat the Parthenon with silicone in order to preserve its crumbling stone. Did we think this was a serious offer or just some hare-brained scheme? We were able to assure Arthur that it was a serious offer. We later learned from Bill that he had made the offer in good faith, but due to slow bureaucratic arrangements, and Bill's later illness, Dow Corning did not carry out the plan.

A MOSAIC FOR THE BELL TELEPHONE COMPANY

Russell Braddon's book *Roy Thomson of Fleet Street* was published in 1965. Inside was a photograph from the early 1940s of Thomson posed in front of *Lands, Lakes and Forests*, the mural he commissioned York to complete for his Timmins Press Building in 1940. It was York's first mural.

More than two decades later, York received a commission for a mural at the new Bell Telephone building on Adelaide Street in Toronto. York completed this project and the Port Arthur General Hospital murals during the eighteen-month period separating our return from Paris in early 1964 and our departure for a world-round trip in late 1965.

York was thrilled at the prospect of a mosaic mural for Bell. He had been interested in mosaics ever since we stopped at Ravenna while en route from Venice to Rome in the autumn of 1957. York had discussed mosaics with architect Ronald Dick and Franklin Arbuckle when they visited us in Paris in late 1963. When the Bell building was contracted to the Marani, Rounthwaite and Dick architectural firm, Ron Dick recalled that

Paris conversation and contacted York. In a letter of April 25, 1964 to Dick, York outlined his theme and declared the mosaic medium desirable "in that it would introduce colour in an unusual way, where it would have value both as decoration and as identification."

The mural was to take the form of five vertical panels, each 20' x 5', installed on the building's exterior facade. The mural's title was *Communications.* Each panel expressed a different aspect of the theme: written, drawn, musical, verbal and electronic. Within the panels are many symbols, including Greek, Moabite and Etruscan letter forms, early Spanish cave paintings, bars of music, abstracted human faces, and a satellite in action.

To execute the Bell mural, York contracted the services of Alex von Svoboda of Toronto's Conn-Arts Studio, a firm specializing in mosaics, murals, designs and sculptures for ecclesiastical and commercial projects. York designed the mural, selected the materials and Conn-Arts did the installation. At the Conn-Arts studio, York enlarged his sketches onto heavy brown paper later marked like the pieces of a jigsaw puzzle. The tesserae were glued face down onto the paper in their final design; when the tesserae were embedded in cement, the brown paper was removed and the panels were installed on the building. Throughout the process, York enjoyed an excellent rapport with Alex and was pleased with the finished mural, installed in July of 1965.

In "Wilson Rings Bell with Mosaics," published in the *Globe and Mail* (June 12, 1965) shortly before the mural's installation, Kay Kritzweiser discussed the project's genesis and execution, and noted that York had been careful to mimic the uneven surfaces of early mosaics, "so that the play of light and shadow during day and night, will become a continuous wonder. Rain will sluice away soot. Sun will catch the glitter of gold leaf impregnated between layers of glass."

These beautiful colour murals, surrounded by white marble, are best appreciated when viewed up close. Unfortunately they are placed so high that one cannot appreciate them fully, and the mosaics are no longer lit at night. Bell's brochure, which featured a colour reproduction of the finished mural, is no longer available. York made a small sample mosaic section which the AIO toured to schools and small towns in Ontario in 1965. At that time numerous buildings in Toronto featured mural decorations. As an article in the *Toronto Daily Star* (August 9, 1965) queried, "What's a Business Without a Mural?" York's works for Imperial Oil, the O'Keefe Centre and Bell were mentioned therein.

MORE INTERNATIONAL EXPOSURE

The art critic Raul Furtado wrote an essay on York Wilson for the US periodical *Arts Magazine* (March 1965), titled "York Wilson's Achievement." The text was accompanied by reproductions of the left side of the Imperial Oil mural and the marvelous triptych *A Propos d'Afrique*, which now hangs in the Ontario Club of Toronto.

The Cardiff Commonwealth Arts Festival, in association with the National Museum of Wales, organized an exhibition of Canadian drawings and prints selected by Professor Norman Yates of the University of Alberta. As he stated in the catalogue, Yates selected the work of individuals whose work was "viable and known to me." York sent *The Lion Hunt*, one of the early mixed-media works he had done in Paris. The exhibition opened in Cardiff on September 18 and continued until October 10, 1965.

York and Clare Bice looking at York's Melun *(1963). 1964.*

XVIII

1965-1966

Around the World: From Hawaii to Japan

ON SEPTEMBER 28, 1965 WE LEFT CANADA on the first leg of a one-year trip around the world which would include more than thirty countries. Our fabulous air tickets, costing about $7,500 each, caused so much excitement at the Toronto airport that several ticket agents gathered to examine our complex itinerary. Our trip ticket had open flights, and we moved on when York felt he had finished sketching in a particular place and was ready for a change. When we were not staying with friends, we arranged for a hotel on arrival at the airport. It worked out well.

The motivation for our trip was of course York's never-ending desire to experience new cultures and vistas. As he wrote a decade later in a letter to a University of Toronto art student, "For me it is continually stimulating to work in a new environment from time to time. The atmosphere, the language, the people, the light, the food, the sound, the entire ambiance, lends a fresh direction to the mind. Working in any one place too long, whether it be Toronto, New York, Rome, or anywhere, tends to deaden the senses, to lessen awareness, to slow down creativity."

Our first stop would be Los Angeles to visit Virginia and her family. It was an opportune moment to visit as Virginia had an exhibition of her paintings opening soon at the Mission Gallery. We were introduced to "happenings" which were just coming into vogue. This one took the form of a few jazz musicians playing during the opening of Virginia's show, while Ted Carpenter projected a film on the outside wall of the gallery. Virginia's exhibition looked fine and she sold a few pieces. Los Angeles' top critic reviewed it as the best exhibition of the month.

HONOLULU

York did collages during our few days in California, and we then left to visit Helen Burton in Honolulu. Helen was an American who had spent years in China, running the Camel-Bell Shop in Peking. She sold Chinese antiques and adapted some of the ancient jewelry to modern use. She had become quite famous through her shop and showed us her thick guest book, inscribed by famous people from all over the world, including Winston Churchill. Helen never married but raised seven adopted Chinese girls; they went to university and some worked in her fabulous shop. When the Communists came to power, she was put in prison but miraculously escaped through her influential connections, and managed to get many of her valuable antiques out of China.

It was heartbreaking for Helen to be separated from her daughters. They had to hide their relationship with her for their own safety, and she relied on friends for smuggled news about them. She was quite sure the elder daughter left in charge of the shop had been put to death because of the connection. P.J. Chang, a university professor and Helen's close friend, had been a great supporter over the years. He too had to escape to Hong Kong and leave his family, relying on word-of-mouth about his loved ones when trusted friends happened to pass through. Helen had written to Chang about our plans to spend time in Hong Kong.

We were astounded at the wealth of Chinese antiques that furnished Helen's Honolulu home. On arrival we joined Helen for a dinner served on a green jade dinner service, which was used only for special friends. While I was helping to dry the jade dishes after dinner, Helen said she was going to leave them to me in her will. I was overcome, when my ever-loving husband piped up that he didn't even like them. Needless to say that was the end of that!

Helen gave us letters of introduction to her Hong Kong friends, P.J. Chang and a Mongolian princess named Helen Wu. On our second and final evenings in Honolulu, Helen took us to her favorite restaurant. As we entered the musicians immediately began playing Helen's "theme song." She was a much-loved, beautiful woman; she must have been about eighty-five at that time but looked years younger. When she died a few years later, we received word that she had left everything to the orphans in Honolulu, and her antiques were to be sold to museums. It was a lovely ending to her fabulous life.

MAKING NEW FRIENDS IN JAPAN

We left for Tokyo on October 7. Upon arrival we went to the Hotel Takinawa, some distance from the city centre. At the first restaurant we tried, the owner spoke English and there were banners of various

Canadian universities and colleges decorating her walls. She explained that she was born in Canada, but during World War II, people of Japanese descent lost their homes and were imprisoned. After the war her parents and their family went back to Japan. However they now understood the reason for this unfortunate happening and her father was in Toronto at that very moment making arrangements for their return to Canada. Of course we ate at her restaurant often and after seeing persimmons in the market, I asked the Japanese name for them. She said, "kaki," which surprised me as it was the same word in Italian!

We took a bus tour of Tokyo in order to learn what to see and made friends with our guide, Sachi. In finding our interest so great she offered to get us prized tickets to enter the Palace grounds and see the Emperor Hirohito. Five hundred workers maintained the Palace grounds and gardens. Most peasants still thought of Hirohito as divine and paid their own way to Tokyo for the honour of working at the Palace. Our sighting of Hirohito was limited to a brief glimpse as he passed by in a large black Rolls Royce on his way home from the Diet (parliament) for lunch. He looked rather glum, not looking right or left.

Helen Burton had given us an introduction to a Mrs. E.C. Kubota, originally from Hawaii but now a powerful Tokyo businesswoman who ran a precision instrument company. She welcomed us warmly, taking us to lunch at a restaurant where foreigners were not able to go without a Japanese escort. It was most interesting; she wanted to know as much about us as we did about her and her life.

Gordon Adamson, our Toronto architect friend, connected us with a Tokyo architect who had visited Toronto, Masakatso Hagi and his wife Eiko. They invited Sachi and us for dinner. We had a great evening with them and Eiko surprised us by saying she had seen York's O'Keefe Centre mural in Toronto, and went on to translate the Confucian proverb which represents Oriental literature in the mural. It translated as, "Thought without learning is labour lost, learning without thought is disastrous." We all laughed and parted good friends.

Guy Carrington Smith, then Canadian commercial minister in Japan, told us many interesting things about Japan during lunch one day. One learns a great deal about a country with contacts such as these.

York sketched every spare moment; he found the Ginza district very interesting and colourful. We took more tours suggested by Sachi, including one to Nikko and to Nara, a beautiful park with tame deer taught to bow to people. At the splendid shrine, one is given a wish on a slip of paper. If one doesn't like the wish, it is tied to a tree outside, where it soon flies away. The trees were fluttering with many bits of paper.

We took the fast train from Tokyo to Miyanoshita and to the Hotel Fujiya, the one-time summer residence of Hirohito in mountainous Hakone, for three days of sketching near Mount Fuji. The area was beautiful and York did many sketches. We then returned to Tokyo, this time sitting in the observation car with its glass surround. It was a thrilling, high-speed ride not unlike a three-dimensional movie. Just when we thought we would crash into a mountainside, the train curved away gently at the last second.

The following morning we flew to Kyoto, a city of much old world charm. We sat and contemplated at the famous Zen Garden—the raked sand symbolizes the sea or waves and the stones represent islands or continents. We visited two royal palaces, permission for which Sachi had obtained for us in Tokyo.

Our Japanese friends in California, Professor Mamoru Iga and his wife Marye, introduced us by letter to their relative in Kyoto, a famous Japanese painter named Kan Hamada, who had been honoured by the Emperor. At the Hamadas' beautiful home, we removed our shoes at the door and sat on cushions on his studio floor, sipping green tea and looking at his tremendous oil paintings of flowers. His young friend with minimal English acted as interpreter; the difficult conversation was accented with rounds of bowing, compliments and smiles. Kan had a library well stocked with art books, which we accidentally glimpsed when a wall panel was opened. His library included some works by Michel Seuphor, which explained why their exhibitions of young contemporaries looked the same as those anywhere else. We had the good fortune to see their annual national exhibition, which featured a few interesting works but consisted mostly of imitations of world-famous painters.

Kan Hamada came to visit us with his son and the same interpreter the following night at our hotel. It was again difficult as the conversation was all about art. After looking long and carefully at a reproduction of the O'Keefe Centre mural, he shook York's hand firmly and long. We had politely waited our turn, giving him the first hour to tell of his painting and honours. The whole family was utterly sweet and charming.

The Igas also introduced us to Bunsho Jyugaku, a professor at Konan University just outside Kyoto. We invited him to dinner at a restaurant of his choice. He brought *The Year of the Monkey*, a book of poetry by the British novelist and poet D.J. Enright, who had recently departed from the university. The limited edition of four hundred was made as a parting gift to Enright. It was a delightful and most interesting evening. He arranged for us to meet an art professor friend at Kyoto University, where we saw the work of the students. They made full use of the meeting by pumping York for information about art.

A BRIEF STAY IN TAIWAN

Our next stop was Taipei, Taiwan, where we stayed at the famous Grand Hotel, bright red with dragons and Mandarin splendour. The National Palace Museum, with its marvelous black and white paintings of Chinese calligraphy, was the highlight for us. We were dismayed by the city's poverty, filth and seeming apathy. Chiang Kai-shek's palace and vast surrounding parkland were beautiful, but surrounded by such abject poverty. We went to Tamuii, a small fishing village, where York sketched.

GRAEME WILSON AND HONG KONG

The next day was November 1st and we flew to Hong Kong where our friend Graeme Wilson met us. Graeme had written to advise us of his new posting, and his furnished five-bedroom apartment, and invited us to help him get settled in. He had lots of room for us, including a studio for York. His two-floor apartment was on the seventh floor of a large apartment building on a high hill on Repulse Bay, overlooking the Repulse Bay Hotel and the distant sea. In the months before our arrival, Graeme had only unpacked some of his furniture and was eating all his meals out. He had a small British car, which we could use when he was covering his vast territory.

Graeme was engrossed in translating the poetry of Hagiwara Sakutaro, a poet called the "Rimbaud of Japan" because of his feeling for the West. Graeme was friendly with Hagiwara's daughter in Tokyo and was recognized as the world authority on his work. On his frequent trips to Japan, he was able to discuss the meaning of Hagiwara's poetry with the poet's daughter and friends. We soon spent our evenings working with Graeme on the translations, fast becoming aficionados. York was absorbing the essence of the poetry and he did a painting each morning related to the previous night's discussions, not knowing that one day they would be used to illustrate Graeme's book on Hagiwara Sakutaro.

Hong Kong was then an island of four million people, connected by a ten-minute ferry with Kowloon on the mainland. Beyond Kowloon is a large area known as the New Territories which borders China, with guards at the frontier. There are huge developments of high-rise apartments along the mountainous coast. We saw all manner of fishing boats, small craft, large merchant and passenger ships, English and American battle-ships, aircraft carriers and submarines right from our apartment windows. It is a great manufacturing centre and a duty-free port with goods from many countries.

P.J. Chang, a delightful, scholarly man who worked in the press unit for the American Embassy, was in touch soon. His job was to check all the Chinese news and report anything of interest. P.J. invited us to dinner in a restaurant with Helen Burton's friend, Helen Wu, a Mongolian Princess and aunt of the Emperor, who would be there with her son-in-law as inter-preter. On meeting, the princess hugged me warmly, a nice start.

The Princess' story, as told to us by P.J. Chang, was that she was allowed to leave China under Mao with only the clothes on her back. Somehow she was able to smuggle out a large diamond, which she sold on reaching Hong Kong. She bought the biggest house possible and started a boarding house to support herself. This was a relatively courageous act for someone raised in such luxury.

A week later our new friends came for dinner to our high perch on the hill at Repulse Bay. The Princess brought me a very personal present, two walnuts from the Royal Garden that she had manipulated in her hands over the years to keep her hands supple. I was deeply touched, and I still treasure this gift. I wondered what I could give her and decided to part with my most special treasure so far on this trip, a hand-made silk flower given to me by Eiko Hagi in Tokyo. It was very beautiful and the Princess was delighted.

Through P.J. Chang we met a famous Shanghai architect then living in Hong Kong, Gin Djih Su and his son Bill, also an architect. When the Hagis came from Tokyo for our Western New Year's we decided to invite Gin Djih Su and Bill as well. It turned out they already knew each other! Gin Djih Su and Bill invited the Hagis and us to celebrate New Year's Eve with them at a nightclub. There was a beautiful female singer entertaining. When York decided to go up on the platform to give the singer a kiss, he found the men at our table had lined up behind him, much to the singer's amusement. Everyone had a lot of fun; it was a wonderful way to usher in a new year.

On arrival in Hong Kong we had applied to the China Travel Service for a Chinese tourist visa but after two months had passed, we made other plans. Permission came through in mid-January of 1966 but we turned it down. We had offers from friends to stay with them in Peking, which was apparently very inexpensive. Charles Taylor of the *Globe and Mail*, on leaving his post in China, had come to visit us before returning to Canada. He told us that travel was limited to certain areas with guides, and that the China Travel Agency asked for $100 a day in advance for hotels and guides. It was too regimented and too expensive, and York would not be able to get where he wanted to paint. We thus decided against visiting China.

In Hong Kong, the main accent is on making money, so it's less developed culturally. There was exhibition space in their new city hall, with shows of all types, even commercial products. There were several commercial art galleries but few local, contemporary painters of any note. We did meet the painter Stephen Cheung, but he had to spend most of his time running a biscuit factory owned by his wealthy father. Stephen was a good painter who also made wonderful sculptures from biscuit tins. He had a fabulous fine studio in a biscuit factory in the New Territory.

We were invited to dinner at the home of Jim Kinoshita, a Japanese-Canadian and brother of the well-known Toronto architect Gene Kinoshita. Bill Su took us there because Jim was born and educated in Winnipeg. Jim's wife Lana was Hong Kong Chinese. Both had graduated from the University of Winnipeg, which was quite a surprise!

Pat and Bob Tow were other interesting friends. Pat was a dancer and did the Tai Chi Chuan for us as a farewell gift. The Tai Chi Chuan is a dramatic dance exercise developed by a Chinese Buddhist monk two thousand years ago. At Christmas time, Pat asked York to play Santa Claus because he wouldn't be known to the small children. She supplied a complete costume, pillow for a big belly, bracelets and belt of jingle bells, white beard and all. There were about thirty tiny tots and one little boy said, "You're not the real Santa Claus because I saw him today at Lanes Department store." York replied, "Oh yes I am, was someone else imitating me?" The little boy gave a quick pull of Santa's beard but fortunately it held. Everyone had a lot of fun; the children were bright and well behaved.

The big celebration in Hong Kong is Chinese New Year on January 21st. Their symbols for decoration are trees, plants, red packets of money, special sweets and cakes. They also display small Mandarin trees in pots, loaded with fruit and a fragrant type of narcissus called "Crab's Claw." It is a time of much visiting; one gives each caller at least two gifts, including a red packet of money. Servants are given a bonus equal to at least one month's wages.

York and I in Graeme Wilson's apartment. Hong Kong, 1965.
Photograph by Graeme Wilson.

XIX

1966

Around the World: From Sabah to Sri Lanka

WE LEFT HONG KONG on January 30, 1966. York shipped about seventy 12" x 16" paintings and extra clothing to Toronto. Graeme, who left earlier, was to meet us in Jesselton (now Kota Kinabalu), in Sabah, a province of Malaysia formerly known as North Borneo. Upon arrival, we checked into the Hotel Jesselton and explored the sleepy, small town on the coast of the South China Sea. There were scores of homes on stilts at the water's edge and islands dotted here and there. York got back to painting at Jesselton, enchanted by the marvelous colours in the batik clothing of women and men.

Graeme arrived from Manila and took us to dinner at the home of the British First Secretary, Rex Hunt, and his wife Mavis. Sir Rex turned up in the news later during the war in the Falkland Islands, where he became governor in 1985. They invited us on several occasions, usually picking us up at our hotel. One night at dinner York said he would like to take a boat and go down the river, but Rex dismissed it immediately because of the danger. He suggested he would get in touch with his colleague in Kuching, on the west coast of Sarawak, who would take us into the jungle to a Land-Dayak village. This sounded like an even better idea so York was placated.

Darkness came fast there, it was a matter of minutes from daylight to total darkness with wonderful brief sunsets. We had many evening walks along the seashore watching sea-life at the water's edge.

A TRIP INTO THE SARAWAK JUNGLE

We left Jesselton for Kuching, Sarawak and found the British information officer. Rex Hunt had indeed contacted him and he had a driver and jeep ready to pick us up in the morning. He suggested we take candies and cigarettes to give to people we might meet at a village of Land-Dayaks, the indigenous people of Sarawak. Our driver, an educated Sea-Dayak, arrived early the next morning with an assistant. They were friendly and full of information. It was a considerable drive into the jungle to reach the Land-Dayak village. We parked the car and walked a long way to the village, which was on stilts.

We climbed the long stairs and saw a giant verandah stretching as far as the eye could see. There were children playing games while the parents sat on their doorsteps eating betel nuts, a mildly intoxicating nut which stain their filed, pointed teeth and mouths red. As we appeared at eye-level, all heads turned. Our Sea-Dayak guide spoke, trying to remember his earlier language, although it was somewhat different from the Land-Dayak language. He seemed to be making headway and asked if we might look into their homes. They agreed but remained sitting while we entered the large bare room with a huge, black fireplace for cooking. We carried on down the verandah, giving candies to the children and cigarettes to the adults.

As we returned along the verandah, I looked over the high railing and saw a large, round building on the ground below. We were told it was the "Head House." We asked to visit, but our guide was told the key had been lost. We waited and waited, and after about thirty minutes, the chief appeared reluctantly with the key, as no outsider had ever been permitted entrance. We entered the house, which housed a large fireplace with a huge iron cauldron in which their victims had been cooked. Our guide explained that the practice of headhunting had been discontinued for approximately fifteen years. The walls were decorated with old skulls and other odd bones hung from the high ceiling.

As we walked back to the jeep we were caught in a sudden downpour. Our guides rushed to cut large leaves with which we covered our heads and shoulders. We spent the next day in Kuching and found the museum quite interesting; the director, a friend of Graeme's, regaled us with stories about the collection.

SINGAPORE

We left Kuching for Singapore. Our friend Leng Leng Liau introduced us to her group of young Malay student friends, just arriving home on holidays from university in Australia. They took care of our every need, providing cars, taking us to sights off the beaten track and even crossing the border to Johore Baharu, at the south tip of Peninsular Malaysia. One unsettling sight in Singapore was Chinatown's "Death Street." If someone dies at home, it is believed to bring bad luck to the house and its occupants, so poor souls about to die are sent to a room on this street, rented for that purpose.

We took a harbour tour and also went to a Malaysian village, where we were invited into the Chief's home, a thatched house on stilts in the water. It was a real tourist set-up with shiny linoleum in bright colours. We also visited the National Museum, and had hoped to meet Graeme's mad friend William Willetts at the University of Singapore museum. Willetts was a leading authority on Chinese antiques; his publications include *Chinese Art* (1958) and *Foundations of Chinese Art from Neolithic Pottery to Modern Architecture* (1965).

A PERPLEXING SIDE TRIP TO DJAKARTA

Our next stop was Djakarta, Indonesia about which we had heard some bad reports. We were advised to take plenty of American cigarettes to help ward off difficulties at the airport. We left Singapore with two small bags, carrying the least possible. We arrived after dark, in the rain, and were relieved when a Japan Air representative approached us, put us in a taxi for Hotel Indonesia, and warned, "Do not leave the hotel tonight. Return to the airport tomorrow and go to Bali." We were not given a reason for these instructions, but we thanked him for his help.

We arrived at the airport the next day, only to discover that no one knew when or if any planes would leave. Out of four or five flights that had taken off already, two had returned with some sort of problem, unloading their passengers and leaving again much later. It was a few hours before our plane took off. We were flying the Indonesian airline "Garuda," named after a mythical bird often shown with the God of Water riding on its back. We finally arrived at Denpasar, Bali.

TO BALI

Denpasar seemed so remote from Indonesia's internal problems! Everyone was smiling and very friendly. Hotel Denpasar was spacious and clean, the cost for two days with meals was about $6. The only other guests were a Spanish-speaking Chilean couple with whom we teamed up to travel. We took an eight-hour tour around the island, seeing people attired in their colourful "sarong cabaya," made from beautiful batiks. Many wear only the sarong, and are nude from the waist up. We visited a large man-made cave in the shape of a cross with stone gods placed in niches.

Families, including the married sons and their families, live together in a compound of thatched huts. There is always a small area reserved for ancestor worship in each compound. One always sees small temples in the clearings, with an occasional large and important structure. We saw a large active volcano bordered by black lava beds for miles. There are rich rice paddies flooded with water on terraced slopes. A primitive plough pulled by cows is used in the mud.

We were fortunate to see a spectacular fiesta, with fabulous street decorations and beautiful dances by Balinese women. The accompanying musicians strike various gongs, making a high-pitched shrill music. This performance occurred outside, on a raised stage in front of our hotel. A native schoolteacher caught up with us to practice his English, telling us many things. There were no tourists and all the tourist attractions were closed. We did not understand why this was the case until leaving the plane in Singapore. I spoke to an English-looking woman who immediately became hysterical, repeating my word "primitive" and throwing herself down to kiss the ground. She then apologized, saying that she had lived in Bali for three years and had seen friends' throats slashed. She wondered if she would ever get out alive.

TO CAMBODIA

We returned to Singapore and then departed for Phnom Penh, Cambodia, where we were to meet Graeme Wilson, who was coming from Burma. A former French colony, Cambodia had gained its independence in 1953. We met Monsieur Nadeau, who had just sold the hotel where we were staying, and was trying to decide what to do next. He did not wish to return to France as Cambodia had been his home for twenty years. He was most helpful, putting his car, chauffeur and himself at our disposal. We had dinner together and then he drove us all over town.

We visited a floating fishing village at about 11:00 P.M. one night. The fishermen opened up their underwater caches to show us their catch while we stepped over sleeping bodies on the wharves. About 3:30 A.M. trucks would pick up the day's haul, taking it to the twenty-five fish markets in Phnom Penh. M. Nadeau took us to the Royal stables at midnight to see the Royal white elephants, considered sacred. We visited the palace, during which time we could hear the music at a ballet being performed for Prince Nor and family. We also saw the royal jewels and treasures. We spent the rest of the morning in the museum.

We flew to Siem Reap, about eight kilometers from the great ruins of the Khmer civilization Angkor Wat, which is surrounded by a tremendous moat. One walks on a long sculpture-lined bridge to reach the first entrance. There is a gigantic temple, fronted by great steps ornamented with stone statuary. The massive front of the temple is made of intricately carved sandstone walls. Inside are endless small rooms, some with altars, through which one emerges onto an open square, and on and on to many other similar rooms. There are high, carved towers connected with each temple, and great bridges over the now-empty moats.

We took a long trip by jeep on a very bad road to see two other distant temples, Bantai Srai and Bantai Samre. Graeme, who knew much of the area's history, added immeasurably to our knowledge, and of course York was doing quick sketches all the time. After five days we flew back to Phnom Penh and on to Bangkok.

BANGKOK

In Bangkok we stayed with the British military attaché, John Turner, and his wife Mary. Their night watchman was a Gurkha, renowned Nepalese warriors who have long served in the British and Indian armies. Every British embassy employs Gurkhas for security. The Turners had a dinner one night; the guests included Sir Anthony Rumbold, the British ambassador, General Songadid, a Thai, and Mr. Holbrook, an American scientist. It was fascinating to observe how hard these three were working to get information from each other while trying to appear casual.

The Turners offered us their car and chauffeur Anzeh, who, with his daughter Toto, took us to interesting sketching spots. Bangkok is not much above sea level, hence canals are everywhere. Everyone has a garden pond, a few feet deep, stocked with fish and full of frogs, toads, water lilies and lizards. The chorus of pond life outside our window every night was soothing as we fell asleep.

Klongs (canals) are the source of water for everything: irrigation, bathing, cooking, washing, and transportation. Houses, farms and small communities all border the canals. We saw water buffalo everywhere, caked with mud. These domesticated buffalo are the work animals of the

East. The canal and river life is the most interesting. The city is ordinary except for many fancy temples, the largest with strange towers sparkling with gold. Some are encrusted with pieces of broken dishes, which came as ballast in ships from China long ago.

We also took a river tour, which turned out to be a most fruitful stimulus to York's painting. Works inspired by this trip include *Chao Phya River, Bangkok* (1966), *Thai Silks* (1966) and *Klong Calligraphy* (1966). Anzeh took us to the dock at dawn, where the produce boats were already lined up. We continued to offshore islands, but found the attractions mostly set up for tourists. We were also fascinated by the "kite fights" in the park, male against female, which were taken seriously and marked on a daily score board. When a female kite brings down a male kite, there is great applause. The kites themselves are fascinating works of art.

Before leaving Bangkok, York shipped his second parcel of paintings to Toronto and we left for Penang, off the west coast of Peninsular Malaysia.

MALAYSIA

In Penang we were met by our friend Robert Heah, a twenty-three-year-old economics student we met in Singapore, who took us to visit his father, a dentist and graduate of the University of Hong Kong. Robert took us on a tour around the perimeter of the island. He stopped to show us beautiful reservoir areas, fishing villages and temples. In one temple there were grass snakes lying everywhere, stupefied by the constant smell of burning incense. A large cobra languished in one corner. Robert invited us to his home that evening for dinner as it was his birthday and he was having a party. The dinner was excellent, with the usual rice and curried foods, followed by games and dancing. The older group played cards. Our romantic hotel, The Pines, served excellent dinners under the "pines."

The third day we were off to the mainland to visit Kuala Lumpur, capital of Malaysia. Henry Richardson of the Canadian High Commission met us, and we later joined him and his wife Nancy for dinner. Henry and Nancy then took us to a big market with batiks, antiques and every imaginable thing. The next day they took us on a picnic in the hills. In the nearby jungle were tigers, leopards and snakes. Henry delighted in telling us frightening snake stories as we were sitting on the grass by the edge of the jungle. I wasn't exactly relaxed! York's serigraph *Kuala Lumpur* (1967), one of the seven "Cities" prints, resulted from this trip.

SRI LANKA

From Kuala Lumpur we left for Colombo in Sri Lanka, then known as Ceylon. York was intrigued with some geometric roof patterns there, and kept busy sketching them. One of the resulting paintings was *Bird and Roof Pattern, Ceylon* (1968), which joined four other of his works in the Simpson-Sears collection in 1972. We were amazed at the dexterity and grace of huge elephants performing in one of the parks. We spent four days in Colombo. It was now early March and we were beginning to worry about the heat in India, our next destination, so we moved on.

York and I at Angkor Wat. Cambodia, 1966. Photograph by Graeme Wilson.

York at work on a study for The Seven Lively Arts *mural, installed in the O'Keefe Centre for the Performing Arts in 1960. Toronto, 1959. Photo by Cunningham, Gilbert A. Milne and Co.*

XX

1966

Around the World: From India to Iraq

WE LEFT COLOMBO FOR MADRAS, on the southeast coast of India. The weather was getting hotter by the day and the next month would be India's hottest. Madras food, served to us by waiters in tuxedos and bare feet, is notoriously spicy and we could hardly eat it. The second day we were off to Mahabalipuram, a seaport with seventh century sculptures—large, impressive animals carved in the round, some of which had already disappeared in the encroaching sea. We returned to Madras and continued on to Bombay, where we were shocked to see homeless people lined up sleeping on the sidewalk each night outside the hotel.

AURANGABAD

After a couple of days we flew northeast to Aurangabad to visit caves at Ellora and Ajanta. The day we spent at each site proved to be one of the great highlights of the whole trip. At the Ellora caves were centuries-old monolithic temples with great pillars carved into the rock. The Ajanta caves, also deeply cut into the rock, are covered with remnants of murals; York found the faded colours so beautiful that he did several sketches there. Another site, Elephanta, on the east side of Bombay harbour had eight chambers hewn from the hard rock. We returned to Bombay for a couple of days and then flew northeast to Jaipur, where the city's odd pink-and-white striped buildings had quite an effect on York, and he made a few sketches. Jaipur kept cropping up in later works, including: *Jaipur* (1967), *Jaipur Revisited* (1969), *Jaipur Bazaar* (1979), and *Jaipur in Blue* (1980).

NEW DELHI

The weather was impossibly hot. We looked forward to New Delhi as Mac Samples, now working for the British Information Services in India, had invited us to stay with him and his wife Elsie in the British compound called Chanakyapuri, a section of Delhi set aside for Britain's high commission and the homes of their ministers. The Samples were delightful and we thrived on a few days of air conditioning, good food, interesting company and nonsensical repartee. York was back in his element with Mac's sense of humour and wit. Mac also turned over his study to York for a studio. Elsie was charming with friendly good humour.

The British compound is a tremendous walled area which one enters through gates with posted guards. Inside are all the buildings and beautiful landscaped gardens. We moved into a wing and life immediately became most agreeable: a superb chef and servants were available for our every need at the ring of a bell. York settled into a daily painting routine.

New Delhi is a large rambling city, with many wide avenues leading to a huge circle at the centre called Connaught Place. One is approached constantly for money and the black market in money is rampant. There are many fine things available at reasonable prices, such as hand-loomed materials including "bleeding Madras" cotton shirts, precious stones, brass and silks. We also met a number of good painters through Mac: Raza, Hosain, Kanna and Ram, for whom Mac procured good painting materials. The Indian government forbade imported goods, in order to provide an impetus to India's industries.

A FIVE-DAY TOUR

It was then early April and the city was growing hotter by the day. The monsoons would come in the next two months, bringing heavy rains and high humidity, and the crops would start to grow. After a few days Mac arranged a car and driver used by the High Commission to take us on a five-day trip south to the Taj Mahal, Agra, Fatehpur Sikri, Gwalior, Khajuraho, Varanasi and Khanjour.

We had a magnificent view of the Taj Mahal under a full moon. Rich carvings, bas-reliefs and sculpture adorn the building. At one point one peers into a dime-sized hole and sees a perfect reflection of the Taj. We stayed overnight in Agra and drove to Fatehpur Sikri the next day. York was charmed with the name, often repeating it, and several paintings emerged from this visit, such as *Fatehpur Sikri Facade* (1967) and *Fatehpur Sikri Memory* (1969). The magnificent ruins there consisted of a mosque and palace, where the ruler played checkers using beautiful damsels as the pieces. We then moved on to Gwalior where there is a second but lesser Taj, a fort and palace.

The temperature during this trip was 107°F; we sat in pools of water in the car, getting out and standing to dry out in the breezes from time to time. Stray animals wandered everywhere on the highway and in crowded traffic in cities. The highways were cluttered with oxen carts, caravans, bicycles and animals. It was an experience to end all.

We drove to Khajuraho, a place famous for its erotic sculpture and some of the most exquisite specimens of Hindu medieval architecture and sculpture. Now a village, it was once the capital of a powerful kingdom, and its ruins cover eight square miles. Only twenty-two of the eighty-five original temples still stand. Each temple stands on a high solid masonry terrace, some as high as 101 feet. Almost every inch is covered with intricate carvings.

We left at 4 A.M. the next morning. Shortly after our departure, a baby tiger crossing the road appeared in the car lights. As dawn came it was not uncommon to see a tree silhouetted against the sky, black with roosting vultures. We saw kites and eagles but the bright green and blue parrots were the most enchanting. Occasionally a tree was filled with flying foxes hanging by their long tails. There were lots of wild monkeys along the roadside, in the fields, trees and on roofs. Camels were common and we also saw a few elephants.

We arrived in Varanasi (Benares) and went to the museum and for a tour of the town with an excellent guide, a Protestant minister originally from Lahore. The museum had a good, small collection which was well presented. We worked our way down to the Ganges river; the route was jammed with people, animals and rickshaws. We planned to return at 6:00 A.M. the following morning, the best time to see thousands of the devout at prayer and dipping in the sacred water.

Our guide helped us arrange to hire a boat which would pass the scene slowly. Returning the next morning, we drifted along the river for more than three hours. York made dozens of sketches as fast as he could. The banks rose very steeply and were protected by cement steps and stones, as the Ganges rises as much as fifty feet at flood time. There are high cement platforms at the river's edge with permanent (and unpopular) cement umbrellas under which sit priests, who preach and teach to the people. One can hear them chanting for great distances. Many people sat cross-legged, praying, looking upward, oblivious to anything around them. Some had washed their clothes and spread them out on the cement steps to dry, having donned a sari in which they bathed, while others bathed in the nude. The priests wash their orange silk robes daily, some spread the yards of material out to dry while others hold them in the wind. The fantastic shapes and colours of materials laid out to dry on the steps and sloping banks with interesting buildings in the background made good painting material.

We left Varanasi early for Khanjour but arrived late and were unable to find accommodation. I was sick, and after trying several places we were directed to a government guesthouse, where after much conversation, they said we could stay if we were out by 6:00 A.M. as they were expecting a General. We were glad to return to New Delhi that day, thankful for the air conditioning, safe water and good food.

BACK TO NEW DELHI

Roland Michener, then Canadian High Commissioner to India, and his wife Norah had heard we were in New Delhi and invited us to dinner. The Samples joked that we would find ourselves out on the street by 10:00 P.M. as Norah was notorious for accomplishing this feat. It was a pleasant, interesting evening and at 9:45 P.M. during coffee, Norah rose, started shaking hands and thanking people for coming. We rose to leave with the others when Norah asked York to wait. When the door closed, Norah said she would like York's opinion on the paintings they had acquired in India. We later had a good laugh with the Samples.

Mac Samples arranged a small exhibition of York's work painted in India and several were purchased by External Affairs people. Mac and Elsie Samples acquired *Tribute to Ajanta* (1966), David Scott chose *Ganja Sanskrit* (1966), the Midgeleys took home *Sixth Century Modern* (1966) and the Micheners acquired *Subheri Varanasi* (1966).

SRINAGAR

Toward the end of March we went north to Kashmir. Mac and Elsie had a friend there, Miss Christie, a Scottish retiree of the British High Commission who lived on her own houseboat. We crossed the Himalayas on our way to Srinagar. The field patterns were fascinating in various tones of brown and grays, and we then came to the mountains, at times so high and snow-covered we seemed to only just clear them. It was spring, with almond and cherry blossoms everywhere, but still too early for tourists. We eventually found Miss Christie and were welcomed. She recommended Mr. Billoo's houseboat next door. We were joined by a young English woman, Betty Horsman, whom we met at the airport. We quickly gained confidence in Mr. Billoo, and rented his two-bedroom boat immediately; our share equaled about $6 a day including food, all services and guiding.

Friday is the Muslim holy day and we took a fascinating ride to Hazrat Bal on Naseem Bagh, an important mosque and market day. We passed under the old Mogul Bridge, which became a subject for a number of York's future paintings. We were the only foreigners among the few thousand people there, and all stared and stared, even touched us, others poked their friends or children to have a good look at us.

In the medieval city of Srinagar, capital of Kashmir, York had made a friend, Mr. Ramzanas, who owned a large three-storey building on the river. It faced a fascinating group of medieval buildings across the river, and Mr. Ramzanas invited York to paint any time from his windows. This scene later resulted in the famous painting *Kashmir Facade* (1971) owned by Dow Corning in Sarnia. On completion he wandered around the town and started to search for a taxi, but none were to be seen. When he tried asking likely prospects, they laughed and a crowd soon gathered, following and pushing him and bursting out laughing each time he opened his mouth. It was all very frightening. Someone finally rescued York, walked with him a mile or two and arranged a horse and cart driver to take him to his destination. The romantic Shalimar Gardens were within walking distance. We left Kashmir and flew back to New Delhi for a few more days. York sent his third shipment of paintings home to Toronto.

TO AFGHANISTAN

We left for Kabul, the capital of Afghanistan, in mid-April, after returning on three successive days to the airport for a plane that finally arrived. It was quite a flight over the Hindu Kush range of mountains, often so high and snow-covered we seemed only to just clear the higher ranges. At five thousand feet, Kabul still had remnants of snow and slush and was very cold.

There were two hotels and one government restaurant in Kabul. They were expensive and ordinary. While we were sitting in the large lobby of the Kabul Hotel one day, our attention was drawn to a large, important-looking woman wearing an enormous amount of jewelry. While waiting together, York and I often played games guessing what unusual-looking people might do for a living. York said, "I'll bet she's a jewelry buyer for Eaton's." I said, "I'll bet she's a receptionist of some grand establishment." York said, "Let's go and ask her," which we did telling her about our game. She was the Countess Kazimiera, from Poland, and was married to an American, Ernest Seaton. She said the Polish people had spirited much of their art out of Poland when the Communists took over. The Polish immigrants bought a huge mansion in New York where much of the art was housed, waiting for the day when they were free again. We later visited her in New York, and were amazed at the beautiful works of art and furniture.

The museum in Kabul had an outstanding collection of coins and a few stunning goddesses delicately carved out of ivory, unlike any I had ever seen. In fact there were many very old and fine pieces, well presented. The attendant, seeing our interest, unlocked and lit each room for us.

IRAN

We left Kabul for Tehran in Iran, a direct two-hour flight on an Iran Air jet, having changed our tickets from Afghan Air. Tehran is a large modern city with a top-notch museum; the wealth from oil is quickly bringing the country up to date. We noticed a great difference in cleanliness, health and comfort.

The many ancient objects housed on the ground floor of the Tehran museum were amazing. We heard that the Canadian archaeologist Douglas Tushingham might be there, so we contacted the Canadian embassy and obtained his phone number. Doug canceled a dinner date and joined us. He spent his mornings in a locked vault with a cameraman and two armed guards, cataloguing the country's crown jewels. He searched old photos, paintings and any mention of the various jewels to find their origin and changes of ownership. The University of Toronto later published his research in *Crown Jewels of Iran* (1968). We spent a lovely evening catching up on news with Doug.

The next day we went to Shiraz and saw the beautiful blue tiles in the mosques, the Khalili Garden and Ghavami Mirror Houses, unbelievably sparkly buildings with lovely Persian painted ornament and a heavenly garden. People were very friendly here, some stopped us on the street to chat in English. Among other works, a beautiful gouache called *Shiraz Blues* (1966) was joyfully painted from our experiences there. Our next stop was Isfahan. I will never forget the astounding beauty of the blue tiles in the mosque there. York was so impressed with the blues that *Isfahan* (1967) became one of the "Cities" series prints.

IRAQ

We returned to Tehran and left the next day for Baghdad, ancient Mesopotamia, meaning "between two rivers," the Tigris and the Euphrates. It was about a two-hour flight from Tehran to Baghdad, where again we noticed a better standard of living. The Baghdad museum was then in the midst of moving into a fine new building. Their large collection of Middle East pieces includes great stone sculptured walls from palaces and giant sculptures, and quite a selection of Luristan and Sumerian bronzes.

Sid Maddocks, manager of Travelworld Tours in Los Angeles, invited us to join him on a couple of tours, first to the remains of an old Sassanid castle at Ctesiphon. A large arch and a four-storey wall still stood then; the arch is said to be the largest unsupported brick arch in the world. The seven-foot thick wall had a dangerous crack.

We came to a small village in the desert and went into a store selling Bedouin clothing. I was intent on looking at things and didn't notice York had disappeared. As I walked out of the store, I paid no attention to a Bedouin man who suddenly touched me from behind. I turned around, amazed that he would be so bold, and realized it was York dressed in authentic Bedouin garb. Sid and York had a good laugh at their prank.

We went to Babylon, where there was little left of this once great city. It was such a fabulous wicked city that the Babylonians were constantly attacked and finally deserted it for this reason. The most valuable objects were removed to Berlin by a group of German archaeologists who uncovered the walls and buildings left standing today.

As for the famous hanging gardens, one has to imagine them, as nothing remains. The story goes that Nebuchadnezzar built the gardens for his wife, who came to this flat plateau from an area with wooded hills and flowers and longed for her homeland. A small hill was built to please her. The trees and flowers planted on the hillside gave the effect of hanging gardens. Nothing remains of the mighty ziggurat or temple tower, which is thought to be similar to the Tower of Babel. One is able to pick up pieces of pottery and stones with markings in the excavated soil and know these pieces can date from 4000-600 B.C.

XXI

1966

Around the World: From Egypt to Cyprus

FROM IRAQ WE FLEW TO CAIRO. York was dehydrated and quite ill from a long bout of dysentery. Fortunately we had old Paris friends in Cairo, the Australian ambassador John Lavery and his wife Rita. John sent his doctor to check on York; the doctor diagnosed dehydration and a skin allergy, and assigned York to bed rest and a restricted diet. After a few days in bed York quickly improved and one of John's ministers, Russell Wilson, invited us to dinner. The following evening we went to see a *son et lumière* (sound and light) performance at the pyramids near Cairo. We had seen several such performances by this time in France, Rome and Athens.

We went to the enormous Egyptian Museum and were overwhelmed by the vast and amazing collections, particularly the monumental sculptures. The sculpture is mostly in pink, gray or black granite and sandstone brought from the Aswan area, as this is the only granite source in Egypt.

In Cairo, the palace and mosque of Mohammed Ali are on a high, impressive citadel. The mosque is still in use. There were many beautiful, enormous copper filigree chandeliers that held countless candles. The floors were covered with hundreds of rugs donated by pilgrims. There is always a fountain or many faucets for the faithful to wash their hands, feet, eyes, ears, nose and mouth before entering.

The Islamic Museum at Cairo contains most interesting examples of beautiful carved and inlaid religious furniture, lamps, chandeliers, pottery and books, among many other things. We visited the opera house one evening and were invited to enter and stay to listen to the Cairo Symphony. The opera would close for the summer the next evening, as the building was not air-conditioned.

We went to the pyramids and made the mistake of entering Cheops' pyramid, the largest. Bent double, we crept up a long, narrow steep tunnel crowded with people. We felt trapped and the air was foul, but at least we could stand up in the tomb, which was just an empty room with a sarcophagus with a mummy in bad repair, before backing down the same frightening tunnel. The pyramids are impressive though and the Great

Sphinx at Giza is magnificently large. It was surrounded by a protective fence for repairs but York was given special permission to enter inside to sketch. He was captivated seeing it at such close range.

We flew south to Luxor and crossed the deep, wide Nile and then drove to reach the Valley of the Kings. It was exhausting in hot weather and it was always hot, and one may have to climb one hundred steps to exit from a tomb. From the middle of April, Luxor, Aswan and points further south become impossible because of the heat. We did not go further south because of this and due to York's illness. He was just beginning to feel well again and had finished a small painting related to the painting in the tomb of Seti, the most outstanding tomb of all.

The tomb of Seti was rich with wall paintings. They used a thick gesso-like emulsion on the stone, and not plaster. The sealed tomb had the entrance stone replaced in the face of the rock leaving no outward trace. On entering one walked down a long rock corridor with walls covered with paintings showing kings and gods partaking in certain ceremonies, areas of abstract symbols, and images of Seti's slaves, in case he needed them in the next life. After the long corridor, we then gradually descended stone steps to a large room with a painted wall that looked like the end of the tomb. The archaeologists tested the wall, found a loose stone and entered another chamber filled with a large boat which must have been assembled inside. We finally reached the tomb with the real sarcophagus, but the mummy and other articles had been removed to the Egyptian Museum.

We had struck up a friendship in Egypt with a Hungarian doctor, Alexander Sos, and his wife Susan, from New York. Sos was not his Hungarian name but as it was difficult for people to pronounce, he had adopted the name of Sos. Our next stop was to be Petra, the ancient rock city. To reach it was a strenuous journey and Dr. Sos felt York should not attempt it until he was stronger. We decided to fly to Beirut with the Soses instead.

LEBANON

Lebanon has a beautiful climate. The fresh green landscape and cleanliness were a welcome change from Egypt. There were elegant shops in Beirut and over three hundred hotels, many of which, like ours, overlooked the Mediterranean. The steep hills with their build-up of houses made an interesting painting subject. The museum in Beirut is well presented but not as interesting as those in Cairo. The unusual things were large ceramic burial jars, each having a piece broken out of the side to insert the corpse, and a large group of white marble sarcophagi with wonderful portrait heads.

We hired a car and driver with the Soses and took a trip to the vast and most impressive Roman ruins at Baalbek, the largest I have seen. The destruction of the huge temple, one of the grandest architectural achievements of all time, was caused by a series of earthquakes in 1759.

SYRIA

We also drove to Damascus in Syria, which turned out to be expensive and of little interest. The large old mosque in Damascus had little of its original mosaics left and was in the midst of restoration. There are over eight hundred room-sized rugs in this mosque.

JORDAN

From Beirut we flew to Aman, Jordan. Aman is an hour by taxi from Jerusalem and as airfield repairs were taking place in Jerusalem, we could not fly there. We stopped at the Dead Sea where York took a swim. We then carried on past the ruins of Jericho and stayed at the American Colony Hotel, under the ownership of Mrs. Vester, a friend of the archaeologist Douglas Tushingham. She immediately inquired about him.

Jerusalem, built on hills, was at that time a divided city like Berlin; many of the Biblical sites were on the Jordan side. Jerusalem's ancient wall was the dividing line and troops were stationed on both sides, with a small area of no-man's land in-between. We walked in the Garden of Gethsemane, and visited the nearby Church of the Crusaders. We followed the stations of the cross, saw where Jesus was betrayed by Judas, and the very spot where he was judged by Pontius Pilate. We felt sadness there. York painted *Jerusalem, Via Dolorosa* (1966) and *Near the Fifth Station of the Cross* (1967) in response to the site.

We went to Bethlehem and saw the actual place where the infant Christ was shown to the three wise men. A very grand and beautiful mosque with a huge area of natural stone inside stands on the Dome of the Rock, where Abraham tried to sacrifice Isaac. Arab Jerusalem is a beautiful city from a painting standpoint, having been built on a hill.

We visited a good museum with a small new section devoted to the Dead Sea Scrolls. Somehow, Arab Jerusalem ended up with a lesser part of the find, possibly because others could pay more. The collection was poor, and most fragments of the Scrolls were small and pieced together under glass. The collection in this museum is well presented and documented. Of course more information is known today. York was very busy sketching there.

ISRAEL

We phoned Ayala Zacks in Tel Aviv, as she was there preparing for the opening of the Zacks' museum at Hazor. She urged us to come and arranged a small seaside hotel for us near her house.

To leave Arab Jerusalem one crosses on foot at the Mandelbaum Gate over a wide section of no-man's land. A Jordanian porter took our baggage halfway, set it down and walked back. Then an Israeli porter came to pick it up while we walked through. It was strange being all alone in this wide empty space and feeling as if guns from both sides are trained on you. We asked to have our passports stamped on a piece of paper, using the lame excuse that our passports were nearly filled. The officials laughed, knowing very well if we had an Israeli stamp in our passports we could not return to another Arab country, such was the hatred.

We were now in Israel. The local museum was a large, impressive white building, and is considered one of the finest anywhere. Marc Chagall's windows, which we had seen in Paris, were now installed in the chapel connected with the Hadassah Hospital. There is much grumbling about them, as some feel they should be in a more important place closer to town. But it was Hadassah that had the idea to commission Chagall and raised the money to pay him!

We took a taxi to Tel Aviv, where Ayala gave us a day or two to rest and then started taking us on trips each day. The Zacks' little-used Tel Aviv house was fabulous—large and elegant with high ceilings, with the main living room designed around an enormous, beautiful tapestry by Lurçat, his first. They have a fine collection of modern paintings and sculptures there.

An amusing incident happened during a dinner at Ayala's. Present that night were Ayala, her mother, her brother Arie Ben Tovim and his wife Stephanie, and us. In honour of their mother the men all wore the yarmulke at the table and York was given one also. Ayala took one look at him and burst out laughing, saying, "My God, you look more Jewish than us!"

R.L. Rogers was then Canadian ambassador; he and his wife June were old friends from our Paris days and they immediately invited Ayala and us to dinner. It was a lovely evening of reminiscences; the Rodgers were enjoying Israel. They informed us that our Paris friends, the Wainman-Woods, then posted in Cyprus, were inquiring as to our whereabouts, as we were overdue in Nicosia.

One day on our way to Hazor, we had coffee in a little café on the Sea of Galilee, beautiful and full of history. Later we lunched at Abu Christie on the Mediterranean. We visited Haifa, a beautiful, hilly city where Ayala's sister, Rachel Graetz had a lovely home on the top of Mount Carmel. Rachel's husband Heinz was the author of an important book on Van Gogh, *The Symbolic Language of Vincent van Gogh* (1963).

The next morning Ayala took us to the kibbutz at Hazor, due north of the Sea of Galilee, where the museum Sam and Ayala were giving to Israel was to be officially opened by André Malraux in a few days. We were impressed by the unusual architecture of this small, simple museum, with a second building as a restaurant. The museum is built at the site of an excavation financed by Baron Rothschild of England. The excavated artifacts were beautifully presented at the museum; large stone pieces were set outside and on the first floor, smaller pieces were found on the second floor, some set in sand and others in well-designed cases. Mr. Horsey, the director and an archaeologist, took us through the kibbutz. The Zacks and Rothschild bequest will make this a more important kibbutz that will undoubtedly bring in tourist revenue.

We met some Israeli painters and sculptors through Ayala, including the famed Russian painter Anna Staritsky, who spent time in Paris but speaks only Russian, and the Israeli artist Rueven Rubin, who had an exhibition at the museum in Jerusalem during our visit. Our friend Constant, a sculptor who lived in Paris, happened to be in Jerusalem then. He had accepted the offer of a house and studio in Israel if he would spend time there each year. We also saw our old friend, the Rumanian-born Dada artist Marcel Janco. He called us and we visited the artists' cooperative in Ein Hod which he started, and where he has taught many artists, including Sorel Etrog. Marcel showed us some of his Dada period works at his home in Tel Aviv.

CYPRUS

Calls were coming again from Tom and Shelagh Wainman-Wood in Cyprus. We decided to leave promptly, thus missing the opening of the Hazor museum the next day. Tom and Shelagh met us at the airport in their chauffeured car with the Canadian ensign. It was a wonderful reunion, and we spent a happy and busy few days with Shelagh and Tom. They kindly put their car and driver at York's disposal, taking him to sketching spots during the day and returning to pick him up at appointed times.

One evening the Wainman-Woods hosted diplomats from various countries; an error in invitations caused a somewhat sleepless night for our hosts. Someone had invited the Israeli and Arab ambassadors on the same evening. When the Arab ambassador arrived, Shelagh rushed to the door, saying, "I must inform you the Israeli ambassador is here, there's been an error in the guest list," at which point the man turned on his heel and left. The next morning, Shelagh said, "I know what to do, we'll send him a large Canadian cheese." The ambassador was delighted!

We did much sightseeing, which gave York an opportunity to go back to sketching. Apart from its interesting history and scenery, there are a lot of Roman ruins on Cyprus. With Canada being neutral, Tom and Shelagh enjoyed many friends among the opposing Greek and Turkish factions, and we seemed to go to one side for cocktails and dinner on the other almost every night. We bid our friends in Cyprus good-bye on May 27 and decided to go to Greece.

XXII

1966

Around the World: Europe and Our Return Home

WE FIRST HEADED FOR ATHENS. After renewing our acquaintance with the museums, the Parthenon and Constitution Square, where we discovered some interesting murals in the surrounding buildings, we decided to get away from the summer heat and headed for the sea port of Piraeus, on the southwest coast of mainland Greece. We caught the first boat to Santorini, and upon arrival in the early morning, faced a sheer facade of rock with a town of pristine white buildings perched on top. Santorini is beautiful from below or above; the white buildings extend down the hillside. Our hotel, the Atlantis, was right at the top. Looking down we saw all sorts of geometric roofs and gardens.

We had a good-sized balcony overlooking distant islands, including a red-hot volcano five minutes from our shore by motor boat. From one side of our room we saw the Sea of Crete and Crete itself, while on the other side we saw some of the other Cyclades Islands. Life was simple and pleasant, and York felt he could paint there a long time, exploring the many subtle shades of white present on the island. York did a couple of small paintings daily and a few drawings. These paintings included *Santorini, Greece* (1967) and *Santorini* (1970), which the new Ontario premier William Davis purchased, along with *Sarawak* (1969), on his first day in office in 1971.

IOS

We left Santorini for Ios, birthplace of Homer. Ios has a beautiful, protected harbour ideal for swimming, and our hotel was right on the beach. On Ios there is considerable life at sea level—hotel restaurants, stores, cafés, houses, and churches. It was very quiet and we slept well, with the doors open to the sea.

There is a tremendous ceramic enterprise on Ios, where special earth is taken from pits and used for porcelain. There are also many old caves. The 366 ancient churches on Ios, all in good repair, are mostly opened on special occasions. I visited a small seventh century structure partly below ground, and a large, isolated thirteenth century church along the shore. Apparently it was the custom for fishermen to promise to build a church if they survived a certain storm. We went with friends to a distant beach. The island is rugged and barren, now and then tiny churches are poised on peaks to be as close to the sun as possible, in the belief that one ascends to the sun in death.

ISLAND HOPPING

After two days on Ios we headed to the island of Siros. En route, we passed hundreds of islands, some scarcely inhabited. We stopped at beautiful Naxos, continued on to the mountainous Paros, and ended up at Siros, where we spent one night at Hotel Hermes, right on the port.

We left for Tinos the next night, an island with a picturesque harbour and hills dotted with the typical white buildings. At the top of the hill was Basilica Santa Maria Virginie, built to the Virgin because legend has it that she freed the island from the Russians.

Miss Sdrin, a pharmacist, stopped us to talk on the street and said she would like to take us to see Aghia Triada, a church out of town. The Brothers welcomed us, giving us chairs and water after the long hot walk and delicious Turkish Delight sweets. The church was simple and clean, with some lovely ancient icons. There was a secret school at the church where the Brothers continued teaching Greek after it was forbidden during the Turkish occupation. Miss Sdrin gave us a parting gift of Turkish Delight; it was unbelievably heavy but delicious. York's *Tinos, Greece* (1966) is a small painting that brings back memories of this lovely island.

RETURN TO ATHENS

We bid our adieus and sailed back to Athens, where we purchased painting supplies and revisited the fine museum. The only interesting contemporary works we saw were murals. There was a tremendous brass and copper mural in a bank, made of brass plates of varied sizes and textures. Another building had a white marble mural with a sculptured bas relief set against a rolling, uneven mat background. The Olympic Air Lines building and bus terminal had a fair mosaic mural, with some delightful aspects but also some tacky figures. Our hotel in Athens had a nice burnt wood mural.

We found we had friends at the Canadian embassy, Arthur and Marcelle Blanchette, whom we met when Arthur was cultural attaché in Paris in 1959. They wined and dined us and we had a nice evening. Arthur was most helpful in finding painting materials and sending York's accumulated sketches back to Toronto.

CORFU

We arrived at the beautiful island of Corfu on June 22, 1966. York was singing on the balcony of our hotel while painting the magnificent scene before him: harbour, boats, islands, sky and the blue Ionian Sea. Ah, what hardships. We seemed to be mostly reading the work of Lawrence Durrell, as he and his family had lived at Corfu in the late 1930s.

ROME

We left for Rome on June 28 and quickly found a small, reasonable hotel. We did very little sight-seeing during this four-day stay, except to reacquaint ourselves with the museums, visit old haunts and see friends. Bill Crean, the Canadian ambassador, invited us to lunch and asked for our opinion on the house they wanted the Canadian government to purchase as their official residence in Rome. The grounds were lovely and spacious but the house was small and unimpressive. We had gone through this exercise with the last three ambassadors in Rome, each of whom did not want the house of their predecessor. We were back again for a Canada Day garden party on July 1. On introduction, we found many of the Canadian guests knew of us and York's work.

PARIS AND THE BIRTH OF YORK'S GEOMETRIC PERIOD

On July 2 we flew to Paris and were quickly installed in Luc and Jenny Peire's studio/home, as they were in Knokke, Belgium for the summer. A strange thing happened to York while sleeping in Luc's studio that first night. He actually dreamt a geometric painting, in colour. It was so clear that he did a pencil sketch of the painting before breakfast, followed by a quick colour sketch. He then intended to get on with his day's work, but he was still completely absorbed in the geometric painting at the day's end. The same thing happened on the second night and day. There were no more dreams but the two had been so forceful that he could think of nothing else. Ideas flowed so fast he could scarcely keep up with them. He was worried, however. Try as he may, he could not get back to his previous work. By the time we left for Toronto three months later, York had done two geometric serigraphs and had designed two geometric tapestries, and had at least fifty plans for further consideration.

We pondered how this compelling new direction could possibly have happened. Although York had many artist friends who painted in a Constructivist direction, he had never felt the slightest interest to do so himself. York took his painting ideas with him to each new locale, using mostly local atmosphere and colour. Op Art had flourished during our previous four-year sojourn in France. Could this have had any bearing? It became a worry for us when York continued week after week in this new direction, with no end in sight.

Exhibitions of York's recent work were scheduled for the spring of 1967 at Montreal's Galerie Agnès Lefort and at Toronto's Roberts Gallery. York had planned on shaping up works during our three months in Paris, based on subjects fresh in his mind from our world trip. He started each morning, intending to work on the blank canvas that had rested on his easel since our arrival in Paris. Against his will he would turn to his side desk and carry on with the geometric sketches that inundated his mind. To make things worse, Lefort Gallery proprietor Mira Godard turned up unexpectedly at the Paris studio, and was not pleased with what she saw, saying there were already too many painters working in this direction. Her comments seemed irrelevant, as York was transfixed with this new style, and he had always painted for himself.

About this time our old friend Dr. Harkavy, a New York psychiatrist, turned up at the studio and York told him about the perplexing situation. "Hark," as we called him, was immediately all ears and said, "Will you tell me the story from the beginning? Don't leave out a detail, I have never been this close to creation." York did and Hark said, "It relates to something in your past—it could have been years ago or it could be recent—something you have repressed and it has been triggered and has surfaced with force. There's nothing you can do about it, this is real creativity."

It took some time before we understood what had happened, but we eventually pieced together the story. After seeing so much Constructivist art in which he had little interest, York had pushed it into his subconscious for four or five years. During the world trip I was conscious on a few occasions of York being attracted to geometric shapes, like a shopping bag with a Mondrian-like design in Hong Kong, so out of place among the many Chinese bluebirds and happiness motifs, the striped buildings at Jaipur and the roof patterns in Ceylon. Arriving in the home of Luc Peire, a Constructivist painter, had triggered the explosion. It had been building all that time in York's subconscious and had come bursting forth with great intensity.

Michel Seuphor recommended Yvette Coquil Prince of Paris' Atelier du Marais as the best person to make two tapestries from his new geometric designs. The completed works arrived in Toronto after our return and York was delighted with them. York also used the same Parisian printer as Jack Nichols, the virtuoso Canadian print-maker. The geometric serigraphs were also shipped to Toronto.

THE FRENCH RIVIERA

During our residence in Paris we had the opportunity to get to know the museums and art galleries on the Côte d'Azur as guests of Ettore and Joanne Mazzoleni. It happened that Herman and Violet Voaden were staying at nearby Menton, and we all chased back and forth along the Mediterranean, on the Upper and Lower Corniches. We visited the striking, new museum dedicated to the work of Fernand Léger.

The Maeght Foundation had opened a museum at Saint-Paul-de-Vence in 1964. The museum's Spanish architect had carefully recorded the site's light patterns for a year, in order to obtain the maximum possible number of daylight hours. A labyrinth garden designed by Miró was full of his sculptures. A long garden wall of stones by the French artist Tal-coat, done in subtle tones of gray, prompted York to say, "How do you get anyone to approve a commission like that?" An ancient St. Bernard Chapel on site featured a window by Braque, in memory of the Meaghts' son, who had died tragically. There was a huge patio of Giacometti sculptures and a fabulous collection of "moderns." The gallery had an exhibition of Kandinsky's work at the time.

We ate at the famous outdoor restaurant at the Colombe d'Or hotel. On the walls were works by artists including Picasso and Dufy. There are many originals in the hotel rooms, a huge mobile by Alexander Calder over the pool, and other sculptures around the grounds. The artists apparently paid for their meals with their work. The collection was stolen a few years back, but was returned, as it was too well-known.

Another attraction was the Biennial at Menton. Each year a different artist is honoured. In 1966 there was a special "Salon de Picasso"; it was a large exhibition and the works of some of our friends were included, including three by Luc Peire. We saw the wondrous Chapel of the Rosary of Dominican Nuns by Matisse, and the striking Picasso museum at Antibes.

OUR RETURN TO TORONTO

We flew back to Toronto on September 27, 1966. We had been gone exactly one year. During our absence, York did 180 sketches (each 12" x 16") and filled numerous sketchbooks, apart from the geometric works done in Paris. York had decided to continue in his new geometric direction for one year, not showing the works anywhere, thus giving him the time to evaluate this new work.

Two months after our return, a solo exhibition of York's recent works opened at Toronto's Roberts Gallery. The show featured seventy-seven small paintings and sketches, often done on the spot in the many countries we had visited. Kay Kritzweiser noted in the *Globe and Mail* (December 3, 1966) that the show was busy and a near sell-out, and reported York's comment that, "It was a year of intensive discipline for me... Not only was there the constant adjustment to colours—from the wild gamut of Japan to the dazzling whites and blacks of Greece—but there was the discipline of painting on 12-by-16-inch canvases." On the other hand, we were to find that much bitterness had developed against York; strangely enough these nay-sayers were all friends of, or had been influenced by, Harold Town.

Robert Fulford published a devastating critique of York's Toronto show in the *Toronto Daily Star* (December 3, 1966), in which he called York the "least talented, least original, least interesting, least serious" artist, in short "the worst of all the successful artists in Canada." Fulford acknowledged the popularity of York's paintings, his large Toronto murals, and his successful career, but called the show "appalling" and declared that York's "layout is careless, his color banal, his insight into subject non-existent." The fact that Toronto audiences consistently purchased York's work signified "a judgment on Toronto taste" in Fulford's opinion. He concluded that "the painter this generation has most enthusiastically taken to its bosom is an artist of whom it can only be said that he is always pretty and he is never offensive." We were gladdened when the *Star* published some letters to the editor in York's defense, including one from Charles Smart, an American professor, on January 3, 1967. Needless to say, it was not an encouraging welcome back to Toronto.

Leonard Brooks, Ayala and Sam Zacks, myself and York at the airport in Morelia, Mexico. Date unknown. Photograph by Reva Brooks.

Group photograph at York's retrospective at the Art Gallery of Windsor. From left: myself, Peter Haworth, Bobs Haworth, Isabel McLaughlin, Yvonne McKague Housser, Betty Burrell, Catie Allan, and York. Windsor, 1979. Photograph by Kenneth Saltmarche.

XXIII

1967-1969

The Geometric Paintings
and an Exhibition in New York

NOW THAT WE WERE SETTLED back in Toronto, York was preparing works
for his exhibition at the Galerie Agnès Lefort, slated for the spring of
1967. The show included thirty-four paintings related to our trip around
the world; most were small 16" x 12" works, but there were a few large
ones. York also included ten of the geometric serigraphs completed in
Paris. Mira Godard wanted more large works, but the geometric phase
had completely monopolised York's attention.

Overall Mira did quite well on sales and the reviews were good. Yves
Robillard of *La Presse* said that York had a "style personnel, affirmé, effi-
cace." In the *Montreal Star* Robert Ayre considered the current exhibition
in light of York's earlier shows in Montreal and found it, "a fresh and lively
show that shares with us a stimulating sense of renewal and discovery."
Ayre compared York's breakthrough to geometric painting to
"Kandinsky's revelation," noting that York "became acutely aware of the
shapes and colours of walls and roofs and their relationship with each
other and the sky, and he painted them for their own sake, leaving out all
other considerations." York agreed with Ayre's comment that, "the places
give the painter somewhere to jump off, into an adventure of
composition, and this is what it's all about." It's obvious that Montreal has
knowledgeable art critics who gave their readers something constructive,
while pure venom flowed from the mouths of Toronto's Malcolmson
and Fulford.

BACK IN THE SWING OF THINGS

York fell back into his usual whirl of activity. The OSA and the Art
Gallery of Ontario combined for the 95th annual OSA exhibition, to
which York sent *Labyrinth* (1966). York's gouache/collage portrait of
Canada's first Prime Minister was included in the special section of the
Centennial OSA, "Portraits of Sir John A. MacDonald." The portrait was

donated to the Canadiana Fund in 1994 for installation in one of Canada's official residences in Ottawa. York acted as juror for the spring exhibition at the Agnes Etherington Art Centre in April, and contributed a painting to an art auction and sale for an Israel Emergency Fund in June. He was honoured with a Centennial Medal on July 1, presented "in recognition of valuable service to the nation." The Arts and Letter Club held a retrospective exhibition of York's work in October.

The Art Institute of Ontario had for many years been touring the work of OSA members to many Ontario venues. Paul Bennett had been in charge of this task, and was doing an excellent job in getting art to the people. The AGO took over the AIO and its funding, which completed Paul Bennett's work. The combined exhibition of the AGO and the OSA in 1966 also concluded the run of OSA exhibitions at the AGO. The artists felt betrayed, as the OSA had founded the AGO.

The RCA and the CGP had already been ousted, and from then on the art societies had to scramble to find annual exhibition space. If the Art Gallery of Ontario's main purpose isn't to support and show Canadian art, one wonders what its purpose is. Its growth was due in part to the devoted work of many artists and their wives. The artists boosted attendance and membership through teaching, demonstrations, discussion panels, lectures and the loan of their works.

ENCOURAGEMENT OF YORK'S GEOMETRICS

York continued experimenting with the geometric direction for a year or so and now the house and studio were filled with large geometric paintings. We lived with them and evaluated them daily. Most of the paintings were based on the Paris sketches. The first larger one was *Labyrinth*, which he showed with the OSA in early 1967, *Fiesta* (1967), included in the 88th annual RCA show late in the year, and *Cybernetics*, shown with the CGP exhibition at the MMFA.

York also completed a series of seven "Cities" serigraphs, in 1967, titled *Cairo, Kuching, Isfahan, Kuala Lumpur, Jaipur, Marrakesh* and *Srinagar*. When the sketches were complete he called me into the studio where he had set them up in a row. He only told me, "These are plans for a series of seven serigraphs related to cities of the world. The only clue is that you have been in all these cities. See if you can name them!" I sat in front of the sketches for some time studying their colours and forms, sensing the city to which each was related. I finally named them all correctly, except that I mixed Jaipur and Marrakesh, the two "red" cities. When York finished the serigraphs in editions of sixty, they were indeed a handsome set. Now instead of fighting the dreams, we both felt so fortunate that they had happened, teaching us so much about colour and form.

During our year of evaluating the geometric works, York had painted nothing else. Sam Zacks phoned to say the New York dealer Rose Fried was in town and that he would like to bring her to the studio. York replied that he had nothing to show her. Sam said they would drop by for a visit anyway. Sam and Ms. Fried arrived, and upon entering, were confronted by large geometric canvases from the front door to the studio. Rose said nothing, just looked, and when she had surveyed the studio walls, she turned around and asked, "When can I have an exhibition?" It was arranged for the fall of 1968.

Sam and Ayala Zacks started a tour of their collection, including York's magnificent *Rome*, to various Ontario venues in March of 1967. The show, entitled "An Exhibition of Modern Canadian Paintings" featured twenty-seven pieces, including work by Alfred Pellan, Jean McEwen, Ronald Bloore, Toni Onley and Kazuo Nakamura.

New York (1967) and *Bleues* (1967), the two tapestries woven in Paris from York's geometric designs, finally arrived in Toronto. We were very pleased with the results of York's experiment in this new medium.

The Sarnia Public Library and Art Gallery acquired York's *Three Women in Blue Rebozos* (1950) and two of the 1967 serigraphs, *Marrakesh* and *Srinagar*. Our Christmas card that year was a reproduction of the sketch for the painting *Longevity* (1966), now in the Robert McLaughlin Gallery in Oshawa.

PLAYING HOST

Toronto hosted an International Sculpture Symposium in 1967, inviting sculptors from other countries to come to Toronto and erect a sculpture on the grounds of our beautiful High Park. Al Latner of Greenwin Construction, a patron and collector of the arts, had just finished an apartment building near High Park and offered accommodation to all the sculptors. The Art Gallery of Ontario delegated certain people as hosts and we were to look after Jason and Clara Seley.

Jason was head of the sculpture department at Cornell University in Ithaca, New York. This was during Jason's phase of using old car bumpers in his work. The Seleys were interesting people and we had a most enjoyable time with them.

A MURAL FOR QUEEN'S PARK, 1968

In 1968 a new building was added to the provincial government complex at Queen's Park. The building was called the Macdonald Block, after John Sandfield Macdonald, Ontario's first premier. The building was purposely designed with long, continuous expanses of wall in its interior, in order to provide room for the installation of large murals. In 1966, Canadian artists were invited to submit proposals to a government-appointed art committee, whose members were Cleeve Horne, Clare Bice and Peter Haworth. All three were experienced jurors with a broad appreciation of art. Jealousies broke out all over with such venom that the government, afraid of criticism, withdrew many of its plans for the opening.

In the end, York was one of twenty-nine artists who received commissions. Other artists represented in the Macdonald Block include Gerald Gladstone, Tony Urquhart, Walter Yarwood, Jack Bush, Franklin Arbuckle, A.J. Casson, Harold Town and Syd Watson. York contributed *Ontario*, a large (8'7" x 16'6") vinyl acetate composition on canvas, and his only geometric mural. In the guidebook "Art at Queen's Park," York stated that although the mural was completely non-figurative it was designed "with thoughts of Ontario's resources in mind," and "does relate to the general contour and form of Ontario."

Of course the press fished around for complaints and came out with a sensational headline, "Has Queen's Park Thrown Away $330,000 on Bad Art?" Toronto is rich in art; regular tours should be arranged for tourists and locals to see its many murals, sculptures and art collections.

1968 ART ACTIVITIES

It seems that the OSA did not have an exhibition in 1968, since their rejection by the AGO. The CGP show, which included York's *Cybernetics*, toured to Regina in February. The O'Keefe Centre showed an exhibition of the work of thirty OSA artists in mid-1968, in which York was represented. York's *Flight* (1968) was included in the 89th annual RCA show, which opened in Hamilton in December. York showed his "Cities" serigraphs with work by A.J. Casson, Albert Franck and Will Ogilvie at the Roberts Gallery in September of 1968. Two walls of York's geometric paintings were installed at the London Public Library and Art Museum late in 1968, in the company of works by Charles Comfort, Albert Franck and Franklin Arbuckle.

RENEWING FAMILY TIES

We spent the winter of 1967-68 in Mexico, with York painting steadily for his New York exhibition in November of 1968. We returned from Mexico by way of Florida to visit my uncle, a retired Methodist minister, who the previous year, at age ninety, had married a fellow resident at the nursing home where he lived. We took a taxi from the Jacksonville airport; the taxi driver had heard of my uncle's marriage in the newspapers! All worked out as planned and we had a delightful two-day visit with my uncle and new aunt. We went on long walks through the surrounding woods, played shuffleboard and talked and talked. It would be my last visit, as my uncle died in 1970.

PREPARING FOR THE NEW YORK EXHIBITION

From Jacksonville we went directly to our New York studio with a huge roll of canvases in early April of 1968. York never shipped his canvases from Mexico. He would roll them with a plain canvas cover and carry them on the plane, where the steward would find a place for his tall parcel.

We settled in the studio and started a long session of hard work. We stretched canvases, nailed painted strips of wood to the stretchers, and then added the long finished strip of wood framing, the front edge of which was painted in dull gold leaf. This piece, projecting well ahead of the black wood, gave the canvas a "floating effect."

Our New York loft was very comfortable. There was no longer any evidence of it being a studio, as Luc Peire had cut a bed-sized hole into the wall storage and slid the bed half in, leaving visible an innocent-looking "couch". No inspectors ever arrived to check on us, and all local artists seemed to live in their lofts. The Bowery area later became less safe. There were no problems with the winos, but drugs had entered the scene and we had to take special precautions at night. We had many trips back and forth that summer and fall preparing for the exhibition. An article announcing the upcoming exhibition appeared in the *Globe and Mail* on May 23.

The opening day of the New York exhibition finally arrived. The beautiful catalogue included three large reproductions, biographical data and a thoughtful, knowledgeable introduction by the Toronto art historian Dr. Theodore Allen Heinrich. Many telegrams arrived from friends, including one from Jules Léger, then Under Secretary of State, which read, "Wish you every success. Sorry not to be with you. A bientôt." The exhibition featured eighteen large geometric canvases and the "Cities" serigraphs. Guy Carrington Smith, Canadian consul general in New York, presided over the opening and later hosted a reception at his home, as many friends had come from afar.

There were some immediate sales. Dr. Alexander Best came from Toronto to buy for his personal collection. Joanne Mazzoleni purchased *Mayan* for her newly formed collection, which she gave to Toronto's Royal Conservatory of Music in honour of her deceased husband, Ettore Mazzoleni. The art historian Laxmi Sihare selected *Guerrero* (1967) and a set of the serigraphs for the Birla Academy of Art in Calcutta, India. William Blair, publisher of *Harper's* magazine, acquired *October* (1968). J.J. Akston, president of *Arts Magazine*, acquired *Tarascan* (1968), the largest canvas (76" x 57"). The Hirshhorn Museum wanted a canvas but offered a fraction of the cost so Rose Fried declined without consulting York. We received a letter dated November 15, 1968 from Evan Turner, director of the Philadelphia Museum of Art, which emphasised his great interest in the show.

The exhibition was well-publicised in American art periodicals. A half-page reproduction of *Teotijuacan* (1967) appeared on the outside back cover of *Arts Magazine* (November 1968); other reproductions appeared in *Art News, Art International, Artforum* and the *New York Times*. The reviewer for *Arts Magazine* (December 1968-January 1969) wrote that York's *Teotijuacan* was "a dazzling zigzag of hot reds and oranges," and "one of the most visually exciting in the show, having a very active optic quality and lively color rhythms."

Zena Cherry reported in the *Globe and Mail* (December 19, 1968) that York was enjoying great success in New York. The *New York Times* noted that "Wilson, a Canadian, is capable of consistently distinguished work. His canvases can be looked at repeatedly with undiminished satisfaction." Cherry also wrote in the Toronto magazine *Gossip* (May 1-14, 1969) that the *Wall Street Journal* said the exhibition was an "unheard of success" for a Canadian's first New York showing.

Rose Fried had great plans for the work of York, but she died within the year. She wasn't well during the exhibition and summoned us one night to witness her will. Martha Jackson and Bertha Schaeffer, proprietors of two other leading New York galleries, contacted us to handle York's work, but he made little effort to oblige. It almost seemed that his goal was to prove his work with the best, and he was satisfied that he had accomplished that goal. He had little desire to become wealthy, and just wanted enough to live comfortably and buy the painting materials he needed.

A SOLO SHOW AT THE ROBERTS GALLERY, 1969

In March of 1969 York exhibited his geometric paintings at the Roberts Gallery in Toronto. We quickly discovered that Toronto was not New York. York was ahead of his time and there was little interest except among an excited few, like the George Benjamins, who purchased *Oriental Dragons* (1969) and *Oaxaca Blanca* (1969). There was more unfortunate bashing of York which now extended to the Roberts Gallery simply because it was successful.

The so-called art critic Jared Sable wrote negatively of York, Grant Macdonald and William Winter. He declared in the *Telegram* (November 8, 1969) that York possessed "just enough panache to disguise his very pedestrian abstracts with a high-gloss veneer. His buyers actually believe that they are getting very advanced art for their money. They're not."

Fortunately the *Globe and Mail* had a real art critic with no axe to grind. Kay Kritzweiser, who had gained an understanding of York's work over the years, wrote intelligently and favourably about the exhibition.

FACE AT THE BOTTOM OF THE WORLD

The Charles E. Tuttle Publishing Company published Graeme Wilson's translations of the poetry of Hagiwara Sakutaro in 1969. The book, titled *Face at the Bottom of the World and Other Poems*, included seven of York's paintings as illustrations. The book won an UNESCO award. It was distributed in many countries and we had the pleasant surprise of being presented with a copy by Sergio Galindo, director of the *Palacio de Bellas Artes* in Mexico City. The Canadian distributor was Edmonton's M.G. Hurtig Limited, but with little promotion it made hardly a ripple, even as it was acclaimed in many other countries.

The staff of Tuttle Publishing in Japan was dubious that a Westerner could illustrate a Japanese poet's work, but were completely won over on seeing the paintings. Graeme cheerily complained that York's paintings were attracting more attention than his poetry! In his introduction to the book, Graeme wrote that York's illustrations did not "relate to any one particular poem or group of poems. They are, in essence, black-and-white representations of 'Hagiwara-ness.'"

Leonard Brooks published another book, *Painters Workshop* (1969) which included three of York's paintings: a colour reproduction of *Kabuki* (1969) on the cover, an image of York's Queen's Park mural from the previous year, and one of the illustrations for the Hagiwara Sakutaro book.

XXIV

1969-1974

The Final Murals, *Four Decades* and a Second Retrospective

IN NOVEMBER OF 1969, York was honoured with a major exhibition of his geometric paintings and figure drawings in the International Salon at the *Palacio de Bellas Artes* in Mexico City. York's serigraph *Kuching* (1967) was used for the exhibition poster, which was posted all over the city. Unfortunately, the posters kept disappearing and after replacing a few, museum staff had to give up. The show featured twenty-two large acrylic paintings; the *Museo del Arte Contemporaneo* acquired *Atotonilco* (1969) for their collection.

The opening was a delightful occasion with Dr. Saul Rae, the Canadian ambassador, hosting a grand reception that included ambassadors and ministers from other countries. Dimitri Diokonov, the friendly Russian ambassador, walked around the exhibition with his arm around York's shoulders, the two of them laughing and obviously enjoying each other immensely. The press coverage was phenomenal; seven or more newspapers published extensive articles, many on the front page, and something almost daily for the exhibition's one-month run.

York was asked to submit an article about his life and work to the local newspaper, *El Universal* (November 2, 1969). In the article, "Mi Obra y Yo" (My Work and I), York focused on the genesis and development of his geometric works. One paragraph in particular is helpful in understanding the conceptual framework of the geometrics.

These recent paintings are abstract space and colour relationships that sometimes can be related to specific experiences. Sometimes they are related to a combination of many places and expressions. Space can be the intervals of music, the distance between buildings, the rhythm of poetry, the beat of marchers, the interval of waiting, the moon exploration, the tick of a watch; it can be audio space, visual space, tactile space, rock and roll space, string quartet space. The definition of space can be and is as limitless as imagination, colour in trees and landscape, sunsets and skin tones and music tones; it is the colour of Bach as compared to Liszt; the prism or the twelve tone scale; it is morning and night, hot and cold, high and low, colour can be fast or slow, happy or sad. The definition of colour can be and is as limitless as imagination.

Dr. Theodore Allan Heinrich wrote a concise essay for the exhibition catalogue. Some of his comments therein were reproduced in the Mexican newspaper *Novedades* (October 24, 1969). Heinrich wrote that York's geometrics were neither "hard edge nor op, even though there are no references of details of the normal visual experience, his paintings are highly evocative. Colours and rhythms suggest the strong sense of a physical place, that has permanence, like the consistent element in all Wilson's work." Heinrich concluded that unlike the work of some of York's contemporaries, "there is no nausea, fear or bitterness in his painting, he avoids the ugly and repulsive and on the contrary thinks of grace, harmony and a calm atmosphere."

The *Instituto Nacional de Bellas Artes* toured the exhibition to San Miguel de Allende, where it opened in January of 1970. The same catalogues and posters were used for the San Miguel venue. After the happy conclusion of the two highly successful exhibitions, we joined the American artists Dorcas and Oliver Snyder for a relaxing sketching trip at Zihuatanejo, then a small and primitive village.

A MURAL FOR THE CENTRAL HOSPITAL, TORONTO, 1970

York's mural for Toronto's Central Hospital came into being through the dreams of two brothers, the Hungarian doctors John and Paul Rekai. The Central Hospital was a place where many new Canadians could be treated in their own language; thirty-five languages were spoken by hospital staff. Professor John Wevers, chairman of the hospital board, chose York to do a mural for the hospital entrance.

Since the hospital's patients came from many different countries and backgrounds, York chose an all-embracing theme, "From the Four Corners," which he executed in four parts, north, south, east and west. The 11' x 12' mural, executed in vinyl acetate on canvas in the studio, was installed at the hospital in mid-1970. As with York's other abstracts, the key to the composition lay in its colour and form. Lotta Dempsey reported Dr. Paul Rekai's comment in the *Toronto Daily Star* (November 7, 1970) that the keynote to Central Hospital's spirit is "expressed sensitively in York Wilson's beautiful mural, which makes an impact on anyone coming in through the front entrance. It expresses a theme…in rich and colourful abstract form. That is, the four corners of the world from which patients…staff and doctors have arrived." The completed mural was featured in colour on the cover of *Canadian Hospital* (November 1971) and a detail was shown in the hospital newsletter, *The Spark* (Autumn 1971).

Years later, Central Hospital staff were still enthralled with the mural. In the Winter 1981 edition of *The Spark*, it was noted that, "This 11 by 12 foot mural remains as one of Wilson's most imaginative and compelling essays in colour and design. It successfully accomplishes its mission as symbolising the wide flung origins of the immigrants to Canada while achieving an authoritative and compelling act of pure visual experience."

THE LOSS OF TWO GREAT FRIENDS

In April of 1970, one of our closest friends, Sam Zacks, lost a valiant battle against cancer. Sam and his wife Ayala did more for art in Canada than anyone else. We never got over the great loss.

The memory of another dear friend, Ettore Mazzoleni, was honoured with an exhibition at Toronto's Royal Conservatory of Music of the "Ettore Mazzoleni Memorial Collection." When Ettore died in a tragic car accident in 1968, York felt the loss so deeply that he completed a painting *Tribute to Mazz* (1970) for himself and later gave it to Ettore's wife, Joanne. This gift inspired Joanne to start a fine collection of paintings, which were later installed in the Concert Hall at the University of Toronto as a tribute to her husband. York and Cleeve Horne had advised Joanne in the formation of her collection, which featured works by artists including Peter Haworth, Borduas, Riopelle, and Bertram Brooker. The opening of the collection was reported in the University of Toronto *Bulletin* and the *Globe and Mail* on December 2, 1971.

York wrote a tribute to his friend Mazz, which appeared in the catalogue presented at the exhibition opening. Apart from his personal recollections, York recalled Mazz's participation in locating a mysterious bar of music to put in the O'Keefe Centre's *Seven Lively Arts* mural.

Mazz was never too busy to take part in a hoax, so when I wanted a musical enigma for the O'Keefe Mural, he was the obvious choice. Typically he set to work as though it were an important commission. In a few days he had worked out an enigma, sufficiently profound to have remained, as yet undiscovered. The hoax is particularly successful in that I have forgotten the exact enigma myself and will have to do considerable research to find it.

A MURAL FOR CARLETON UNIVERSITY, OTTAWA, 1970

During York's exhibition at Rose Fried Gallery in 1968, an Ottawa resident, Jean Grant, read a review of the show in the *New York Times* and telephoned the gallery, asking to speak with York, who was fortunately there. Jean Grant was planning on funding a mural for Carleton University in memory of her late husband. She knew she wanted York to do the mural, but she didn't know how to contact him. On our return from New York months later, she visited us in Toronto to discuss the project.

The mural would be installed in the student lounge of the new University Centre, then under construction and designed by Matthew Stankiewicz, one of the architects of the Canadian Pavilion at Expo '67. The building's art/sculpture committee approved the choice of York as the muralist.

York proposed a mosaic mural, *For Peace*, a brilliantly-coloured abstract composition more decorative than representational. In his execution of the 4' x 55' mural, York again worked with Alex von Svoboda of Toronto's Conn-Arts Studio. The mural composition was composed of various geometric patterns, the meanings of which York explained to the building committee on May 21, 1969. The upright "Y" represented the "expectant soul," while the reversed "L" or angle symbolized the "meeting of celestial and terrestrial" and the "bird-shaped configuration" the dove, symbol of peace. While the various symbols did not convey a cohesive narrative, York declared, "they should tend to direct through toward peace and understanding."

For Peace was officially unveiled at the University Centre's grand opening on September 25, 1970. The famed American engineer and inventor Buckminster Fuller delivered the keynote address. "Bucky," as he is referred to, again mounted the podium after dinner to address the students, saying, "Before I begin I must answer a call of nature" and then disappeared for several minutes. When Bucky was still talking an hour later, we decided to slip away to return to Toronto.

The reviews of the new University Centre in the Ottawa press seemed to focus on the negative. An article in the Ottawa *Citizen* (September 26, 1970) highlighted the $4.5 million cost of the building, Buckminster Fuller's $3,000 fee, and the building's "costly frills," namely *For Peace*, and Gerald Gladstone's *Electronic Light Mural*. Matthew Stankiewicz replied to the article in a letter published in the *Citizen* on September 30. He wrote that, "The attitude of 'if it's cheap enough, it's good enough' is largely responsible for our present sterile environment and perhaps your energies might be more usefully directed toward encouraging any attempt to rise above the currently-prevailing mediocrity."

E.L. Mortimer, the Centre's new director, was meanwhile thrilled with York's mural. He wrote us on August 19, saying:

> To my delight last week I was present when your own beautiful
> mural was installed, and to say that I am impressed and pleased is
> an understatement! In all conscience I cannot pretend to be knowl-
> edgeable about abstract works of art, but when I stood in the main
> lounge and looked at your mural for the first time I felt very keenly
> a sense of delight in the form and colour before me. I would like
> you to know that I think the work is beautiful and extremely rele-
> vant to our centre.

1970-71 ART ACTIVITIES

A solo exhibition of York's work opened in late October at Roberts Gallery. The invitation featured a colour reproduction of *Kabuki* (1969), a large acrylic geometric purchased from the show by the Japanese firm Nissho-Iwaii Canada Ltd. In her review of the show in the *Globe and Mail* (October 24, 1970), Kay Kritzweiser noted a "loosened paint" and a suggestion of representation in York's recent geometric paintings, such as *Serendipity at San Miguel* (1969). She also found his New York abstracts more cool and formal than those done in Mexico. Peter Wilson of the *Toronto Daily Star* (October 23, 1970) gave the exhibition a positive review, saying York "always carries out these pictorial blandishments with integrity, with sound balanced craftsmanship, and his achievement has been a consistent quality for two decades."

The Birla Academy of Art and Culture in Calcutta held a ceremony inaugurating their new Gallery of International Modern Art on

November 12, 1970. Kenneth B. Keating, then U.S. ambassador to India, performed the inauguration. The collection catalogue includes artists from many countries and one lone Canadian, York Wilson, represented by the "Cities" serigraphs and *Guerrero*, purchased from the 1968 Rose Fried Gallery exhibition.

The Gallery of International Modern Art is housed on the fourth floor of the beautifully-designed eleven-storey Academy building. As the gallery pamphlet indicated, the collection contains paintings, drawings, sculptures and prints "by eminent artists, both Indian and international." York was the only Canadian represented in the painting section, while Sorel Etrog and Jacques Besner had sculptures in the collection. Other artists represented included Joseph Stella, Jean Arp, Frank Kupka and Louise Bourgeois. The museum planned to tour the exhibition throughout India as a teaching tool.

York still enjoyed his involvement with the Arts and Letters Club in Toronto. He spoke to the club in mid-October, calling his lecture, "Reminiscences in Prospect." The following year he presented a copy of *Face at the Bottom of the World* to the Club. He had inscribed the poetry book, "To the Oriental Department of the Arts and Letters Club."

The Canadian Irish Studies Committee at the University of Toronto invited York and our dear friend Marshall McLuhan to speak and open an exhibition of the Irish artist Miceal O'Nuallain, at St. Michael's College on February 11, 1971. The show was held in conjunction with the Fourth Canadian Seminar in Irish Studies. It was a hilarious opening, with York and Marshall tossing witticisms back and forth.

York University presented a fine exhibition, "African Sculpture," drawn from private collections in Toronto, in April of 1971. We loaned eleven African pieces from our collection to the exhibition; our stunning "Baga Crocodile Mask" was reproduced on the cover of the catalogue.

York had recently been somewhat disappointed in the quality of the OSA exhibitions, and decided to resign in March of 1971 from the society for which he had worked so hard in the past. He was, however, still contributing to the RCA shows. His *Tribute to Lawren Harris* (1970), painted in memory of the great Canadian painter who died in 1970, was included in the 91st annual RCA exhibition in Montreal in 1971. A review of the show by Terry Kirkman and Judy Heviz published in the Montreal *Star* (March 26, 1971) declared York's painting a "beautifully sober work that recalls in a completely abstract form the latter's Northern landscapes of the late 20s." The reviewers wrote in support of the RCA exhibitions, noting that the shows had "gradually grown wider in their scope, more catholic in taste, and increasingly of the present day."

A MONTH IN EUROPE

We left for a month in London and Paris in late May of 1971. We joined Mac and Elsie Samples in London and stayed in the now-famous house of Sir John and Lady Casson in Chelsea. The Cassons are renowned in the world of theatre; John is the son of Dame Sybil Thorndike and their daughter Jane is known to Canadian audiences at Stratford. The plaque of the ancient Chelsea Pottery Works was originally affixed to the house next door, but when the Victoria and Albert Museum dug up the Casson garden, they found many pottery pieces that confirmed their garden as the actual site of the works.

We checked in at Canada House, where Ian Christie Clark, the cultural counsellor, offered York an exhibition for April of 1972. We also called on the British Council and had a delightful visit with Miss Luce and John Hulton, but we were disappointed in their offer of representation in the Venice Biennial of conceptual art. They kindly gave us a list of local galleries for York to approach. We received a nice welcome at most galleries; Harry Miller at the Redfern offered their 6000-name mailing list for York's Canada House exhibition, but few galleries handled work that York felt was compatible to his own.

We visited the National Gallery, the Marine Museum and the Tate Gallery, where York enjoyed the work of Morris Louis, Mark Rothko and Yves Klein. At the British Museum, York found the Elgin Marbles alone to be worth the trip.

On June 12 we headed for Paris. We saw François and Marie Madeleine Thépot; François was on vacation from the Ontario College of Art and tried to maintain his art connections in France during the summers. Luc and Jenny Peire were away for Luc's exhibitions in Milan and Stuttgart, so we moved into their place on Rue Falguière. This is where York had experienced his important but initially upsetting dreams of geometric painting. We rushed around, seeing friends, and visiting the Louvre and other museums. York particularly enjoyed the Georges Rouault exhibition at the *Musée National d'Art Moderne*.

BACK IN TORONTO

A letter from the AGO informed us that the gallery had acquired two more of York's works through the gift of Sam and Ayala Zacks, the geometric oil painting *Blue Music* (1969) and a small untitled mixed-media collage (1964) which York had given to Ayala.

Rothmans of Pall Mall invited York to open their collection of contemporary French tapestries at the O'Keefe Centre in September of 1971; the show was stopping in Toronto on a nation-wide tour. The exhibition included thirteen pieces by the late Jean Lurçat, who was responsible for restoring the art to its rightful place after a century of dormancy. Some of the other celebrated artists represented in the show included Le Corbusier and Alexander Calder.

At that time I was in the hospital with unbearable pain. This was later diagnosed as polymyalgia rheumatica. It was a little-known affliction then; the cause and cure is still unknown. It can only be treated with cortisone, which eases the pain immediately and eases aching muscles gradually. Unfortunately, however, it usually leaves one with arthritis.

York was now exhibiting regularly with Ottawa's Wallack Galleries. His solo show in late 1971 received good reviews in the Ottawa papers. *Le Droit* (November 6, 1971) called it an "exposition stimulante," while the *Citizen* (November 6, 1971) noted York's "intelligent abstracts in which the haphazard has been avoided" and the *Journal* (November 4, 1971) asserted that "few contemporary artists have a wider appeal or work with such professional competence."

We spent six months in Mexico in late 1971. The CBC came to San Miguel to do a film on York, Leonard Brooks and Fred Taylor. Footage included the artists at work, their paintings, the scenic town and countryside, and the exceptional climate. During the filming the sunny weather suddenly changed to a cold wind and even snow flurries! We all laughed at the irony of the situation.

The editors of *PHP*, an international magazine published in Tokyo, invite people from all over the world who excel in their field of endeavour to write articles about their work. York was asked to contribute a text; he wrote about his oil sketch *Shalimar Bagh* (1966), inspired by our travels to Kashmir, and discussed how his sketches could serve as a visual travel biography, in the February 1972 issue of the magazine.

Sketching has become a means of recording a variety of visual reactions to places and people. These impressions assist in developing quite abstract paintings, often several years later.

Kashmir is unbelievably strange and beautiful. The mirror-smooth lakes, the Shalimar Gardens, the strange medieval people and buildings, the mountains and blossoms—all combine to become visual poetry.

CONTINUED COMMUNITY SERVICE

The secondary school at Napanee, near Kingston, decided to have seven murals by senior art students installed in different areas of the school. York was invited in November of 1971 to select the final seven works from a pool of forty-two designs. He would be videotaped as he discussed his reasons for his selections. Two art instructors later brought the students to Toronto for a mural tour. York hosted them at his studio, explaining his own work and answering questions, and then carried on to the O'Keefe Centre, where he explained *The Seven Lively Arts*.

At that time, a large tract of farm land east of Toronto was selected by the federal government as a site for a second airport. The government had been quietly buying the land from farmers in the area, and soon people became aware of the planned use. They formed a "People or Planes" committee to fight this waste of land. To raise funds, the committee invited artists to donate paintings for sale, and the works of many leading artists were auctioned at Brougham Community Hall during the Spring Festival in May of 1972. York donated an early work, *Celaya Market* (1959). "People or Planes" was eventually successful and the government put the purchased land up for sale again.

NO MORE GEOMETRICS

By late 1971, York's geometric period was coming to an end. During this phase, initiated by his startling dreams in 1966, York had only painted geometric works. Yet he found that the geometric impulse left him as suddenly as it had descended. York felt he had learned much in the areas of colour and form in the last five years. He was now entering his final period of pure abstraction, which his work had indicated from the beginning.

York's new non-geometric works, featured in a solo show at Roberts Gallery in October of 1971, prompted Kay Kritzweiser to write in the *Globe and Mail* (November 4, 1971) that, "York Wilson's paintings are not so much a return to landscape as an emergence on canvas of the sights, sounds, colours and forms which have saturated the subconscious of the painter for 20 years." Kay commented in particular on *Corfu Music* (1971), *Kashmir Facade* (1971) and *Things Roman* (1971). She noted that York used "collage to give richer depth to several paintings and it works with golden results in *Thanksgiving*" (1972). Joan Murray, then a curator at the AGO, wrote us to say she had seen York's show, and that it made her again aware that, "York is such a fine colorist and the work I saw is so very elegant compared to many other artists today."

The Sarnia Public Library and Art Gallery acquired the excellent 1943 portrait that York did of *Hedley Rainnie* in his studio. Our dear friend Alec Panton had passed away in 1954. He was remembered in an exhibition at the Arts and Letters Club in 1972, to which members loaned their works by Alec. When Alec retired as Club president, York had drawn his official portrait, which joined the frieze of exalted past presidents.

FOUR DECADES

Four Decades: The Canadian Group of Painters and Their Contemporaries, 1930-70 was published by Toronto's Clarke-Irwin in 1972. The book, written by Paul Duval, was instigated by York during his tenure as president in 1965. The quality of the colour plates is largely due to the perseverance of York and Syd Watson. *Four Decades* remains the definitive book of that period. It won the 1973 Leipzig Gold Medal for the "most beautifully designed book in the world" and medals in Toronto from the Art Director's Club and the Book Promotion and Editorial Club.

Harold Town became very difficult during the assembling of material to be included in *Four Decades*, even threatening to sue if any of his work appeared in the book. His work of course belonged in the book, but it was necessary to limit his inclusion to a brief mention in the text, in order to avoid any problems. The *Globe and Mail*, ironically, asked Harold to review the book. Harold of course delivered a vicious critique, published in the *Globe* on November 25, 1972. As one letter to the editor, published in the *Globe and Mail* three days later concluded, "Harold Town's piece on Paul Duval's *Four Decades* was not a book review, but an unrestrained emotional ramp."

THE FIRESTONE COLLECTION

On May 10, 1973, the Ontario Heritage Foundation accepted officially Professor O. Jack and Mrs. Isobel Firestone's gift of their gallery/home and their magnificent collection of Canadian art. The collection is now housed in the Ottawa Art Gallery, in Ottawa's former court house.

Jack Firestone had been collecting York's work over the years. The Firestone collection originally contained forty-nine of York's works, but now includes forty-seven. When the collection catalogue, *Firestone Art Collection*, was published in 1978 in conjunction with a major exhibition at Toronto's Campbell House, forty of York's works were listed. I believe Jack Firestone sold or traded some works in order to obtain others. The collection contains a large body of some of York's finest drawings of the female nude, some sketches and a major canvas, *Paean to Autumn* (1971). The collection also includes a 1964 mixed-media study for the Bell Telephone mosaic mural that York executed in 1965. This is somewhat unfortunate, as I have tried to carefully keep all the mural studies intact, with a view to donating them to the right museum at the right time.

YORK'S FINAL MURAL COMMISSION, TORONTO, 1973

Douglas Peacher, president of Simpson-Sears Ltd., in Toronto commissioned York to design a tapestry for the directors' dining room in 1972. York proposed the theme *Game*, which the Board approved. His design included stylised animals such as fish and bears or any other food that might appear on the table.

As York had been so pleased with his two 1967 tapestries, *New York* and *Bleues*, he again asked Yvette Coquil Prince of the Atelier du Marais in Paris to execute his designs. By the time the completed tapestry arrived in 1973, Douglas had forgotten about the commission, saying "What tapestry?" Nevertheless, the 4' x 9' mural was installed in the dining room, much to the delight of the company's directors. *Game* proved to be York's only tapestry mural, and his final commission.

The Peachers were good friends. In 1973, Douglas, a former American army colonel, donned his uniform at a dinner given for the occasion and performed the ceremony of inducting York and Maestro Ernesto Barbini into the "Honourable Order of Kentucky Colonels." It was a highly humorous evening and eventually resulted in York receiving a certificate with a large gold seal, signed by the Governor of Kentucky and Secretary of State.

THE GIRLS

In 1972 Clarke-Irwin published Rebecca Sisler's *The Girls*, an overview of the lives of Frances Loring and Florence Wyle. York was asked to review the book for the *Globe and Mail*. As we had known Frances and Florence well, York was perfectly suited to the task. In his review, published in 1973, York wrote that the project was made doubly interesting because the period of these women's lives was little documented, and that the book was well-researched and filled with Sisler's detailed reminiscences.

York reasoned, however, that the book just did "not work." He felt the title was derogatory and the cover featured poor examples of their work. He also disagreed with the concept of a composite biography, which "creates the unfortunate impression that they were artistic Siamese twins." "With all due respect to this publication," York concluded, "we can only hope that in the future a more scholarly evaluation will be done of these people who we consider two giants in the world of sculpture in their time and in the Canadian arena."

FRED POWELL

Leonard Brooks drew our attention to Fred Powell, a Canadian sculptor working in San Miguel who was then unknown in Canada. Fred was in the Canadian Armed Forces but after the war went directly to the States. Fred had a studio full of wonderful carved wood sculptures but no money. York was so impressed with Fred's work that he asked Jack Wildridge to give Fred an exhibition at Roberts Gallery. Fred had an old, patched truck that he loaded with his sculptures in San Miguel and somehow drove to Toronto without a major breakdown.

We introduced Fred to Cleeve Horne, Sorel Etrog and other friends who realised Fred was a very important sculptor. We publicised him as much as possible before the exhibition. At the opening we quickly purchased the largest piece, *San Remi*, to ensure a little money went into

Fred's pocket. Sorel Etrog also bought a piece, as he was really enthusiastic about Fred's work. With these two well-known names buying work the public gained confidence in Fred, and he did very well for a first exhibition in Toronto. We later purchased *School* and *Mexican Door*, and received *Sunflower* as a gift from Fred.

We worked hard to promote Fred because we believed in his great work. Fred, however, had a problem with alcohol. When a friend of ours, a collector from western Canada, was visiting his daughter in Toronto, we told him about Fred's work and he said, "If York Wilson says it's that good I will promote him in the West. Bring him to dinner." We told Fred, and he promised not to have a drink and the dinner went well. The collector's daughter would visit Fred's studio the next morning. By the time she arrived, Fred had already been drinking, and she was so disgusted that the deal ended. We realised we could not promote him further, as it jeopardised our own reputation.

Fred went on to have exhibitions with the Dresdnere Gallery and the Moos Gallery in Toronto. Walter Moos was so excited about Fred's work that he intended to present Fred to New York and the world, and the Powell exhibition at the Moos Gallery was the stuff of genius. Both galleries, however, had in short order had enough of Fred's instability. We ourselves had to make the rule that he was not to come to our house if he had a drink. When the Canadian writer Scott Symons did a documentary film on Fred, York was invited to speak in the film about Fred's work. York was frail and ill during Fred's last visit in the 1980s. Fred sadly passed away, much too young.

A NEW HOUSE IN SAN MIGUEL

York had a solo exhibition at Ottawa's Wallack Galleries in November of 1973; the beautiful painting *YingYang* (1973) graced the cover of the invitation. I was just recovering from pneumonia and York thought three weeks of sun in Mexico would help. We took our packed bags to Ottawa, and flew from there to Mexico.

We stayed with Dr. Francis and Letitia Echlin in San Miguel. While sitting in the town square one day, a Mexican real estate agent approached us to ascertain our interest in a house she thought was very special. We went to see it and ended up buying it. It was large and spacious, with five bedrooms with baths and patios, and had a good, remote studio on the second floor. The guest quarters and an acre of patios were also on the second floor. We returned to Mexico in July of 1973 for three months to take possession of our new home. York started painting immediately and I began alterations that included a real roof garden with trees, bougainvillaea and long rows of climbing geraniums. We were back again from December 1973 to April 1974. Everything had been left in place.

Jules Roskin and his wife Phyllis, a concert pianist, used their great entrepreneurial abilities to start a series of lectures at *Bellas Artes* in San Miguel, taking advantage of the wealth of visiting talent. Jules invited York to start off the venture with three lectures on abstract art. Jules' suggested title was "All You've Ever Wanted to Know About Abstract Art But Were Afraid to Ask." This was a subject dear to many, and the large auditorium was filled each night. Jules was an excellent host and the lectures carried on weekly during the winters until the late 1980s. Phyllis gave many a recital, sometimes as part of a duet. Jules and Phyllis were greatly missed when they returned to the States.

YORK'S SECOND RETROSPECTIVE

The Sarnia Public Library and Art Gallery organised the first Canadian retrospective of York's work in 1965, a touring show presented at four other venues in Eastern Canada. Sarnia is in a strategic position on the border of the United States; many of its members and support comes from Michigan. In 1974, Sarnia mounted their second retrospective of York's work; the show toured to Stratford, Oshawa and London.

It was a pleasure working with director Reg Bradley and curator Margo Street. Sarnia purchased *Candelaria* (1974) from the exhibition. Margo had first seen the painting while it was still wet in York's studio. We received a lovely telegram at the show's opening from Yvonne McKague Housser, who wrote that, "I am sad to miss the opening of the retrospective exhibition of an artist whose creative integrity has been an inspiration to me through the years."

The show featured thirty-six works created by York from 1927 to 1973. Most of the works were paintings, from *Burlesk No. 2* (1939), *Indian Harbour* (1946), *White Figures of Acambay* (1951) to *A Propos de Shaka* (1960), *Mayan Dimension* (1963) and the tapestry *Game* (1973). The catalogue included an introduction by Margo Street, a text about York by Paul Duval excerpted from *Four Decades*, and York's extensive commentary on numerous paintings included in the exhibition.

York began his text with a brief overview of his art training and commercial art career. "By 1938," he wrote, "not only was I ready to paint larger works, I felt I had something to say and was ready to begin exhibiting." York recalled his destruction of *Burlesk No. 1* and the subsequent success of *Burlesk No. 2*, accepted for the 1939 OSA exhibition and later shown with the Canadian Group of Painters at the New York World's Fair.

York summarised his concern of the 1940s as "a very realistic 'social commentary' type of painting." Such works included *Welfare Worker*, *Public Library*, *Local Dance*, *Blood Donors*, *The March Past*, and *Beauty Contest*. He singled out *Beauty Contest* as different from the other social paintings because it was a strong caricature. Looking back, York concluded that caricature rendered a painting "ludicrous and thereby makes a work less acceptable as a serious painting." The only major landscape of that period was *Indian Harbour*.

Of his ballet paintings, represented in the show by *L'Entrechat*, York noted that "the subject became so popular that if I continued, the public would never allow me to paint anything else."

York asserted that "the meaning of abstraction became amazingly clear" when painting *Sunlit Street, Acambay*. "Even though today this painting seems to be very slightly abstracted," York wrote in 1973, "nevertheless for me it was the key to abstracting form. This later led to my ability to also abstract colour."

From there, York made specific comments about several more works, touching on the first collages, the many sketches done on our round-the-world trip, the birth and death of the geometric period, and the new ideas and concerns that occupied him in his most recent work.

There were pages of complimentary reviews from both sides of the border; it hardly seemed like Canada! William MacVicar wrote in the *Globe and Mail* (November 16, 1974) that, "talking with York Wilson is like hearing a young artist with talents he hasn't even begun to test…He makes theory sound as vivid and engaging as gossip. His serene enthusiasm makes one forget that York Wilson is one of Canada's most successful artists, certainly its foremost muralist, and that he began to paint almost half a century ago."

York's mural, For Peace, *installed in the student lounge in the University Centre at Carleton University. Ottawa, 1970. Photograph by Hans L. Blohm.*

XXV

1975-1980

Potpourri

A SOLO EXHIBITION OF YORK'S RECENT ACRYLICS AND COLLAGES opened at Toronto's Roberts Gallery on October 23, 1974. The opening was announced in the *Globe and Mail* (October 22, 1974) and *Toronto Week* (Oct. 26-Nov. 2, 1974). York was then sixty-seven years old and his solo shows were a regular feature of the Toronto art scene. During this busy autumn, I was occupied preparing the annual exhibition of well-known artists' works to raise funds for the Toronto Symphony. My daughter Virginia, now back in Toronto, was a great support in giving us ingenious lighting for these events.

The Sarnia Public Library and Art Gallery must be given credit for mounting exhibitions of some of the artists who achieved fame in the decades following the Group of Seven. In 1995 the National Gallery of Canada brought out another exhibition and catalogue on the Group, *Art for a Nation: The Group of Seven*, even though they have never given proper recognition to equally-worthy Canadian artists. Some of these artists have been accepted internationally with the world's best, except in Canada, and York is a case in point!

Dr. O.S. Pokorny of Sarnia, a devoted collector of York's work, organised a combined posthumous exhibition of the work of Syd Hallam, who had died in 1953, and Alec Panton, who had died in 1954, at the Sarnia Public Library and Art Gallery in 1975. In the exhibition catalogue, Dr. Pokorny wrote that Syd "credited York Wilson with loosening up his painting approach which enabled him to reach out with considerably more freshness." York wrote the introduction to the catalogue, and the show toured to Woodstock and Owen Sound.

Wallack Galleries in Ottawa presented a York Wilson exhibition in November of 1975; the invitation featured a reproduction of *Etruscan Impression* (1975). This painting represents York at his best in abstraction, and the Wallacks quickly bought it for their own collection. The Ottawa *Citizen* (November 8, 1975) published an excellent, lengthy review of the show accompanied by photos, but there was little that hadn't been said before, with the exception of York's comment that, "I used to hate pink. But then I gradually came to see that pink could do all sorts of things other colours could not. And now I like it!"

I presented my annual Toronto Symphony silent art auction in 1975 at the Del Bello Gallery on Queen Street. Some of the twenty-eight artists in that auction included Ronald Bloore, Ken Danby, Doris McCarthy, Alfred Pellan, William Winter and Ruth Tulving. Liona Boyd, the internationally famous guitarist, gave the opening address. On the night of the final sale we moved to the ballroom of the Harbour Castle Hotel. Because of the quality of works I had assembled, many of the reserve bids were exceeded.

Roberts Gallery opened an exhibition of York's fine acrylic abstracts in October of 1976. The monthly newsletter of Toronto's Arts and Letters Club, where York had another solo show that year, reported of York's Roberts' opening that, "the art world is really pulsating in Toronto." Someone at the Club overheard an eminent New York art critic, then visiting Toronto, say that "abstraction was dead. But that was before he went to see York Wilson's show. He was reconverted…"

We spent six months in Mexico in 1976. During our residence there, Vivienne Wechter, of Fordham University in the Bronx, who had a regular program on New York radio, interviewed York. To get the conversation flowing, she asked York to talk about anything, and so he started talking about art in general. She found York's observations so interesting that she signalled him to continue. On completing the tape, Vivienne said she would contact York again to talk specifically about his work. We heard the program had gone well in New York, and that a repeat broadcast was requested, but our paths did not cross again. Fortunately a few short audio recordings of York discussing his work still exist.

Oshawa's Robert McLaughlin Gallery mounted a retrospective of the work of Dennis Burton in 1977 that toured to ten galleries across Canada. Dennis had studied in California with Rico Lebrun. Dennis wrote in the exhibition catalogue of his rigorous drawing lessons with Rico, and how upon his return to Toronto, York and Cleeve had visited the studio he shared with Gord Rayner and Bob Smith: "York Wilson and Cleeve Horne came to see my work; Wilson had been sent a letter about me from Rico Lebrun. Rico had said York was the most important artist in Canada, and that he should help me. So Wilson and Horne came over to our studio and saw our abstractions. They thought we were doing terrific things and they told us about how tough art was. They said nothing terribly critical; we felt pretty good."

WORK BEGINS ON THE *YORK WILSON* BOOK

In 1977, John and Claire Wallack of Ottawa's Wallack Galleries decided to go ahead with their idea to publish *York Wilson*, a limited edition book on York's work accompanied by a colour lithograph, *Blue Opus*. The sale of the limited edition book and print would pay for the costly colour plates, the services of Paul Duval, who would write the text, and all the other costly things that make publishing a commercial high-quality art book nearly impossible. If enough of the limited edition would sell, it would be possible to go ahead with a commercial edition at a reasonable price.

Claire was a brilliant art entrepreneur and she and John began getting the ball rolling to produce the book, which was published in November of 1978. Paul Duval got to work on the text, the Wallacks initiated promotional activities and York started doing lithographs at Toronto's Open Studio. He completed four lithographs that year before he was satisfied that he had the right one to accompany the book. We were excited when pre-publication orders for the $300 book and print set started to come in.

Some years after York's death in 1984, I came across an interview with the excellent printmaker Otis Tamasauskas, who worked with York at the Open Studio that year. "When I was 21," Otis recalled, "I was working with the painter York Wilson, who, at the age of 74, was still full of good concepts and was constantly experimenting. That surprised me because I had worked with a lot younger artists, including some pretty great Canadian artists, who were amazingly rigid."

The Wallacks mounted their biannual exhibition of York's work in the fall of 1977; the invitation showed a fine reproduction of the exciting painting *A Canaletto Day* (1977), an acrylic abstract based on our Venice experience years earlier. The Arts and Letters Club included a fine reproduction of York's painting *Backdrop For a Corroboree* (1976) in their 1977 calendar.

SKETCHING IN MEXICO AND GUATEMALA

On Christmas day of 1977 we flew to San Miguel for a couple of days, where we joined Dudley Baker and Fleta MacFarland on a driving trip to Guatemala in Dudley's van. Dudley had been loaned a house and servants in Antigua, the former capital of Guatemala. York was captivated by the Indian villages in Chiapas country, just before the Guatemalan border, and did some excellent watercolours inspired by these scenes, including *Fiesta at Zinacantan* (1977), *Chiapas* (1977) and *Chouinvalvo, Chiapas* (1977).

Once across the border we drove hard to make Antigua that night, passing through Guatemala City, and arrived exhausted that evening. York was up early, exploring the surroundings from the roof, when he suddenly came rushing down to tell us that smoke was erupting out of the nearby volcano. The cook laughed and told us this was a common event, so we relaxed. After breakfast York went to the Antigua market which, with the mountain backdrop, offered good sketching.

We had friends in Antigua and quickly met a few of the permanent foreign residents who felt Antigua was a Shangri-la they wished to keep secret. Among our new acquaintances was the American archaeologist who excavated Tikal and remained to retire in Antigua. He had a vast workshop full of fragments that he said would keep him busy for the rest of his life. The famous market at Chi Chi Castenango is the best place to see the crafts and clothing of Guatemala. When driving one day we came upon Lake Atitlan suddenly and were so impressed with the strong blue and beauty of the lake that we were compelled to stop. The Indian population is enormous and there seems to be a small loom and weaver in almost every yard.

On our return to San Miguel we stopped for York to sketch at Chamula in Chiapas territory, as there was a fiesta in a large park around the church. We bought our tickets at the entrance to the fiesta and progressed in the direction of the church, but were definitely made to feel unwelcome. We felt it was dangerous to take another step and quickly left.

BACK IN TORONTO

In 1947 York had sent *Beauty Contest* to the RCA exhibition in Montreal. When Roger Selby, director of the Winnipeg Art Gallery, came to York's studio in 1977, he selected *Beauty Contest* to represent York's early work in the permanent collection of the Winnipeg Gallery. Once he saw York's geometric paintings he became very excited and said that if York would donate about eight geometrics to the gallery, they would permanently dedicate a York Wilson room.

Shortly before the Winnipeg proposal, we had offered our home, contents and finances at time of death to Heritage Ontario as a York Wilson Museum. Having lived in Europe, particularly France, for some time, we were conscious of the many small museums and felt Canada had also developed to that point. We were both born in Ontario and felt York should be represented in his own province, and particularly in Toronto, his birthplace. Larry Ryan of Heritage Ontario came to talk it over with us and promised an immediate answer. We didn't feel free to accept Roger Selby's tremendous offer and said we would let him know. We waited and waited, a year went by, and still no answer from Larry Ryan. York was very discouraged, especially when we read in the newspaper that Roger Selby had resigned from his Winnipeg job to return to the United States.

In May of 1978, the Arts and Letters Club and the Heliconian Club combined to present two "York Wilson evenings." His works were installed, he gave lectures both nights and Imperial Oil sent a film technician who showed "Mural," the Imperial Oil film. Both evenings were highly popular. Chuck Matthews, an eager and supportive member of the Arts and Letters Club, proposed that York have an extra ten colour reproductions made from each of the colour plates from the *York Wilson* book. These would then be signed by York and sold by Chuck for the Club at an agreed price. York did not agree to this scheme, for ethical reasons.

Crown Life Insurance featured a fine reproduction of *Mountain Cut* (1978), a work based on our Guatemala trip, in their annual report that year. The company had purchased *Mountain Cut* for their permanent collection of more than sixty works by Canadian artists, installed in their Home Office building.

Mona and Kenneth Campbell gave a garden retirement party for Mac and Elsie Samples. Mac had been British Consul-General in Toronto from 1969-78. The guests contributed to the purchase of a *York Wilson* book, soon to be published. We were very pleased as the Samples were among our dearest friends.

York gave his print *Mayan* (1977) to the Herman Abramowitz Chapter of Hadassah in Montreal to raise funds for Israel, and was delightfully surprised when it won first prize in the graphics section. He again contributed to the Canadian Opera Art Exhibition at the O'Keefe Centre by sending his oil painting *Ontario Lake* (1977).

In October of 1978, Roberts Gallery mounted a solo exhibition of York's work, one of the finest shows of abstractions seen anywhere. York was at his peak. His lifetime search and experimentation had culminated in paintings like *Oriental Interior* (1978), featured on the invitation and snapped up immediately by a collector, who already owned five other works by York. He certainly knew what he was buying. My hope is that these works will end up in a museum.

PUBLICATION OF THE *YORK WILSON* BOOK

The deluxe limited-edition book *York Wilson*, by Paul Duval with a foreword by our dear friend and neighbour Marshall McLuhan, was finally ready. The book contains nearly one hundred superb reproductions, mostly in colour. In his essay, Paul Duval covered York's various periods with understanding and perspicacity. I don't think the book could have materialised without Claire Wallack's vision and expert handling. Toronto subscribers were invited to a champagne party at the Rosedale home of our daughter Virginia and her husband Jon Kieran, where they could pick up their books, being signed by York, Paul and Marshall that afternoon, a blustery winter Sunday.

We were of course honoured that Marshall McLuhan had agreed to contribute the foreword. He was a man before his time and is only beginning to be understood today. In his essay, Marshall focused on the role of art in the nuclear age. "The work of York Wilson," he wrote, "is a notable manifestation of the new awareness of nuclear man, the shift from sight to insight." Tracing the rise of painted representations of things and the gradual move to abstraction in the twentieth century, Marshall asserted that York was a "key figure in relating us to both the old visual world of realism and to the new resonating world of touch and echo and pattern." He acknowledged York's "joy in the intellectual exploration of the very complex world we share," and concluded that "the painting of York Wilson is not based so much on new skills and techniques as on a new way of seeing and knowing the world."

MEXICAN WATERCOLOURS

We spent less than two months in Mexico during the winter of 1978 and York brought back sixty-six watercolours. The artist Enrique Cervantes, our first Mexican friend in San Miguel, died in February of 1979. Enrique's wife Sonia asked York to write a few words for the catalogue of Enrique's exhibition at *Bellas Artes* in San Miguel the following November.

The Honourable Donald Cameron, Nova Scotia's Minister of Culture, Recreation and Fitness, opened York's exhibition of Mexican watercolours on March 22, 1979 at the Manuge Galleries in Halifax. The invitation featured a reproduction of *On Road to Guanajuato* (1979). Halifax gallery-goers were primed for the exhibition in articles in Halifax papers. Elizabeth Manuge wrote to say that an art historian from Georgia University was most impressed with the exhibition. There were many positive reviews, most of which reiterated old news, but one thought published in the Halifax paper *The Mail Star—The Chronicle Herald* (March 17, 1979) caught my eye: "he feels comfortable in Toronto, but he does not want to feel too safe when painting. He wants to be a nervous painter, in search of new visual ideas and concepts."

A WINDSOR RETROSPECTIVE

The Windsor Art Gallery mounted a carefully selected retrospective exhibition in November of 1979. The show featured works ranging from York's 1946 Arctic sketches to pieces completed in 1979. Included were *Mexican Girl* (1951), reproduced in Paul Duval's *Canadian Drawings and Prints* (1952), the oval painting *A Propos de Shaka*, shown at Sao Paulo in 1963, some geometric paintings including *Aguas Calientes* (1970), and two geometric tapestries, *Gidai Matsuri* (1970) and *Monte Alban* (1970), later renamed *Totem*.

David Quintner wrote in the *Windsor Star* (November 2, 1979) that York was "one of Canada's most consistently brilliant and durable painters." He also declared that what York had "given us in his 72 years, as a muralist, tapestry designer, painter in water-colours, oils, gouache and acrylics, with pencil and conté, should assure him of perpetual studio space and eternal northeast light in the Canadian art firmament."

York's 1979 solo show at the Wallack Galleries in Ottawa included his *Borneo Batiks* (1979), a subject that interested him at the time. York often looked over his sketches from our world trip, seeking inspiration for new paintings. That year, he was attracted by his colour studies of the bright, wonderful designs in the batiks worn by the people of Sabah and Sarawak.

A SKETCHING TRIP TO THE WEST INDIES

It had been thirteen years since our last trip to the West Indies in 1966, so we decided to return in 1979. We visited our friends Margo Moser, the actress, and Bill Cohen, a doctor from Connecticut who had built a charming house overlooking a bay on the island of St. John. York enjoyed several days of painting there and on nearby islands. Some of the lively works resulting from this trip included *Sir Francis Drake Channel, V.I.* (1979), *Caneel Bay Plantation, V.I.* (1979) and *Little Cruz Bay, V.I.* (1979).

COMMUNITY SERVICE

York again supported the Canadian Opera's fund-raising sale of art with three paintings. He gave a drawing, along with many other gifts from artists, to Toronto journalist Kay Kritzweiser on her 70th birthday. York took part in the art decoration for the Arts and Letters Club's spring review "Out Of Your Mind." He participated in a group exhibition organised by the Roberts Gallery, which featured the work of twenty-two academicians they represented. He acted on the jury to select the students awarded an Ontario arts award, given each year by F. Javier Sauza of Mexico. A Sauza award includes the fare to Mexico, a course of study in the arts, living expenses and spending money.

TRIBUTES FROM BOB PATERSON, LEONARD BROOKS, AND FRED TAYLOR

York was no longer well, and was in the hospital from time to time because of his unstable heart. When he was unable to attend Arts and Letters Club functions, we received invitations, autographed menus and programs in the mail from our many friends there, letting us know how much they missed York's presence. During these years we sometimes received tribute letters from various friends.

Bob Paterson, York's assistant on the Imperial Oil and O'Keefe Centre murals, wrote a particularly poetic letter.

> Lives are interwoven like threads of a weaving, moving in and out, affecting and being affected by others as they go. My own life-thread was altered when I came into contact with York Wilson in the autumn of 1956.

Bob related in detail his experiences working on the two murals and concluded that:

> Little did I realise that the opportunity to assist on the Imperial Oil mural was to be involved with one of the more important works in Canada. Even at the time there was a pervading sense of historical meaningfulness, which added greatly to the excitement and intensity of the operation.

The artist Fred Taylor wrote of York in a letter of July 12, 1982 in a humorous and lively vein:

> No one has ever seen paintings signed by him which might be attributed to anyone else. Yes, he has style, plenty of it, whether you refer to his line or design, his bangs or his ties. York is emphatically York and don't let anyone think that they might talk him out of any of his convictions! They are legion and fiercely held.

Fred also included a lovely paragraph that touched on my place in York's life and career:

> Just as it is impossible to think of York without smiling and chuckling with him, it is impossible to think of him without thinking and smiling about Lela—about "The Wilsons," for they are a team, an inseparable force which it would be very difficult to think and speak of otherwise. All through the history of painting since Rembrandt there have been painters whom one cannot consider without also considering their wives and the supporting roles they played in those illustrious lives which certainly would not have been as renowned without them. Such partners are not a matter of luck and chance: they have been strong teams by design—the design of the partners, and the credit must be shared equally. All successful people are remembered and in the history of painting in Canada York and Lela will always enjoy special loving remembrance.

Our long-time friend Leonard Brooks sent a lovely letter in March of 1983. Leonard wrote of first meeting York, and of their many experiences together over the years, in Canada, Mexico, France and Italy, some of which Leonard had already recounted in his numerous art books. Looking back over their friendship, Leonard wrote:

> It has been a privilege and a joy for me to have spent the time we have had together—never competing, enjoying each other's successes. To paint something "good," "worthwhile," a little better than the *last* one, and nearer to what we hoped and knew could be the real thing—a work of art. Braque said: "Painting is a compromise with the impossible." I salute York whose work over his lifetime has made that "impossible" less formidable for himself, for us, and others to come. He is fulfilling himself as a genuine, creative spirit and has contributed a legacy of work which has added lustre to Canada's art image in the world.

York at his retrospective at the Art Gallery of Windsor. Windsor, 1979. Photograph by Kenneth Saltmarche.

XXVI

1980-1984

The Final Years

IN LATE 1980 THE ART GALLERY OF WINDSOR presented an exhibition of over three hundred Pre-Columbian clay objects and textiles drawn from our collection and that of Virginia and Jon Kieran. Our Pre-Columbian works are now in the permanent collection of the Carleton University Art Gallery.

Rosalie Cohen opened the Atelier 19 gallery in Montreal in October of 1980. Several of York's prints were included in the opening exhibition of "Original Limited Edition Prints." Roberts Gallery opened a solo exhibition of York's work that same month. We received affectionate notes from André Biéler and Doris McCarthy, the latter writing that, "The show is exhilarating and I am enchanted by the small landscapes." The O'Keefe Centre celebrated its twentieth anniversary in 1980. A short overview of York's mural and the union scandal was included in the anniversary program.

Rebecca Sisler's book *Passionate Spirits: A History of the Royal Canadian Academy, 1880-1980* (1980) came in for much criticism in a review by Gary Michael Dault in the *Toronto Daily Star* (December 20, 1980). The book included a reproduction of each academician's work chosen by Sisler; York was represented by his 1950 painting *Toluca Market*.

Among the eleven academicians Dault had selected to vilify, York headed the list. In defence of York, the reproduction of his *Toluca Market* was poor and dark, and certainly not a flattering example of his work. Completed the first year York began painting full-time, *Toluca Market* was an important work in his career. It won the J.W.L. Forester Award and was the first pyroxylin painting shown publicly in Canada. The art scene had moved quickly in the ensuing thirty years and York had continued to progress with the times. By 1980 he had been the toast of New York, had been offered a retrospective in a French museum and was represented in at least six foreign museums. A 1950 painting should not have been chosen to represent York in 1980.

York rejoined the OSA in 1980, convinced that president Kemp Kieffer was doing a good job. Among many other accomplishments, Kemp founded the OSA awards in 1980. The awards were initiated to honour "Canadians who have made a distinguished contribution to the vitality and stature of the visual arts in Canada either as artists working in a wide range of disciplines or as patrons of the arts whose vision and support had been significant for the cultural heritage of this country."

In 1981 the presentation took place during a dinner, with an exhibition and sale of members' works. York was pleased that his oil sketch *Whale Cove, Cape Breton* (1980) brought in considerably more for the OSA than his asking price. The artists honoured with awards included Jean-Paul Lemieux, Isabel McLaughlin, Jack Nichols and Jack Shadbolt. The actual award was a fine, characteristic piece of sculpture by Gord Smith.

York again supported the Canadian Opera, Appleby College, Windsor Art Gallery and the Toronto Symphony Orchestra with paintings for their fund-raising efforts. Eight of York's drawings were reproduced in the Arts and Letters Club newsletter in December of 1980.

THE RCA IN THE WEST

Since the 1981 Royal Canadian Academy exhibition opened in Vancouver in November we decided to go early, stopping off in Calgary and Banff, which was a marvellous experience. It was also our first trip to Vancouver and Victoria. I think the Vancouver RCA contingent thought the easterners were cheapskates because the cash-strapped Academy had asked the Vancouverites to trim expenses. We were not treated well in Vancouver.

It was a different story with the Victoria artists, who were excellent hosts. We simply couldn't understand the Vancouver attitude; in Toronto we had always gone to great trouble to make visiting academicians' sojourns as pleasant as possible. The same with our visits back and forth to Montreal, it was always a joy to see each other. We need more involvement with our western colleagues for better understanding.

THE MCLUHANS

One of our greatest pleasures in life has been our long friendship with Marshall and Corinne McLuhan. While Marshall was working as the Schweitzer Chair for a year at New York's Fordham University in 1967-68, he developed a tumour under his brain. He had a successful operation in New York, which left him sensitive to noise for some time. One day he phoned from New York to see if York could find them a house in Wychwood Park. Rarely was there a house for sale, but good luck was with us and one that was perfect became available through a chance conversation. That is where the McLuhan family has lived ever since.

Our friendship flourished throughout the years. We went on many evening walks with Marshall and Corinne, or watched a particular television program with them at their home, during which Marshall often fell asleep! Marshall and Corinne once visited us in San Miguel in 1976, as Marshall was delivering a lecture in Mexico City. The four of us were invited to a banquet for the new governor of the State of Guanajuato. Marshall received a great deal of attention from the Mexican press.

Less than six months before Marshall's death on December 31, 1980, the University of Toronto talked about closing the Marshall McLuhan Centre for Culture and Technology, which infuriated York sufficiently to write a letter to the editor of the *Globe and Mail* (June 12, 1980):

> The closing of the Marshall McLuhan Centre for Culture and Technology on June 27, is probably the biggest blunder Canada has made in many years.
>
> Marshall McLuhan is one of the Canadian names that is respected and quoted all over the world. Many countries have made attractive offers to Dr. McLuhan, but he has remained faithful to a country that has no appreciation of greatness.
>
> It is ridiculous to say that there will be an $18,000 saving by closing the Centre, when the Canada Art Bank spends at least that much for a couple of pieces of garbage annually in the name of Art.
>
> There is no excuse or reason why we should let an international name, and a great person be ignored and forgotten. I, personally have known people from Japan, United States, France, England and Mexico, who envy us this great Canadian.
>
> Let us make sure that some tangible recognition of Dr. McLuhan is assured before it's too late.

Teri McLuhan, daughter of Marshall and Corinne, presented her film "The Third Walker" in Cape Breton in September of 1980 at the Savoy Theatre in Glace Bay. We were invited to the premiere, and decided to make

it a painting trip also. We attended the many functions given by Premier
Donald Buchanan and the mayors of Glace Bay and Sydney. It was Marshall's
last trip, a year after the stroke which left him without speech but did not
affect his mind. By some strange quirk, just before the trip, he came out with
"Oh boy, Oh boy" with a big smile, which seemed to serve well in introductions. During one of the functions he had a beautiful dance with Corinne.

During Marshall's last illness, when he was unable to speak, read or
write, he appeared at our door, all smiles, offering York a little painting as
a birthday gift. Corinne had put a row of dots to show where he was to
put his "X" and she signed his name. It was one of York's great treasures.

We were greatly saddened in December when Marshall died. York
wrote of the death in his diary on December 31, 1980:

> Marshall McLuhan died last night in his sleep. The immediate
> feeling is a sense of emptiness—a loneliness, depression and even
> pessimism. What is the use of anything? What matters?" What to
> do, where to go? A sense of uselessness—I want to paint a tribute to
> Marshall—where to start? He is too great a mind, too close a friend.
> Maybe as time goes by I'll know what to do. Not now.

HONOURS FROM BOB PATERSON

Bob Paterson published *Abstract Concepts of Drawing* in 1981, in which
he included mention of York in some very distinguished company:

> Cezanne, Wyeth, Whistler, Rothko, Vasarely, Picasso, Pratt, York
> Wilson and others have used Composition Ideas to provide a firm
> structure to their work, and we can learn from them. To look only at
> the subject matter would be to miss the true Visual Meaning and
> essence of what the artist is communicating. One must come to
> realise that meaningful works of Art do not just happen by chance,
> but are thought out and developed by the artist with a particular goal
> in mind for each individual piece.

THE GUILD OF ALL ARTS

Spencer and Rosa Clark had long worked on their dream of assisting
artists in need and rescuing sculpture that had embellished early Toronto

buildings slated for demolition. They bought a huge property on the top of the Scarborough Bluffs in Toronto, called "The Guild of All Arts" and built an inn that was known for years as "The Guild." Spencer carefully placed the historic sculptures on the spacious parkland surrounding the inn. An engineer, Spencer made this his life's work. The Guild of All Arts was one of the most beautiful parkland areas in Toronto, with sufficient interest to attract tourists.

Spencer sold this unique cultural museum to the city of North York under the aegis of Heritage Ontario. The name was changed to "The Guild Inn" and the Delta Hotel chain was brought in to manage it. This turned out to be a strictly commercial enterprise and the board of directors seemed unable to safeguard this great treasure.

Spencer was in the midst of forming a group of influential cultural people, including York, to manage the property. One of the threats was to remove the fences, put refreshment stands on the grounds and open it to the general public. Spencer knew vandalism would soon destroy his life's work. He worked tirelessly the next few years trying to protect his dream.

SYMPHONY ART AUCTION

My most successful Toronto Symphony art auction occurred in 1981. The Arcadian Court at Simpsons donated their huge gallery space and we were able to obtain eighty-one works of art, including one work each by LeMoine FitzGerald and A.J. Casson. We were grateful to our generous artist friends, the media and the hard-working committee. York donated a $1,000 sketch as his contribution.

YORK IN THE UFFIZI

In 1981 we were very excited to learn that the Uffizi Gallery wished to commission York to do a self-portrait which would enter their permanent collection, and be installed with other self-portraits by acclaimed world artists in the gallery's "Vasari Corridor." Among many artists from around the world who are represented in this collection, York and David Blackwood are the only Canadians.

Zena Cherry reported this great achievement in the *Globe and Mail* on November 23, 1981 and Kay Kritzweiser wrote us to say, "Bravo! Great! and other expressions of delight to see your photograph and story in Zena's column. I think it's a great tribute to you—and to staunch Lela as well—to receive this international recognition when we can all proudly share it with you." The portraits, including York's and David Blackwood's, are reproduced in a publication of the gallery entitled *Gli Uffizi* (5 March 1983).

Central Hospital's publication, *The Spark*, (Winter 1981) celebrated York's Uffizi commission with a short essay on the honour "bestowed to artist of our mural," along with a photograph of York and myself with the completed portrait. In 1982, the Central Hospital hosted an exhibition of the Sculptors Society of Canada, during which the two existing busts of York were borrowed and placed in front of his mural at the entrance. One bust was that done by Cleeve Horne in 1949, the other was by Linda Keogh, well-known Canadian puppeteer, sculptor and actress who often used York's head as a model for her puppets. Linda later donated her work to the hospital.

SUN UMBRELLAS

York's solo show at Wallack Galleries in November of 1981 featured thirty-seven acrylics and one gouache. *Sun Umbrellas* (1981) was reproduced on the invitation. The Canadian writer Philip Kreiner thought this painting so beautiful that he asked permission to reproduce it on the cover of his book *Heartlands*, published in Ottawa by Oberon Press in 1984.

HOMETOWN TIES

In 1981, my hometown school, the Aurora Public School, was turned into the Aurora Museum, administered by the Aurora and District Historical Society. That year, I attended a reunion and fund-raiser at the school. I donated the *York Wilson* book and *Blue Opus* lithograph set, which was happily accepted. Years later when I visited Aurora, I realised that their collection was very small, so I immediately offered our Pre-Columbian and "primitive art" collections. Although the Royal Ontario Museum had expressed interest in our collection, I felt they already had so much material. The Aurora committee discussed it with the town council and decided to maintain their original policy of collecting only local items, as they had neither the money nor the resources to look after such a collection.

NEW GALLERY REPRESENTATION

By 1981, York was represented by Hamilton's Moore Gallery. York and Ron Moore, the gallery's proprietor, had hit it off immediately. Ron had been buying two or three works each year, and when his gallery opened in 1980, York joined Ron's stable. With his regular shows at Roberts in Toronto and Wallacks in Ottawa, the Hamilton representation further increased his exposure in Ontario.

In late 1981, the Moore Gallery released their pre-Christmas exhibition schedule, which listed the excellent group of artists in their stable: Appel, Bellefleur, Bloore, Chadwick, Danby, Dunford, Ferron, Fournier, Jenkins, Kahane, Kurelek, Martin, Nakamura, Perehudoff, Riopelle, Rogers, Ronald, Sarafinchan, Town, Wilson. The Moore Gallery moved to 80 Spadina Avenue in Toronto in April of 1997, opening with an incredible exhibition of Canadian talent rarely seen elsewhere.

TWO FINAL SKETCHING TRIPS

We took what turned out to be our last major sketching trip together to Spain and the Canary Islands for three months in the winter of 1982. We stayed with our old friend Dr. Carlos Pinto Grote in Tenerife. York did some exceptionally fine watercolours there, such as *Taganana, Coto de Caza* (1982), *Sauzal, Isla Canarias* (1982) and *Igueste, Tenerife* (1982).

Our artist and architect friends there bestowed many honours on him, and the Yacht Club made us honorary members, commemorating thirty years of friendship. The famed art critic Eduardo Westerdahl, among others, paid homage to York at the various affairs. York gave one of his finest watercolours from the Canary Island trip, *Puerto de Guimar* (1982) to the Montreal Hadassah fund-raising auction.

In the summer of 1982 Stephanie McLuhan gave her mother, Corinne and ourselves a beautiful painting holiday in East Hampton on Long Island, where she hosted us at her lovely house for the summer. It was a short walk in the sand to the sea and we enjoyed very fine evening sunsets. Stephanie later purchased York's lovely watercolour, *Long Island Summer* (1982). When she made a film about her father in 1983, the film crew visited us to record some of York's memories of Marshall. York's contribution was of necessity small, as he was then having difficulty speaking.

SPECIAL BIRTHDAY PRESENTS

The imaginative family of Jim and Mildred Harris, our old friends from York's commercial art days, wanted to give Jim an unusual 70th birthday present and decided on a book written by his friends. Jim was a friend of York's for more than forty years, so York did a humorous essay entitled, "Do you remember when?"

> When we had a hockey game between *Liberty* magazine and Ronalds Agency?
>
> When we had a stag party for Russ Mayo and we did a pseudo *Liberty* magazine for him?
>
> When we had a stag for Ray Avery at the Prince George Hotel, when we put his bow tie in a full bottle of beer and capped it?
>
> When we checked all his clothes at the Checkroom downstairs? [A revenge for Ray's many misdemeanours.]
>
> When Vic Murray tried to stab Sammy Sales' [a maddening comedian employed for the occasion] hand with a fork?
>
> When we had separate parties to invite C.J. Harris and Jack Kent Cooke but Lela forgot and invited them the same night and one sat in the living room and the other in the recreation room all evening?
>
> Do you remember Drooling T. Creepalong Fondle Bum Snide? [A secretive name among the friends for someone they didn't like.]
>
> When the beautiful waitress in the coffee shop responded to Hutch's [Charles Lee Hutchings] question: "Did you make the cake with your own lily-white hands?" "No, my father made it with his lily-white hands."

Another request for a 70th birthday gift came from our Wychwood Park neighbour Jack Sword, a retired University of Toronto professor, for his wife Connie. The gift could take any form, and York did a tiny 3" x 4" painting called *Age of Wisdom*.

YORK AND THE ART GALLERY OF ONTARIO

On learning that the AGO had done nothing in recent years to honour York's work, Ayala Zacks Abrimov wrote to us from Jerusalem on March

11, 1984, saying, "I am dumbfounded about the AGO's behaviour. It is so unfair that York's works are not the calling card of the Art Gallery." Senator David Walker, whose portrait York had painted, wrote to AGO director William Withrow, asking why a retrospective exhibition of the work of York Wilson hadn't taken place. Withrow replied (December 10, 1984) to Walker:

> Thank you for your letter concerning the work of York Wilson. You may be interested to know that I have been very familiar with this artist's work for over 25 years. There are many homes in this city where his work is enjoyed. Perhaps outside of Toronto he is not as well known.

Where has Mr. Withrow been? There are over two hundred of York's works in every major art gallery in Canada and at least nineteen works in foreign museums!

IMPORTANT DONATIONS

In November of 1982 Edwin Stringer, a lawyer, donated *Labyrinth* to the Hamilton Art Gallery. This excellent work, York's first geometric painting, was done from a Paris sketch. York was pleased, as it was an important piece and his first in that gallery.

The gallery has since received a donation of York's *Celaya Market* (1959) and purchased his remarkable oval oil painting, *Encore de Shaka* (1963), so York is now well represented there. About the same time, York's *Lexicon of Pinks* (1982) was included in Hamilton's 14th Annual Arts Exhibition. In 1981 Mrs. C.B. Munson donated York's *On the Beach* (1952), a work inspired by our 1952 Canary Islands trip, to the Edmonton Art Gallery.

ONGOING ACTIVITIES

In 1982, the Lakehead Board of Education published a brochure with an article by York titled "Contemporary Canadian Art," accompanied by many reproductions. The international art critic Raul Furtado wrote a fairly complete coverage of York's work for *Real Estate News* (December 10, 1983) titled "York Wilson Brings Art to the Man in the Street."

The Montreal gallery La Collection Tudor, at 1538 Sherbrooke Street West, asked for a few paintings and the *York Wilson* book by way of reintroducing York, as he hadn't shown in Montreal for many years. The gallery then presented an exhibition of his work titled "A New Way of Seeing," in April of 1983.

The show was a certain success; among several good reviews was an excellent piece by Jean-Pierre Duquette published in *Vie des Arts* (September-November 1983). Duquette's comments were wide-ranging: he wrote of the "loveable mastership" of York's nude studies, the "free and atmospheric" quality of the watercolours, the harmonious "balance of masses" seen in the acrylics, and noted the "tragic intensity" of York's "fascinating portrait of the writer Scott Symons." "On the whole," Duquette concluded, it was "an interesting exhibition certainly testifying to a vigorous métier, but also a personal vision, always alert and attentive."

In mid-1983, Central Hospital mounted a fine exhibition called "Fibre Art 1983." York was represented by two large tapestries, *Gidai Matsuri* (1970), and *Totem* (1970), which sold to Toronto artist Isabel McLaughlin for $8,000. The sale caused so much excitement that Dr. Paul Rekai himself phoned to tell York. The exhibition later toured to the Cambridge Public Library and Arts Centre in Cambridge, Ontario. The exhibition was opened by Mayor David Crombie at Toronto's St. Lawrence Art Centre in March of 1984, in celebration of Toronto's 150th and Ontario 200th anniversaries.

FIFTY YEARS OF MARRIAGE

On July 13, 1983, York and I celebrated our fiftieth wedding anniversary at the Guild of All Arts in Scarborough. Spencer Clark gave the opening remarks, in which he asked the guests to take a special look at York's portrait of Scott Symons, one of thirty-eight of York's works installed for the occasion, and drew their attention to Virginia's special anniversary gift to us. Virginia had searched out and gathered fifty-one different flowers, one to mark each of our anniversaries and one more to mark the day of our marriage. Each flower was presented in an individual vase; the effect was quite spectacular!

Our anniversary party was reported in the *Globe and Mail* (July 16, 1983) by Zena Cherry and by Stasia Evasuk in the *Toronto Daily Star*

(July 16, 1983), who noted that the guests from Jerusalem, Belgium, France, San Francisco, Mexico and Toronto constituted a virtual "International Who's Who." She also mentioned a special honour accorded York that night. Spencer had arranged to have the Guild Inn's Coral Room officially renamed the York Wilson Room, where a permanent collection of York's works from different periods are on display. The works installed there include *A Poetic Face* (1968), *Medieval Rites* (1974) and *The Loch Ness Visitation* (1977). A plaque was affixed over the door of the new York Wilson Room, while a photograph and biography were installed nearby.

In 1987, Heritage Ontario removed York's paintings and put them in storage, saying the steam table was damaging them. The steam table was later removed but the paintings have not been replaced. This is contrary to the wishes of Spencer Clark, and to myself, the guardian of York's interests.

The anniversary was such a happy occasion for us. I had been anxious because of York's fragile state of health, but he was determined to see all his friends. Maybe he had a premonition that it would be the last time! Corinne McLuhan was our constant companion as she had been invited to spend a week at the Guild with us.

A HAMILTON RETROSPECTIVE

In the autumn of 1983, Hamilton's Moore Gallery presented a major retrospective of York's work. The show, which featured works covering forty years of York's career, included many pieces from our collection. This important exhibition was covered in numerous newspapers and periodicals. Grace Inglis wrote in the *Hamilton Spectator* (October 1, 1983) that the exhibition's "stunning visual effect" proved the "remarkable history of a productive and disciplined artist."

While Joan Murray commented in *artmagazine* (November 1983) that York was one more candidate for Painters Eleven, Lois Crawford wrote in the *Burlington Post* (October 1, 1983) that York's strong individualism was "a characteristic shared by Varley, Jack Bush...and every great painter of the modern world. Fads in art did not deter him from his search for his own expression." In the *Globe and Mail* (October 4, 1983), Kay Kritzweiser saw the show as the "unfolding of a painter's subconscious creativity. This one moves to the measured tread of an artist unaffected by the bandwagons and isms which eddied around him."

AN OSA AWARD

The OSA honoured York with an OSA Award at a dinner held on November 3, 1983. The other recipients that night were Yvonne McKague Housser and Saidye Bronfman. As York was not well enough to attend, I accepted the award on his behalf. 1983 was a noteworthy year for York; many honours came his way. It was fortunate indeed, as he passed away within four months of the OSA award night.

YORK'S DEATH

At 4:00 A.M. on February 10, 1984, York died in the Toronto General Hospital. Over 250 letters of condolence arrived from many countries, obituaries appeared in many newspapers, and memorial essays were published by the various art societies, the Arts and Letters Club, and the Central Hospital. All attested to the fact that this brilliant, gentle man was well-loved.

Since thirteen had always been our lucky number, I planned to sprinkle York's ashes in thirteen of his favourite countries to commemorate the fact that he was truly a world citizen. Leon Katz took some to Israel and put them in the soil when he planted a tree in the Peace Forest in remembrance of York. Corinne McLuhan tossed some in the Pacific Ocean in California, hoping they would touch many shores with thoughts of peace. Leonard Brooks buried some under a tree in his garden near his studio in Mexico, during a little ceremony held by York's friends. Luc Peire sprinkled some in his garden in Paris. Dr. Carlos Pinto placed some in his Tenerife garden, in the presence of our many friends there. I threw some with a prayer from the Rialto Bridge in Venice, and worked some into the garden of our home on Alcina Avenue.

Before York's death, he said, "What pleases me most is to have my work in the Uffizi Gallery." What he didn't know was that they later requested a copy of the *York Wilson* book and *Blue Opus* print. He also didn't know that he had been awarded the 1984 "Statue of Victory Personality of the Year" by the Centre of Study and Research of the Nation in Italy. This "World Culture" prize was awarded in "acknowledgement of cultural and professional zeal shown in your field of activity, and of your important contribution to the improvement of present-day society."

Of the many letters I received after York's death, those from Scott Symons and Graeme Wilson were particularly memorable. I include excerpts of them here as a final tribute to my dear husband and lifelong companion. Scott Symons wrote from Morocco (March 27, 1984):

> So he's gone. Charles Taylor has sent me the newspaper clippings announcing dear York's death even as they belatedly celebrate his life and work. Of course I grieve with you!
>
> But if I certainly feel the hurt of York's death, I also feel almost a sense of relief—because York suffered in a prolonged way in those final months. This I know from various friends, including Leonard and Reva Brooks. York confronted for many weeks the spectre of oncoming death. He must have known there was little likelihood of any enjoyable reprieve, given the state of his health. So for him it is a mercy. And that is what counts, isn't it!
>
> There is, Lela, the final irony of all the newspaper accolades, given after his passing. Yes—but by and large Canadian art critics (with some distinguished exceptions) did precious little for York during his life! Indeed, many critics seemed almost to overlook York, studiously ignoring him, and his ever-evolving art. And doing so in favour of trendy younger artists whose work will not last, except as visual sociological data of a time and place.
>
> The fact remains, that York as a person, and as an artist, is larger than any of the media and its variable critics. And his work will stand, and his reputation will grow! He knew this; and he deserved to have the confidence of knowing it.
>
> But you know, Lela, it is York's personality that remains with me as a standard. Ebullient, witty and witful, horrendously irrepressible and loyal! He was a fighter, a scrapper and a civilised host. He combined many opposites, well!
>
> He could be termagant, yes, as you know better than any of us, dear Lela. But if and when termagant, it was always on the side of the angels—sometimes even despite York.

Graeme Wilson wrote from Brunei (June 19, 1984):

> Your sad letter reached me here today and, though Mac had earlier told me of York's death, I now at last am able to settle down and send you all my heart's condolences.

I know from your earlier letters that, in a very real sense, York's actual dying was a release and that he himself was content to go. I realise, too, that York had grown to see his fantastic personal contribution to Western art as something like a failure. In that, he was quite and entirely mistaken. I do not know all the ins and outs of his struggles with competitors and denigrators; only that York was too fine a man to match muck with muck, and too sensitive a man to believe in himself with the same total commitment as I, for one, believe in him and in the imperishable worth of his life-work.

It's hard to say that something is to be valued even more than the life-work of a great artist; but I do value York as a man more highly than his astonishing creations. He was, in the most complete sense, a giver of life. Just to have chatted with him for a quarter-hour, made a whole week lively. And his sense of fun, perhaps more exactly, his sense of frolic remains, in my experience, unsurpassed.

As you know, I loved him very dearly and, having seen so little of him over the last few years, I still feel that, just over there, "old Cocker" will be up to his larks again. In that sense York has, to me, always been, and still is, immortal. Yet most of all I'll miss knowing that, at any time, I'll be able to see, through his painter's eye, his truth of the world as he saw it. For he saw, and saw truly, what anyone can see once York had shown him how to look. And that's the mark not just of a master-painter, but of a master spirit. This little verse says a little of what I feel.

My friend is dead. His death has blinded me,
Not merely with the tears such deaths compel
But with the losing of a way to see.

For York could show, and no man else as well,
A particular, truth of colourings and shape
Not grasped by any other, heart or mind.

Tears blind me with their temporary escape,
But my lost York-sight no man can unblind.

The following text is the foreword that our dear friend Marshall McLuhan wrote for the *York Wilson* book in 1978.

In the nuclear age abstract or non-objective art is plainly prophetic. On the phone or on the air the user of electric services has no physical body. We are discarnate people, figures in an instantaneous and invisible ground of energy and vibration. This resonant and acoustic ground is discontinuous and man-made, deeply involving and subjective yet minus any point of view or personal stress. The work of York Wilson is a notable manifestation of the new awareness of nuclear man, the shift from sight to insight.

The paradox of visually representative art, the art of the copy, had been that the visual faculty had first to be abstracted from the human sensorium before the matching or copying of the environment could begin. The Greeks began it with their innovation of the phonetic alphabet. Twenty-four semantically abstract and meaningless sounds began the translation of the acoustic world of speech into the visual world of writing. This matching process of sound and sight had begun in Greece in the sixth century B.C., leading at once to the abstractly visual forms of Euclid and to the copy art of Plato's time. After the ages of iconic and multi-sensuous art of pre-literate man, visual representation was itself extremely abstract and novel.

E.H. Gombrich reminds us that *mimesis* or copying the pictorial effects of things, "the world of mirrors that deceive the eye", this new skill, was a recent invention of Plato's day which evoked his scorn as mere illusion. Plato was condemning "the great awakening of Greek sculpture and painting between the sixth century and the time of his youth toward the end of the fifth century B.C." (p. 116). The ground for this great awakening had been created by the spread of the unique form of phonetic literacy in the same period. Prior to literacy there had been centuries of non-representative art, which induced Gombrich to remark "Making comes before matching." The world of the audile-tactile is multi-sensuous and of age-old experience before the emergence of the alphabetic abstraction of the visual.

If a massive cultural innovation promoted the rise of visual and representational art in the fifth century B.C., an equal revolution in our twentieth century environment and perception must have occurred to create a bias in favour of non-objective art in the age of phenomenology. From the time of Hegel to Husserl, and from Faraday to Einstein, there has developed an increasing awareness of the ground behind the phenomena we perceive. Our new environment is electrical and resonant rather than visual, evoking a sense of primal involvement and touch, rather than the visual sense of objective spectatorship. In the new acoustic ground we naturally tend to relate by pattern-recognition of *figures in a ground*, rather than by the matching of objects according to verisimilitude.

York Wilson is a key figure in relating us to both the old visual world of realism and to the new resonating world of touch and echo and pattern. His own words explain the transition we have experienced in the twentieth century from the pictorial to the iconic and the patterned:

> *Sunlit Street* was the major turning point in my painting. Before this time I could appreciate abstract painting, but unable to find the exact point of departure for myself. It was while doing the sketch for this painting that the meaning of abstraction became amazingly clear. The whole scene in front of me became visually a related environment. The mountains had the same basic form as the roofs of the houses. The rebozos on the figures in the street repeated the same form. The markings on the street and sky and all the elements of the scene seemed to complement one another. Even though today this painting seems to be very slightly abstracted, nevertheless for me it was the key to abstracting form. This later led to my ability to also abstract colour.
>
> It was shortly after this discovery that I began to study picture construction per se. Prior to this time, a composition was limited to what could only be described as "tidying up the elements". But now there was a conscious effort to orchestrate each painting so that even without any recognizable subject the painting would be complete as a work of art. En route to the Canary Islands in 1958, we spent many days at the Louvre in Paris and the Prado in Madrid. It is a fact that during the time spent in these museums I developed an insight into abstraction through the work of artists like Uccello, Piero della Francesca, Breughel, etc. The understanding that I derived from them was much clearer than from my contemporary painters.

Behind this dramatic account of a transition there is a rich story of experiment and discovery and dialogue that emerged in an art that is calm, serious, and splendid.

Those acquainted with York Wilson recognize his joy in the intellectual exploration of the very complex world we share. That is why his work opens doors not only on art but on science. Anyone reading Lewis S. Feuer's *Einstein and the Generations of Science* (Basic Books Inc., New York, 1974) will see how the work of York Wilson offers many vistas into the world of Linus Pauling and Sperry and Bogen. Each of his paintings and murals is an encounter with current science and technology, and with the intense conversations they engender. Feuer makes it clear that the abstract science of Einstein's generation was built on a direct struggle to dislodge the old establishment of continuous and connected and rational space. The work of York Wilson represents a major endeavour to comprehend and to replace the established verities of visual space. Going along with this effort to update our awareness of the new scientific world was his sharing an intellectual dialogue with the educated people of his milieu. He also shared in the artistic benefits of his time of scientific change. As Feuer comments in words which apply to modern art:

> Generational rebellion is a powerful motivating force in the progress of scienceIn science generational rebellion widens the imagination, deepens the intuition, proposes challenging hypotheses, provokes laborious calculation and patient observation; but additionally, science has the common discipline and criteria of scientific method, which bind into a joint enterprise both intergenerational and intersubjective, the diverse hypotheses and emotional standpoints. (pp. 88-89)

The painting of York Wilson is not based so much on new skills and techniques as on a new way of seeing and knowing the world. Such changes in perception go with long debates and questioning and doubting of our personal identities. The nisus toward creativity in art and science is generated by strong emotion. Einstein wrote:

> The normal adult never bothers his head about spacetime problems. Everything there is to be thought about it, in his

opinion, has already been done in early childhood. I, on the contrary, developed so slowly that I only began to wonder about space and time when I was already grown up. In consequence, I probed deeper into the problem than an ordinary child would have done.

York Wilson has been driven by the desire for precision, yet this has not diminished his capacity to individualize and to render his abstractions dramatic and majestic.

York and I at our 50th wedding anniversary celebration at the Guild of All Arts. Scarborough, 1983.

Myself at approximately 4, Toronto, 1914. Photo by Mickelthwaite, Toronto.

York and his sister Dorothy, Toronto, c. 1908-09.

York's parents, Maude and William Wilson. Toronto, date unknown.

A portrait of York as a young man. Toronto, 1942.

York and Virginia at home at 28 Hambly Avenue. Toronto, c. 1937.

Charles Lee "Hutch" Hutchings and York. Toronto, early 1940s. Photo by Movie Snaps, Toronto.

York at work on his first mural, Lands, Lake and Forests, *installed in the Timmins Press Building in 1940. Toronto, 1940.*

An advertisement designed by York, appearing in Bus and Truck Transport
in Canada. *Toronto, early 1940s.*

A bon voyage party for us before leaving for Mexico in 1949, at Jean and Cleeve Horne's. Clockwise from lower left: Marion Panton (in sombrero), Jean Horne, Tome Riley, Herbert Palmer, Virginia, York, myself, Alec Panton. Toronto, 1949.

Mariachis and the city's mayor welcome us to San Miguel de Allende.
Leonard Brooks and the mayor are standing next to York.
San Miguel de Allende, 1949.

York sketching in the vicinity of San Miguel de Allende during
Peregrinations *1949. Photograph by Reva Brooks.*

Rushka Pinto and myself crossing a river in the vicinity of San Miguel de Allende during Peregrinations *1949. Photograph by Reva Brooks.*

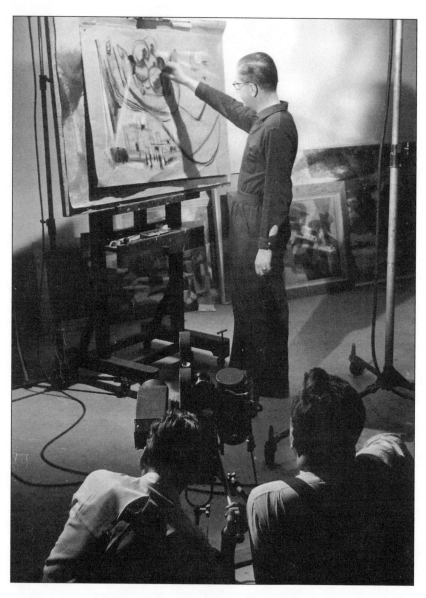

York at work on a study for the Imperial Oil mural, The Story of Oil, *in his studio at 41 Alcina Avenue, during the filming of "Mural." Toronto, 1957. Photograph by Crawley Films Ltd.*

York and Jack Bechtel at work on The Story of Oil *mural in the Imperial Oil Building. Toronto, 1957. Photograph by Imperial Oil Limited.*

Our home at 41 Alcina Avenue in the autumn; York's studio is at the front of the house. Toronto, c.1957-58. Photograph by Fednews, Toronto.

York and I with Fulvio Ara. Rome, 1958.

Wilson family group portrait at our 50th wedding anniversary celebration at the Guild of All Arts. Clockwise from centre: York, Virginia Kieran, myself, York's niece Anne Terwillegar, York's sister Dorothy Gillespie. Scarborough, 1983.

Group picture taken after the scattering of York's ashes around a tree near Leonard Brooks' studio. From left: Dr. Frances Echlin, myself, Letitia Echlin, Fred Taylor, Reva Brooks, Leonard Brooks, Spencer Clark. San Miguel de Allende, 1984.